Professor Elisabeth Porter teaches politics and peace studies in the international relations major at the University of South Australia and is Director, Centre for Peace, Conflict and Mediation in the Hawke Research Institute. Prior to this, Lis was Head of School of International Studies at the University of South Australia. She has been Research Director at INCORE, the International Conflict Research Institute in Northern Ireland. She has also taught at Flinders University, the University of Ulster and Southern Cross University.

Dr Anuradha Mundkur is a lecturer at Flinders University of South Australia. She is Associate Director of the Gender Consortium, Centre for Development Studies, at Flinders University. She has experience in gender research, training, policy-making, and monitoring and evaluation of gender mainstreaming.

Other titles in UQP's New Approaches to Peace and Conflict series
Reporting Conflict: New directions in peace journalism
by Jake Lynch & Johan Galtung

When Blood and Bones Cry Out: Journeys through the soundscape of healing and reconciliation
by John Paul Lederach & Angela Jill Lederach

Peace-making and the Imagination: Papua New Guinea perspectives
by Andrew Strathern and Pamela J Stewart

Also by Elisabeth Porter
Peacebuilding: Women in international perspective
Feminist Ethics
Building Good Families
Women and Moral Identity
Mediation in the Asia-Pacific Region: Transforming conflict and building peace (co-ed.)
Activating Human Rights (co-ed.)
Researching Conflict in Africa: Insights and experiences (co-ed.)

NEW APPROACHES TO PEACE AND CONFLICT

PEACE AND SECURITY:
implications for women

Elisabeth Porter & Anuradha Mundkur

UQP

First published 2012 by University of Queensland Press
PO Box 6042, St Lucia, Queensland 4067 Australia

www.uqp.com.au
uqp@uqp.uq.edu.au

© 2012 Elisabeth Porter & Anuradha Mundkur

This book is copyright. Except for private study, research,
criticism or reviews, as permitted under the Copyright Act,
no part of this book may be reproduced, stored in a retrieval system,
or transmitted in any form or by any means without prior
written permission. Enquiries should be made to the publisher.

Cover design by i2i Design
Typeset in 11.5/16 pt Minion Regular by Post Pre-press Group, Brisbane
Printed in Australia by McPherson's Printing Group

Cataloguing-in-Publication entry is available from the National Library of Australia
http://catalogue.nla.gov.au

ISBN (pbk) 9780702249228
ISBN (PDF) 9780702247866
ISBN (ePub) 9780702247873
ISBN (Kindle) 9780702247880

University of Queensland Press uses papers that are natural, renewable and recyclable
products made from wood grown in sustainable forests. The logging and manufacturing
processes conform to the environmental regulations of the country of origin.

This book is dedicated to all the women and men peacebuilders and their organisations who met with us and generously shared their knowledge and experiences.

Note from Series Editor

UQP's New Approaches to Peace and Conflict series builds on the wisdom of the first wave of peace researchers while addressing important 21st century challenges to peace, human rights and sustainable development. The series publishes new theory, new research and new strategies for effective peacebuilding and the transformation of violent conflict. It challenges orthodox perspectives on development, conflict transformation and peacebuilding within an ethical framework of doing no harm while doing good.

Professor Kevin P Clements
Chair in Peace and Conflict Studies
Director of The National Centre for Peace and Conflict Studies
University of Otago, New Zealand

Contents

Abbreviations	viii
Introduction	1
CHAPTER 1 Peace and security for women	10
CHAPTER 2 UN Security Council resolutions on 'women, peace and security'	33
CHAPTER 3 Protecting women and girls from violence, and preventing conflict	53
CHAPTER 4 Ensuring gender perspectives in peacekeeping	81
CHAPTER 5 Increasing participation of women in decision-making and peace processes	111
CHAPTER 6 Gender-inclusive relief and recovery	141
CHAPTER 7 Timor-Leste	167
CHAPTER 8 Fiji	195
CHAPTER 9 Sri Lanka	224
Appendix	252
Acknowledgements	258
Endnotes	260
Bibliography	270
Index	295

Abbreviations

ACCORD	African Centre for the Constructive Resolution of Disputes
Apodeti	Timorese Popular Democratic Association
AusAID	Australian Agency for International Development
AWAW	Association for War Affected Women (Sri Lanka)
BPFA	Beijing Platform for Action
CAVR	Commission for Reception, Truth and Reconciliation in Timor-Leste
CEDAW	Convention on the Elimination of All Forms of Discrimination against Women
CENWOR	Centre for Women's Research (Sri Lanka)
CIVPOL	Civilian Police Force
DDR	disarmament, demobilisation and reintegration
DRC	Democratic Republic of Congo
FPSPI	Foundation of the Peoples of the South Pacific International (Fiji)
FPU	Formed Police Unit
Fretilin	Revolutionary Front of Independent East Timor
FRSC	Forum Regional Security Committee
FWCC	Fiji Women's Crisis Centre
FWRM	Fiji Women's Rights Movement
GAD	gender and development
GAPS	Gender Action for Peace and Security (UK)
GDI	Gender Development Index
GenCap	Gender Standby Capacity Project (Australia)
ICC	International Criminal Court
ICES	International Centre for Ethnic Studies (Sri Lanka)
ICISS	International Commission on Intervention and State Sovereignty

ICRC	International Committee of the Red Cross
ICTR	International Criminal Tribunal for Rwanda
IDP	internally displaced person
IHR	Institute for Human Rights (Sri Lanka)
INTERFET	International Force for East Timor
IWDA	International Women's Development Agency
JSMP	Judicial System Monitoring Programme (Timor-Leste)
LRC	Law Reform Commission (Solomon Islands)
LTTE	Liberation Tigers of Tamil Eelan (Sri Lanka)
MDG	Millennium Development Goal
MONUC	Mission in the Democratic Republic of the Congo (UN)
NAP	national action plan
NDI	National Democratic Institute
NGO	non-government organisation
NIWC	Northern Ireland Women's Coalition
NPC	National Peace Council (Sri Lanka)
PCP	Pacific Centre for Peacebuilding (Fiji)
PFAW	Pacific Foundation for the Advancement of Women (Fiji)
PIFS	Pacific Island Forum Secretariat
PKO	peacekeeping operation
PNG	Papua New Guinea
PNTL	Policia Nacional de Timor-Leste
PPC	Pearson Peacekeeping Centre
PRADET	Psychosocial Recovery and Discovery in East Timor
R2P	responsibility to protect
RAMSI	Regional Assistance Mission to Solomon Islands
SEPI	Secretary of State for Promotion of Equality (Timor-Leste)
SGBV	sexual and gender-based violence
SGI	Sub-Committee for Gender Issues (Sri Lanka)
SSR	security sector reform
STRWN	Sinhala Tamil Rural Women's Network
UDT	Timorese Democratic Union
UN	United Nations

UNAMET	UN Mission in East Timor
UNDAW	UN Division for the Advancement of Women
UNDP	UN Development Programme
UNDPKO	UN Department of Peacekeeping Operations
UNFPA	UN Population Fund
UNGA	UN General Assembly
UNHCR	UN High Commissioner for Refugees
UNIFEM	UN Development Fund for Women (now UN Women)
UN-INSTRAW	UN International Research and Training Institute for the Advancement of Women
UNMIL	UN Mission in Liberia
UNMISET	UN Mission of Support in East Timor
UNMIT	UN Integrated Mission in Timor-Leste
UNMO	UN Military Observer
UNOMSA	UN Observer Mission to South Africa
UNOTIL	UN Office in Timor-Leste
UNPOL	UN Police
UNSC	UN Security Council
UNSCR	UN Security Council Resolution
UNTAET	UN Transitional Administration in East Timor
VPU	Vulnerable Persons Unit (Timor-Leste)
WAC	Women's Action for Change (Fiji)
WDP	Women Defining Peace (Sri Lanka)
Weavers	Women and Theological Education Committee of South Pacific Association of Theological Schools (Fiji)
WFP	Women for Prosperity (Cambodia)
WID	women in development
WIN	Women in Need (Sri Lanka)
WIP	Women in Politics
WMC	Women and Media Collective (Sri Lanka)
WPS Fiji CC	Women, Peace and Security Coordinating Committee

Introduction

Wars, armed aggression and violence continue to rage. Peace and security for many women, men, girls and boys remain elusive dreams, vague hopes, something to cling on to despite the surrounding conflict in which no-one feels safe. Everyone suffers incredible trauma, loss and pain during the ravages of war. However, people's experiences of insecurity often differ. For women living in conflict-affected communities, there are gendered aspects to their experiences. Hence, the United Nations Security Council Resolution (UNSCR) 1325 on 'women, peace and security' (UNSC 2000a), adopted in 2000, is of immense international importance. It is historic in being the first Security Council resolution to recognise the impact of conflict on women and girls, address the special needs of women and girls in relation to security and acknowledge the significant role that women play in bringing about peace and security.

It is ironic that, at the time of writing, eleven years later, we are still introducing the idea of why this resolution is necessary. In this book, we analyse the extent to which UNSCR 1325 (and to a lesser degree subsequent resolutions) has been implemented in ways that foster positive changes that make a difference to peace and security. In this vein, our aims overlap with the goals expressed in a significant edited collection titled *Women, peace and security* by 'Funmi Olonisakin, Karen Barnes and Eka Ikpe (2011), who state that 'what has not been explored is the *impact* that UNSCR 1325 has had since it was passed in 2000' (Barnes & Olonisakin 2011, p. 3, italics in original); thus, their book is the first to have undertaken this critical scholarly assessment.[1] They too explore what actually makes a difference in advancing gender equality and seek to examine the lessons learned. Like us, they are concerned that 'while the amount of research and anecdotal evidence about the implementation of UNSCR 1325 has proliferated over the past ten years, understanding of the process whereby it is translated from a rhetorical commitment at the UN level into concrete progress on the ground is still lacking' (2011, p. 4). The authors in this edited collection are concerned with the framework of UNSCR 1325 within peacekeeping missions and assess relationships between formal and informal local peacekeeping structures. While our focus in this book is specifically on assessing the efficacy of UNSCR 1325 in instigating positive change for peace and security, we also look broadly at how women across the globe are influencing changes aimed at building sustainable, peaceful communities.

This book stems from a project that was funded by the Commonwealth of Australia, Australian Agency for International Development (AusAID) to examine the efficacy of UNSCR 1325 in AusAID partner countries, which include Papua New Guinea (PNG), South Asia, East Asia, the Pacific, Africa and the Middle East.[2] Our research included semi-structured interviews with grassroots women's groups, non-government organisations (NGOs), representatives of donor organisations, government officials and legislators in Timor-Leste, Fiji and Sri Lanka with whom we explored a series of questions on the implementation of UNSCR 1325. Specifically, we investigate practical benefits of its implementations, as well as hurdles and challenges it confronts. We evaluate strategies that are successful and try to understand the importance of gender equality, empowerment and security to these strategies. Men's responses to women's participation in political decision-making on peace and security matters are taken seriously in assessing what is needed to increase women's capacity for leadership in peace and security decisions.³ Part of our intention in investigating these matters is to gain insight into the role of international development agencies and the donor community in conflict-affected countries.

We highlight good practices on how to advance women's leadership and decision-making in conflict resolution, peacemaking and peacebuilding. It is not surprising, then, that our use of the term 'good practices' is explicitly normative. We understand good practices as being innovative, creative, effective strategies to meet local challenges. The policy implication of good practices is that such initiatives may be adaptable to suit other local contexts. Each conflict-affected country has different needs, so a flexible, holistic approach is required. For example, for rural Nepalese, food and poverty concerns are part of peacebuilding considerations. This is because the lack of food and water can lead to unrest and violent conflict. Improving access to basic amenities is part of developing a holistic response. Thus, talking about food and water may be an entry point to peacebuilding. Locally based inclusive and plural solutions are important. Non-written forms of communication draw in those who are unable to read or write. Or, involving people from different ethnic, religious and rural groups creates partnerships so that good practices are locally based and integrated into communities.

In the following six thematic chapters – on the global context of gendered insecurities, the significance of UNSCR 1325 (and related resolutions), protection against and prevention of violence, peacekeeping, participation, and relief and recovery – we provide a broad, generalist overview of what is being done in conflict-affected countries. Our focus is specifically on what is happening to advance peace and security through women's participation in preventing conflict and in peace processes, peacebuilding and post-conflict reconstruction. Many of our examples are from the Asia-Pacific region because they derive from our initial funded research, but our analysis has wider implications for understanding what has worked to assist women's security beyond this region. Accordingly, we also provide examples from elsewhere, including countries in Africa in particular. The in-depth case studies on Timor-Leste, Fiji and Sri Lanka draw on our fieldwork experiences.

Chapter 1 explores why we should be concerned about global insecurities and, in particular, gendered insecurities. The human tragedy of violent conflict is enormous. Wherever there is armed conflict, sectarian tension, ethnic or religious rivalries, the occupation of territories or militaristic violence, men and women suffer deeply. We start by explaining the changing nature of war that affects men as well as women and demonstrate how women are disproportionately affected by violence in multiple ways. We explain what it means to talk of gender-specific experiences of conflict that prompt the urgency of a response, our feminist responses to these experiences and the priority we place on a feminist approach to gender equality and justice, culturally appropriate empowerment, human security and a broad understanding of peacebuilding.

Chapter 2 explains the relationships between UNSCRs 1325, 1820, 1888, 1889 and 1920, and, in particular, it examines the achievements and challenges in implementing UNSCR 1325.[4] We highlight some key features of certain national action plans (NAPs) on the implementation of UNSCR 1325. A critical evaluation of the limitations of these resolutions is given. The book's central argument that the implementation of UNSCR 1325 is not simply a women's issue but is about furthering sustainable peace and human security is reiterated.

The next four chapters cement the theoretical parameters of this book by examining the four pillars of the resolutions on 'women and peace and security':

- protection (of safety, health and human rights);
- prevention (from structural and physical violence and sexual-based violence);
- participation (in decision-making processes related to the prevention, management and resolution of conflicts); and
- relief and recovery (of specific needs in conflict and post-conflict situations).

Chapter 3 examines ways to protect women and girls from violence and also indicates what is entailed in preventing conflict. We begin by explaining what is meant by 'protection'. Protecting civilians from violence, especially during conflict, is an important concern for international organisations. The International Committee of the Red Cross (ICRC) and the Office of the UN High Commissioner for Refugees (UNHCR) play leading roles in the issue of protection in conflict zones. However, the changing nature of conflict and a broadening of our understanding of what constitutes security mean that there is an increase in the number of actors enthusiastically working in the area of protection. UNSCRs 1325, 1820, 1888 and 1889 perform a significant role in highlighting the need for comprehensive action to protect women and girls from violence both during and after conflict. Any discussion of protection is tied inextricably to preventing conflict, and we argue that preventing conflict is a proactive approach to protecting the rights of women and girls. Hence, we review the implementation of UNSCRs 1325 and 1820 with respect to the protection of women and girls and the prevention of conflict. Drawing on the work of the UN, national governments and civil society organisations, we review what is being done to include women as gender focal points or as Special Representatives on women, peace and security. The emphasis in this chapter, as in all chapters, is on highlighting good practices. For example, raising awareness of the necessity to prevent violence against women and girls is an ongoing process, and we highlight community-based approaches. We emphasise the importance of working with men. Early warning systems have gendered dimensions and yet rarely are taken seriously, so we examine them. Access to justice includes building the capacity of the judicial system, particularly judges and police, truth and reconciliation commissions and engendering traditional justice systems. Dealing with impunity and monitoring evaluation of indicators of protection remain important challenges; we explain what is involved in setting targets, mobilising political will and monitoring peace agreements.

Chapter 4 explores ways of ensuring that gender perspectives are adopted in peacekeeping. Peacekeeping is a multidimensional undertaking that has involved changes within the UN, UN peacekeeping missions, troop-contributing countries and host countries. These changes are instigated through external and internal pressures. UNSCR 1325 is used as a focal point for creating this pressure, though change is also fostered through the work of groups that are doing '1325 work' but do not identify it as such. In this chapter, we review the implementation of UNSCR 1325 by UN troop-contributing countries and host countries in relation to peacekeeping and gender-sensitive training. This review focuses on what has been done and which groups and institutions are active in achieving these changes, and evaluates what still needs to be done to incorporate gender training, improve gender equity and build capacity for gender-responsive peacekeeping. We briefly discuss the need for women to be active participants in all aspects of security sector reform (SSR).

Chapter 5 examines women's participation in decision-making. Much has been written about women's roles in grassroots peace processes and the important roles they play in brokering peace and rebuilding conflict-affected societies. However, it is also widely acknowledged that their wisdom and expertise are not similarly recognised in formal peace negotiations and processes. Rather, women are alarmingly absent from high-level peace processes. Since 1990, in 585 peace agreements, only 16 per cent 'have contained at least one reference to women or gender' (UNIFEM 2010, p. 18). We explore how women's absence from peace negotiations undermines the possibility of sustainable peace. We also review barriers to women's participation in peace processes and use a variety of examples to explore women's participation in peace processes and decision-making. These examples highlight heterogeneity and understanding of what is involved in creating a peace process that is truly inclusive. We also stress the need for women's participation, not just in peace processes or as elected Members of Parliament but in all levels of decision-making, to prevent, manage and resolve conflict, as peacemakers, peacekeepers and civil society peacebuilders.

Chapter 6 explores what is entailed in gender-inclusive relief and recovery. We begin by making explicit connections between development, women's rights and gender-inclusive security. The practice of gender mainstreaming is subject to a critical analysis to explore whether mainstreaming, integrating or engendering peace and security with justice is preferable and to see how each approach differs. We suggest that while some progress in including gender issues is better than excluding these issues, attention to women-specific needs must be part of a truly gender-inclusive relief and recovery. A brief appraisal of the indicators to monitor and evaluate progress in securing a peace that empowers women is given. We also scrutinise the concept of empowerment; this term is used frequently in development literature in particular (UNDP 2008a), and we tease out cultural variations in what equality and empowerment mean in differing cultures, through drawing on the words of our interviewees. Throughout the text, unsourced quotes are from the interviewees and are in italics.[5] What does empowerment really mean? Is it understood in all cultures, and what are some cultural differences in understandings? What does empowerment lead to? We rethink some of the traditional ideas on empowerment in order to suggest one as a practice that is transformative, releasing previously inhibited capacities to allow the unfolding of full human potential.

Chapters 7 to 9 give in-depth case studies on Timor-Leste, Fiji and Sri Lanka, respectively. In these countries, we conducted interviews with some key women's groups, civil society peace groups, local grassroots groups, significant NGOs, aid workers and, where possible, UN personnel and government officials, speaking with men as well as women. The interviews in Timor-Leste and Fiji were carried out in late 2009 and those with Sri Lankans in early 2010. Each of these case studies adopts a similar format. We begin with a brief background of the country's conflict, with a particular focus on instability triggers and gendered experiences of insecurity. This enables us to see more clearly what urgently needs to be done in the different countries in order to improve gender equality in peace and security matters. Gendered insecurities are linked to development issues. We explore the extent of awareness of UNSCR 1325 and assess the degree of its implementation in each country. Next, measures adopted to protect women and girls from violence are outlined. Examples of how women contribute to conflict prevention are provided. We explain what is needed to ensure that gender perspectives are adopted in all aspects of peacekeeping and SSR, and give examples of measures taken to increase the participation of women in political decision-making and peace processes. The significant remaining complications in engendering peaceful relief and recovery efforts in order to achieve effective security are summarised. Wherever possible, we use direct quotations from the voices of local people. We suggest key actions that might assist policy-makers, donors, development agencies and international peacebuilders to work with local communities to overcome some of these challenges in gender-inclusive relief and recovery.

In this book, we argue that UNSCR 1325 and the related UNSCRs 1820, 1888, 1889 and 1960 provide an important set of lofty aims, but the failure of indicators to measure progress since the adoption of UNSCR 1325 is a major shortcoming. In many conflict-affected countries, lack of knowledge of the resolutions or failure in their implementation means that it is difficult to assess whether women's participation in peace and security issues is leading to enhanced gender equality and justice and the empowerment of women. Despite this limitation, we argue that while the obstacles to the implementation of UNSCR 1325 remain significant, evidence that emerges from our fieldwork and research allows us to offer some suggestions that address the remaining challenges while being optimistic about progress made. These resolutions are about transforming inclusive peace and security; they are not simply about women's issues. Our central argument is that it is possible to provide concrete examples of good practices that show what really makes a transformative difference in women's lives in furthering peace and security.

CHAPTER 1

Peace and security for women

In this chapter, we build the case for why special attention to women's insecurities is justified. We begin by explaining how the context of international relations is altering. The changing nature of war, with a predominance of civil wars, affects men as well as women. Not only is the enormity of armed conflict significant, but so too is the relationship between conflict and poverty. Understanding a little about the context of global insecurities is crucial for grasping the significance of the chapter's second section, in which we explain the severity of gendered insecurities. The human tragedy of violent conflict is extensive, and everyone suffers deeply, but women are affected disproportionately by violence in multiple ways. In particular, they are subject to sexual violence, material hardship and shifting family responsibilities. Despite women's persistent informal peacebuilding, they are marginalised or excluded from formal peace processes. Finally, we outline a feminist response to peace and security. We offer arguments to explain why we give priority to gender equality and justice, culturally sensitive empowerment, human security and broad understandings of peacebuilding.

Global insecurities

The UNSCRs emerged in the context of a shifting geopolitical landscape and international relations. The end of the Cold War saw changes to superpower relations and to the nature of armed violence. Reasons for current violence vary. Conflicts in Kashmir, Sudan and the Democratic Republic of Congo (DRC) continue from the post-colonial period. Other conflicts are armed insurrections against the state, such as in Sri Lanka, the Chechen Republic and Colombia. In Burundi, Somalia and Indonesia, local clan or ethnic leaders contest territory or resources. The wars in Afghanistan and Iraq are invasions of sovereign states in the name of a war against terrorism conducted by the United States and its allies. Violent conflicts within states 'now make up more than 95 per cent of armed conflicts' (Mack 2005, p. viii). Triggers to violent conflict are numerous; they include disputes over territory and resources in which western capitalists, hungry for diamonds, minerals, oil or a market for weapons, sometimes provide backing to insurgents or those who provoke such conflict. Other triggers are ethnic, religious and sectarian animosities. Many of these conflicts reflect long historical bitterness with deep religious, ethnic and cultural roots. They lead to insurgencies, tribal and clan rivalries and revenge killings. 'Control over lucrative and sometimes illicit trade, such as in drugs and arms' (UNRISD 2005, p. 210), drives other conflicts. State actors, while rarely admitting culpability, also are part of the landscape of conflict, in examples of external invasions and terrorist attacks. Peace itself seems to be more militarised, with soldiers acting as peacekeepers. Indeed, Cynthia Enloe (1993, p. 73) talks of the presence of 'militarised peace'.

What Mary Kaldor (2007) calls 'new wars' take place in contexts of the disintegration of old authoritarian states, in which distinctions between combatants and non-combatants are loosened, so that the exact end of war is hard to define. The war zone has changed from battlefields to ordinary living spaces of markets, villages, schools, churches, temples, mosques, trains and homes. The fighting method of aerial bombardment invariably hits civilians, and the use of the term 'collateral damage' to rationalise civilian deaths is a morally repugnant attempt at abstraction, depersonalising the cruelty of war. More typically, these new wars draw on the ease of gaining small arms and light weapons such as pistols, handguns, rifles and grenades; gangs, militias and paramilitary groups can readily conduct ambushes and raids, and children can use weapons easily. Civilians make up a substantial number of casualties of contemporary violent conflicts, with about ninety civilian deaths to every ten military losses (Kegley & Blanton 2010, p. 509). While 'the direct impact of violence falls primarily on young males ... women and children often suffer disproportionately from the indirect effects ... [W]omen and children are close to 80 per cent of refugees and those internally displaced' (World Bank 2011, p. 6).

The problem is huge. Including those countries that experienced war between 1987 and 2007, where war is defined as 'an armed conflict with at least 1,000 battle-related deaths in a given year, over the past 20 years' (Bastick, Grimm & Kunz 2007, p. 23),[1] the list is shocking. In Africa, it includes Algeria, Angola, Burundi, Chad, Côte d'Ivoire, the DRC, Eritrea, Ethiopia, Guinea-Bissau, Liberia, Mozambique, the Republic of the Congo, Rwanda, Sierra Leone, Somalia, South Africa, Sudan and Uganda. In the Americas, Colombia, El Salvador, Guatemala, Nicaragua and Peru experienced armed conflict.[2] In Asia, degrees of conflict continue in Afghanistan, Burma/Myanmar, Cambodia, India, Nepal, the Philippines, Sri Lanka and Tajikistan. In Europe, armed conflict occurred (and continues in parts) in Azerbaijan, Bosnia and Herzegovina, Croatia, Georgia, Russia and Serbia (Kosovo). In the Middle East, Iraq, Israel and the Palestinian Territories, Kuwait, Lebanon, Turkey and Yemen experience violent conflict. *Peace and conflict 2010* is a ledger that examines the legacies of wars and the prospects of rebuilding states (Hewitt, Wilkenfeld & Gurr 2010). Its authors show how, 'of the 39 different conflicts that became active in the last ten years, 31 were conflict recurrences' (2010, p. 1). The challenges of living in failed or failing states are enormous, with economic repercussions including costs often borne by neighbouring states, some of which are failing states themselves. What is disturbing is that, with the exception of Afghanistan, Iraq and Nepal, 'the twenty-five states with the highest risk of new failures are in Africa' (2010, p. 2).

In the global south, there is a direct relationship between conflict and poverty. Countries within the area 'have a low gross national income and rate low on the Human Development Index. The UN describes Africa, Asia (excluding Japan), the Caribbean, Central America, Oceania (excluding Australia and New Zealand) and South America as "developing regions"' (Valasek 2008, p. 20). For example, over three-quarters of Australia's major bilateral aid programs operate in countries that are experiencing, recovering from or vulnerable to conflict (AusAID 2002, p. 6). Many of these countries are fragile states, in which government and state structures lack the capacity to provide security, sound governance and economic growth. Conflict is a central reason for fragility: it reverses development gains and can cause poverty, which then increases the risk of provoking further violent conflict. 'Evidence shows that fragile states also generate substantial and complex social costs including conflict' (Anderson 2005, p. 2). Conflict and fragility affect national and regional security. Ian Anderson's research shows that when considering fragile states, 'leadership matters' (2005, p. 4). He draws attention to the political elite, while we draw attention to the significance of women's leadership as integral to nation-building because 'fragile states have high gender disparities' (AusAID 2007a, p. 23).

The Paris Declaration on Aid Effectiveness (2005) model offers indicators as ways to measure progress in addressing this relationship between conflict and poverty. It focuses on supporting country-led policies to attain growth, reduce poverty and promote the Millennium Development Goals (MDGs). It 'is most appropriate in contexts with capable, accountable and legitimate states. Where these conditions do not prevail, there has been a tendency within donors to work "around" conflict and fragility, rather than addressing them head-on' (DFID 2009, p. 3). In the following chapters, we see why greater attention needs to be given to fragile states so that building peaceful states becomes fundamental to donor responses. State-building is an integral part of peacebuilding because it develops the capacities, resources and legitimacy of state institutions.

Peaceful societies

After examining the nature of global insecurities, it is useful to outline briefly the nature of peaceful countries. The *Global peace index* (Institute for Economics and Peace 2009) defines 'peace' as Johann Galtung (1964, p. 2) defines 'negative peace', that is, as 'the absence of violence, absence of war'. Structures and institutions that help to resolve the root causes of conflicts begin to create 'positive peace', which is a long-term sustainable peace. Notions of positive peace imply how a society should be, which entails realising ideals of equality and inclusive, participatory and democratic structures with open, accountable government. 'Working towards these objectives opens up the field of peacebuilding far more widely, to include the promotion and encouragement of new forms of citizenship and political structures which will develop active democracies' (Pankhurst 1999, p. 6).

In 2010, the *Global peace index* registered New Zealand as the most peaceful country, followed by Iceland and Japan, with Pakistan,

Sudan, Afghanistan, Somalia and Iraq ranked as the least peaceful (Institute for Economics and Peace 2010). This index investigates drivers that influence the creation of peaceful societies.[3] A summary of the 2010 findings provides a useful snapshot. Western Europe is the most peaceful region, with the majority of the region's countries ranking in the top twenty overall. The Asia-Pacific exhibits wide variation, with New Zealand, Japan and Australia peaceful, but there are significant differences in South-East Asia, with Taiwan, Vietnam and Indonesia in the top seventy,[4] and security concerns with Cambodia, Thailand and the Philippines. Afghanistan, Pakistan and North Korea are ranked the lowest in this region. War-ravaged Iraq is the lowest ranked, in addition to occupied Palestine/Israel and Lebanon. 'Sub-Saharan Africa is the region least at peace' (2010, p. 17). Clearly, these annual rankings change as internal and external drivers impact on security. One chief message of this index confirms our argument: that gender inequality is an important indicator of how well countries divide resources and opportunities among men and women, and thus gender equality enhances the possibility of enduring peace and security.

Gendered insecurities

Given this brief overview of global insecurities, what does it mean to talk of gendered insecurities? It means that armed conflict sometimes affects men and women in similar ways, in subjecting them to trauma, devastation and loss; and sometimes it affects women and men differently, in the consequences of war, in choices to fight or to build peace and in opportunities to be involved in peace processes. In conflict-affected countries, many men are warriors, resistance fighters, warlords, militia, paramilitaries, guerrilla fighters, rebels, tribal soldiers, mercenaries or trained military personnel. Some wars include disenfranchised youth (mainly boys) who become soldiers or are forced to be child soldiers. Those men who are not directly involved in fighting often make decisions about conflicts, including giving orders to kill, rape, plunder or destroy property. Particularly in rural or mountainous areas, older men are left behind with women, children, the ill and the disabled, and many people are reduced to a state of radical insecurity brought on by the devastation and consequences of war, including extreme poverty.

Certainly, some women and girls choose to be combatants or active supporters to resistance fighters or soldiers, while others are cajoled or forced to become soldiers or sex slaves attached to fighters. 'Women and girls have fought in armed conflicts in Afghanistan, Bosnia and Herzegovina, Colombia, the DRC, East Timor, Ethiopia, Eritrea, Guatemala, Iraq, Lebanon, Mozambique, Namibia, Palestine, South Africa, Sierra Leone, Sudan, Uganda' (Mazurana et al. 2005, p. 2). Other women have been (or continue to be) involved in liberation struggles in Colombia, the DRC, East Timor, El Salvador, Eritrea, Guatemala, Mozambique, Namibia, Palestine, Sierra Leone and Uganda. Girl soldiers are used particularly in the Central African Republic, Chad, Colombia, Côte d'Ivoire, the DRC, Liberia, Nepal, the Philippines, Sri Lanka and Uganda (Coalition to Stop the Use of Child Soldiers 2008). However, in most conflict-affected countries, women are the primary carers of children and adults who need care and thus bear the brunt of the destruction of crops, food supplies and community networks that result from armed conflict. There is ample evidence that, in sharing this responsibility for nurture, many women are willing to thrust aside, even temporarily, ethnic, tribal, clan, religious and sectarian differences that underlie conflicts in order to work together to ensure that everyday needs can be met. In visiting many conflict zones, Sanam Naraghi Anderlini (2000, p. 20) found that women often adopt strategies 'to take a unified stance on issues that affected everybody'.

In addition to family and community support, women also share the reality that in militarised cultures in which guns, uniforms, checkpoints and fear are normal, protection and aggressive masculinity overlap and extend from the battlefield into the home. Domestic violence often is extreme in militarised cultures, part of the prevailing 'structural violence' (Vlachová & Biason 2005). Increasingly in wars, many women are targeted for sexual assault. This is part of a deliberate strategy of ethnic cleansing, seeking to impregnate women from a different culture group, and 'is meant to humiliate, demoralise, and eventually destroy an ethnic group' (Wolff 2006, p. 103). It also is viewed as a natural spoil of war in which women are used, abused, assaulted and raped as part of attacks on villages (Anderson 2010). Shockingly, it is also part of the abhorrent behaviour of some security forces, including peacekeepers (Bastick, Grimm & Kunz 2007). Stories of sexual violence during war are horrifying. It is important to address issues of violence against women, while Srebrenica and Kosovo give horrible reminders of systematic killings of men and boys: gendered insecurities can affect anyone. However, women suffer disproportionately and in different ways.

Gendered insecurities include:

- economic insecurities with poor access to economic development and lack of land and property rights;
- sexual insecurities with sexualised violence;
- children born as a result of war rape;
- child abductions and trafficking;
- health insecurities with HIV/AIDS and lack of attention to specific health needs, particularly in childbirth;
- social insecurities with women-headed households, girl-headed households and orphans; and
- psychological insecurities with gender-based persecution that accompanies asylum status, trauma and gendered hardships faced as refugees, returnees and internally displaced persons (IDPs).

Landmines also continue to endanger lives, particularly those of women and children, who traditionally traverse long distances to collect firewood and water. In attending to these extensive concerns, the interdependence between gender inequality, women's access to justice and specific needs for security must be carefully analysed as part of a holistic approach to human security.

Specific attention to sexual violence is essential. A global overview that documents conflict-related sexual violence in fifty-one countries that have experienced war over the past twenty years in Africa, the Americas, Asia and Europe, including the Middle East, notes that 'armed conflict has involved sexual violence against women and girls, and also against men and boys' (Bastick, Grimm & Kunz 2007, p. 13). In 2009, sexual brutality was reported as severe in Burundi, Chad, Côte d'Ivoire, the DRC, Liberia, Myanmar, Rwanda, North and South Kivu, Somalia and Timor-Leste (UNSC 2009a, pp. 2–3). Conflict-related sexual violence occurs at all stages of conflict – during peak times of violence, during population displacement and also during transitions to democracy. Sites of violence are many: homes, fields and forests where women collect firewood, beside creeks where they collect water, in detention or refugee camps and on military sites. Sexual assault is a routine part of a fighting culture, with women as strategic targets. Perpetrators of violence are wide-ranging, potentially from militia, paramilitary groups and official armed forces to peacekeepers and humanitarian workers. HIV/AIDS is spread when sexual violence is rampant. While all women potentially are targets, 'in some armed conflicts, certain people, such as single women, homosexuals, women heads of household and displaced women and children have been particularly vulnerable to sexual violence' (Bastick, Grimm & Kunz 2007, p. 14). In places where there has been a long history of resistance movements, such as in Northern Ireland, South Africa, Argentina and Timor-Leste, women who are part of movements or have known partners in these movements are vulnerable. The next chapter examines how to prevent violence and protect women and girls from such violence.

Responding with resilience to insecurities

War changes the social dynamics of a society. Some women lose their professional and business occupations – as happened to many women from Bosnia and Herzegovina – as a result of which many sink into poverty. Women in African conflicts such as in Angola, Rwanda and Uganda lose workable land. Yet, ironically, through the process of having to learn new ways of surviving and adjusting to new forms of hardship, some women gain new experiences in wartime that they would not necessarily have in peaceful times. This growth can come from working with the international community on aid, relief and reconstruction work; women in refugee camps gain from education programs or from being exposed to new experiences; and when men are away fighting or hiding, or are displaced, interned or jailed, women accept new responsibilities. In post-genocide Rwanda, with so many men killed or across the border in Burundi, about '45,000 households were headed by children, 90 per cent of them girls' (UNRISD 2005, p. 224). In addition to different experiences of violent conflict, there also are gendered experiences that influence decision-making on peace and security.

Typically, women and men play different roles in armed conflict as victims and as agents, and, also, their approaches to and priorities in securing peace often differ. While some women are involved in wars as combatants or through supporting male family members' involvement, women rarely make decisions as to when to fight and how and when to cease fighting. Importantly, while women globally are active in informal peacebuilding roles in ways we outline in the following chapters, it seldom translates to official recognition, so they rarely are visible in negotiations and political decision-making about the construction of new, just laws and policies needed to ensure sustainable peace. This persistent absence from peace tables is of deep concern. In a sample of twenty-one major peace processes since 1992, the UN Development Fund for Women (UNIFEM, now UN Women)[5] found that while 'women's participation in negotiating delegations averaged 7.6 per cent of the 11 cases for which such information was available' and details are not easy to collect accurately in war zones, 'only 2.4 per cent of signatories to peace agreements were women and that no woman has ever been appointed as "chief mediator" with the exception of Graça Machel who was one of three mediators appointed by the African Union for the Kenyan crisis' (UNSC 2009a, p. 4). John Paul Lederach's (1997) framework for peace identifies the importance of top and grassroots leadership for sustained peace. Top leadership involves the military, political and religious leaders; middle-level leadership includes those respected in ethnic, religious, academic and humanitarian sectors; and grassroots leadership comes from local leaders of indigenous NGOs, community development workers, local health officials, educators and refugee camp leaders. There are no good reasons why women should not be represented in each level of leadership.

When women are included in peace processes, prospects for more durable peace agreements improve. Indeed, as developed in Chapter 5, 'the higher its level of gender inequality, the greater the likelihood that a state will experience intrastate conflict', and 'peace agreements are more durable when women formally participate in their negotiation' (Caprioli, Nielsen & Hudson 2010, p. 93). Our emphasis is on understanding the impact of women's transformative participation on the full gamut of peace processes at all levels of leadership. In each chapter, we highlight the differences that occur when women are involved in decision-making on peace and security matters.

A feminist approach to peace and security

In the following chapters, our approach stresses five fundamental aspects: a feminist methodology, the importance of gender equality and justice, the need for culturally sensitive understandings of women's empowerment, the foundational nature of human security in the resolutions with which we are concerned, and a broad-based understanding of peacebuilding. We include examples in which men assist in furthering peace, but our emphasis is on women and girls because they are the focus of UNSCR 1325. This group of women and girls is not homogenous. Culture, age, ability/disability, ethnicity, religion, employment status, health, sexuality, presence or absence of children and involvement in both conflict and peace processes impact on different experiences of security. A focus on women and girls does not mean that we ignore gender as an analytic tool, where gender is understood as the socially constructed characteristics, expectations and opportunities associated with being male or female. It is simply that we highlight how gendered power relations and cultural constructs affect men and women differently and seek to redress the lack of scholarly attention on what happens to women and girls in war and in peacebuilding, as consistent with UNSCR 1325. So often in UN, NGO and aid programs, 'gender is still commonly used as synonym for "women"' (Moran 2010, p. 262). There is an enormous diversity among women, and we seek to provide cross-cultural examples of this.

Feminist methodology

To begin with, we adopt a feminist methodology. This does not entail essentialist assumptions about women being natural peacebuilders. As mentioned, some girls and women are aggressive combatants, guerrillas, 'bush brides' for rebel fighters, resistance fighters, spies or part of paramilitary organisations (Miranda 2006). Some combatants choose their role as a means of forging independence, or, more typically, they become fighters to defend ideological or political positions. Girl soldiers usually are cajoled, forcibly taken from families or sometimes sold by families; other young women see combat as their only survival option. As already alluded to, in most communities, women are primary caregivers and often unwittingly find themselves playing crucial activist roles in conflict resolution and sorting out grievances, particularly responding to their household tasks to satisfy practical needs for food, water, shelter, education, health care and preservation of families' everyday lives.

We adopt a straightforward understanding of feminism to include all those (women and men) who challenge oppressive, restrictive, unequal and unjust gender relations and advocate free, just and equal rights (for women and men).[6] This understanding has both a critical function in challenging gendered inequalities and a political function in seeking social transformation. In our fieldwork, we sought to listen carefully to the voices of women (and men) in order to heed local understandings of what is required for women to gain equality, justice and human rights. It is extremely important to encourage men to become active partners with women in the pursuit of peace and justice. Men, like women, are not a homogenous category, so including them in activities that strengthen the nexus between peace and security for women as well as men involves considering different strategies. There are new entry points to engage young men on the importance of respecting women through using sport, music or multimedia. Sometimes, it is possible to groom seemingly unlikely champions of specific feminist causes, including the implementation of UNSCR 1325, such as a male Chief of Police, which happened in Nepal. The resolutions discussed in this book should resonate with men because ultimately they are about the human face of war and the need for human security.

Gender equality and justice

Our notion of gender equality accepts the need for 'equal rights, responsibilities and opportunities for women and men, girls and boys' (AusAID 2007a, p. 36). Practically, gender equality means a range of different things. For example, women and men need equitable access to resources provided in conflict-affected areas – to economic resources, assets of land, property information, income, financial services and skills in leadership and training (2007a, pp. 8–9). Without ways to measure equality, definitions lack bite. The Standardised Indicator of Gender Equality Strategies draws on measures of well-being (Dijkstra 2002). One measure designates education as a vital indicator as appraised by literacy rates and enrolments in primary and secondary education. Another focuses on life expectancy, in which the ratio of female to male life expectancy reveals different cultural responses to equality, particularly to nutrition and health care. Relative labour force involvement quantifies equality in the extent to which women share technical, professional, administrative and managerial positions. The number of women in Parliamentary seats also acts as a crucial indicator of gender equality. Ways to enhance gender equality are crucial, given that 'there is no region of the world where women enjoy equal rights and benefits of development' (AusAID 2007a, p. 7). This inequality is stark when one examines political representation. 'Women hold an average of three per cent of seats in national Parliaments in Pacific island countries, and an average of 19 per cent of seats in East Asia' (AusAID 2007a, p. 7). As elaborated more fully in Chapter 4, 'five of the ten countries in the world with no female representation are in the Pacific' (AusAID 2008a, p. 12).

Throughout the book, we argue that equality of respect and dignity is bound intrinsically with the results expected in a just, sustainable peace. For example, an anticipation of demilitarisation enhances prospects of security and increases the capacity of local leadership to assume responsibility for peace. This in turn empowers civil society, including the involvement of women's groups. With these initiatives, war economies may be converted from black market operations to sustainable economies, a conversion that helps to extend trust in political and legal systems as well as increase the capacity of these systems to function (Canadian International Development Agency 2001). Sustainable economies open avenues for women's participation in labour markets. Hierarchical, patriarchal societies can build peace, but this is a limited, exclusive peace. Instead, we argue that gender equality and justice are fundamental to inclusive peacebuilding. This means that when women and men enjoy such equality and its accompanying opportunities, rights and responsibilities, it should extend to the exercise of leadership. Where it does not, equality can be said to be only hypothetical, enshrined in beautifully worded constitutions, policies and laws, but in reality insubstantial.

The protection of women and girls from violence, as we elaborate in Chapter 2, improves the chance of women and girls realising their rights, accessing resources, making decisions and living without fear. Strategies to address this protection are needed urgently, given that outrageous atrocities continue to occur, particularly through war rape. 'Issues of women's equality with men, and women's participation in decision-making, have traditionally been more contested than issues of women's protection' (Tryggestad 2010, p. 161). We are arguing that a heightened awareness of gender helps to tackle cultural practices that cement gendered inequalities, including violence against women and girls. As the following chapters reinforce, there is a link between equality and justice, where 'gender justice refers to the protection and promotion of civil, political, economic, and social rights on the basis of gender equality' (Anderlini & Stanski 2004, p. 9).

Although we link gender equality with the inclusion of women in the full range of peace and security practices, we adopt a critical stance to any inclination to utilise a 'use-value' of women approach. Such an approach ignores the dominant masculine security discourses and the systematic 'overuse' of men. In defence of a rights-based approach, 'what is potentially lost with the "use-value" approach is that women should be there because they have a right and a reason as individuals, people, as human, not simply or solely because they are somebody's vision of a peace-maker' (Cohn, Kinsella & Gibbings 2004, p. 137). Having qualified a critical approach to the 'use-value' of women, we consider favourably the 'added value' of women's perspectives when they break down the rigidity of dominant, hegemonic stereotypes, making their contributions genuinely transformative, an argument elaborated in later chapters.

Women's empowerment

Our research builds on the former UN Secretary-General (1997–2006) Kofi Annan's 2005 statement that 'study after study has taught us that there is no tool for development more effective than the empowerment of women' (in AusAID 2007a, p. 4). But what exactly does women's empowerment mean? An Australian government development donor and policy-maker defines it as 'a process of transforming gender relations, so that women gain the skills, confidence and ability to make choices and decisions about their lives' (2007a, p. 36). Vivienne Wee and Farida Shaheed (2008, p. 16), writing about a program called Women's Empowerment in Muslim Contexts, define 'women's empowerment' as 'an increased ability to question, challenge and eventually transform unfavourable gendered power relations, often legitimised in the name of "culture"'. These researchers note as an important qualifier that the term 'empowerment' varies widely in differing cultural and linguistic contexts. In some countries there may be a close approximation, but the term may not be in common usage.[7] We urge caution in assuming culturally homogenous notions of empowerment, but, given its importance as a way to increase women's self-confidence in their own ability to make decisions, influence others and instigate social and cultural change, we recommend seeking culturally relevant understandings of the concept from local communities and, in particular, from local women's groups.

Human security

We implicitly criticise traditional realist notions of security for not being adequately responsive to women's specific security needs. Traditional notions of security concentrate on national security, territorial integrity, sovereignty, economic might, military power, border controls, intelligence and defence capabilities. These generally assume the inherent insecurity of states, all-pervasive competition, inevitable state conflict, the importance of a defence of the state and the paramount importance of the doctrine of sovereignty. Ironically, conventional security 'may make women less safe. This is symptomatic of the fact that matters of war and peace have been measured in terms of bullets, bombs and blades, rather than whether women can access markets or girls can get to school safely' (Anderson 2010, p. 246). We accept the crucial importance of national security but explicitly develop broad notions of 'human security', a term popularised by the UN Development Programme (UNDP 1994) in response to practical security concerns with economics, food, health, environmental, personal, community and political security as well as the need for freedom from violence. In many ways, the institutionalised acceptance in the UN of human security discourse influenced the writing of UNSCR 1325.

Our understanding of human security is based on the premise that there are multiple interrelated insecurities, the root causes of which require illumination. Root causes of insecurity include the violation of human rights, gender-based violence, all forms of inequality and injustice, women's lack of access to land and property, poverty, disease, organised crime, sexual trafficking, political corruption, environmental degradation and terrorism. Strategic peacebuilding attends to all forms of insecurities. For example, in Fiji, the femLINKpacific (2009, pp. 3–6) policy initiative on women, peace and security highlights seven main areas of human security: economics, health, food, the environment, and personal, community and political security. This multifaceted initiative is important because 'it is not clear that the UN-directed understanding of any kind of security, including human security, that is incorporated into UN policies and programs in fact matches local perceptions of security' (Barnes & Olonisakin 2011, p. 6).

Understanding of security's entanglement with gender need not be nebulous: there are actually ways to measure gendered insecurities. Mary Caprioli (2004, pp. 418–21) offers some practical gender equality measures. For example, personal and health security can be measured by assessing fertility rates, recorded rapes and births attended by health staff. Economic and political security can be measured by numbers of women in the labour force and in Parliament. To gauge levels of social and cultural security, data on education and literacy are needed. Human rights and democracy indicators include levels of human rights abuse. For many women, security is grounded in the immediate fulfilment of ordinary daily needs. Women cannot feel secure when they live in a context of gendered violence, face gender-based discrimination, live in poverty or are unaware of their human rights. The first recommendation of the Second International Women for Peace Conference, held in Dili, Timor-Leste, in 2009, was for an understanding that 'peace is not just the absence of war but also requires that people have food and shelter, are healthy, educated and secure' (Women for Peace 2009, p. 2). Conditions that enhance human security broaden the parameters of peacebuilding to include all practical measures needed to build peace with justice. Women's security is seldom a priority in efforts to reform, rebuild or rehabilitate security and justice systems. We attempt to show that through the UNSCRs under discussion, 'gender concerns have emerged as a legitimate and widely accepted normative framework of relevance to peace and security matters' (Tryggestad 2010, p. 168).

As feminists, we have an explicit commitment to emancipatory goals like gender justice, equality, human rights and sustainable peace with security. Realising these goals requires practical solutions for men and women that address root causes of insecurity and empower women in culturally appropriate ways. As Susan Pakoi from Bougainville says, '[e]very time they shout at me that I am trying to change custom I tell them that I am not trying to change custom; I am merely asking them to recognise women's rights' (in femLINKpacific 2008, p. 6). Those who stress human security as the context for empowerment tend also to adopt both a human rights and a human development framework. Goals of development are measured not in income per capita, but rather in terms of capacity development (Nussbaum 2000). 'In this sense, the Gender Development Index (GDI) is not a measure of gender inequality as such, but rather a human development measure that takes into account gender gaps in well-being.' An additional gender empowerment measure 'captures the extent of gender equality in economic and political power' (UNRISD 2005, p. 57). This contextual interpretation of human security is directed towards developing a holistic understanding of complex relationships and pays attention to the degrees of human suffering and ways to enhance equality, rights, development and justice.

To summarise, human security initiatives tackle the abusive power of individuals and structures that cause insecurity. They prioritise the protection and empowerment of individuals and their communities. They focus on the sources of people's insecurities by linking everyday life with broader political processes such as the role of the state and global governance structures, as well as non-state actors (Hudson 2005a). As Desmond Tutu writes, 'human security privileges people over states, reconciliation over revenge, diplomacy over deterrence, and multilateral engagement over coercive unilateralism' (in Mack 2005, p. iii). Within UN Security Council (UNSC) discourse, human security makes 'certain aspects of human rights and humanitarian concerns relevant to the peace and security agenda', and, thanks to UNSCR 1325, it has 'declared that attention to gender is integral to "doing security"' (Cohn, Kinsella & Gibbings 2004, pp. 135, 139).

Peacebuilding

The final common theme running through the following chapters is an explicitly expansive view on peacebuilding. There are different visions of peacebuilding in pre-conflict, conflict and post-accord transitional justice periods. What is typically called a liberal peace approach includes democratisation, economic liberalisation, neoliberal development, human rights and the rule of law (Richmond 2007). A peacebuilding from below approach is communitarian and stresses 'the importance of tradition and social context in determining the legitimacy and appropriateness of particular visions of political order, justice, or ethics' (Donais 2009, p. 6). We adopt broad understandings of peacebuilding that deal with everyday insecurities and also are more likely to recognise women's informal activities as peacebuilders. For example, one broad definition adopted throughout this book is that '[p]eacebuilding involves all processes that build positive relationships, heal wounds, reconcile antagonistic differences, restore esteem, respect rights, meet basic needs, enhance equality, instil feelings of security, empower moral agency and are democratic, inclusive and just' (Porter 2007, p. 34). This type of peacebuilding involves long-term, sustainable processes, and, consistent with holistic views on human security, the processes should be culturally sensitive. Such processes take into account cultural practices that respect equal rights and dignity.

A qualifier is needed. The terms 'post-conflict' and 'peacebuilding' frequently are paired. However, we suggest that 'post-conflict' is a problematic term; it implies the end of violence when combatants cease to engage officially in war. This period does not guarantee security when a culture of 'gendered violence is supported and legitimised by structural violence' (Caprioli 2004, p. 413). The conditions that contribute to an escalation of violence – 'fear and hatred, a criminalised economy that profits from violent methods of controlling assets, weak illegitimate states, or the existence of warlords and paramilitary groups – are often exacerbated during and after periods of violence' (Kaldor 2007, p. 185). Additionally, while peacekeeping operations (PKOs) are deployed to create and sustain security, as mentioned, we are too familiar with the reports that implicate some peacekeepers in the exploitative use or rape of local girls and women (Higate & Henry 2004). Nevertheless, we continue to use the term 'post-conflict' cautiously and with the reservations noted above, given its common usage in UN and government aid policies, simply to mean the period after violent conflict has ceased. This period can vary from being a momentary stage after which violence flares again to partial ceasefires with some groups and not with others, to agreed ceasefires between all parties and to the processes within a transitional justice period.

We prefer, however, to emphasise the ongoing processes that are intrinsic to peacebuilding. This endorses the recognition that countries emerging from armed conflict and ongoing violence have opportunities for transformative conditions in which to advance the human rights of women. Thus, the work of development and donor agencies offers real opportunities to promote gender equality.

For example, increasing women's participation in leadership positions and supporting economic livelihood programs do not merely advance gender equality, but also are part of the strategy for the prevention of violence that sustains peacebuilding processes. This is partially because when women can stand up for their right not to be violated, this in turn promotes conflict prevention work. Yet, the responsibility for change must not be placed solely on women's shoulders. A gendered approach recognises that women should be encouraged to stand up for their rights and men should be encouraged not to be silent on the implicit aggressiveness that is part of stereotypical masculinity. Adequate responses to the prevention of violence against women require concerted outcomes involving national governments, civil society, NGOs, international partners and men and women in local communities, with coordination across sectors in law and justice, health and education programs (AusAID 2009, pp. 5–6).

This book deals with the significant challenges that women face in demonstrating leadership in peace and security matters. Our emphasis highlights good practices of four active pillars that hold up the UNSCRs on 'women and peace and security', and we outline them accordingly:

- protecting women and girls from violence and preventing conflict;
- ensuring gender perspectives are included in multidimensional peacekeeping missions and in SSR;
- increasing participation of women in decision-making; and
- ensuring that there are gender-inclusive relief and recovery processes to mainstream gender and increase women's empowerment.

We acknowledge the multidisciplinary nature of transitional justice and peace initiatives, and contend that issues of peace, security, justice, truth, development and recovery in the fullest sense are intertwined. It makes a difference to peace and security when women participate in leadership.

CHAPTER 2

UN Security Council resolutions on 'women, peace and security'

In this chapter, two central issues are explored. First, we provide clarification on the content of the resolutions on 'women and peace and security' and contextualise these within significant UN conventions. Second, we provide a short, selective overview of several NAPs on UNSCR 1325 to date and offer a critical analysis on the importance of using indicators to evaluate successes in implementing these plans. Our central argument consolidates the point that these UNSCRs are not merely concerned with women's issues but are about inclusive peace and security. As we will see in the following chapters, 'women are crucial partners in shoring up three pillars of lasting peace: economic recovery, social cohesion and political legitimacy' (UNGA 2010, para. 7).

Why are resolutions on 'women, peace and security' significant?

With the overview given in the previous chapter of gendered insecurities in mind, why are UNSCRs on 'women and peace and security' significant? When talking about protecting women and girls and encouraging the participation of women in all aspects of peace processes, there are already significant related UN resolutions and conventions. For example, the Geneva Convention of 1949 and the Additional Protocols of 1977 are international treaties limiting the barbarity of war and protecting those who do not fight, such as civilians, medics and aid workers, and those who cannot fight, like the wounded, sick and prisoners of war. The Convention on the Elimination of All Forms of Discrimination against Women (CEDAW) (1979) and its Optional Protocol (UNGA 1999) define what constitutes discrimination against women and enables the CEDAW committee to hear cases of violations of rights brought by individuals against their states. The Beijing Platform for Action (BPFA) of 1995 combines rights and development.[1] It identifies twelve areas of 'critical concern' that remain stumbling blocks to women's progress: poverty, education and training, health, violence, armed conflict, economic considerations, power and decision-making, institutional mechanisms for the advancement of women, human rights, the media, the environment and the girl-child. The 'armed conflict' concern is foundational to this book, but we concentrate on the importance of women's 'power and decision-making' (Porter 2003). The MDGs of 2000 include the need to promote gender equality and empower women, which clearly are prerequisites to involving women in peace processes and decision-making. The Rome Statute of the International Criminal Court (ICC) of 2002 includes a series of court crimes of sexual and gender violence codified in international treaty: rape, sexual slavery, forced prostitution, forced pregnancy, enforced sterilisation and other forms of sexual violence. These crimes are listed as 'crimes against humanity' and 'war crimes' in international and internal armed conflicts. Gender-based persecution is also included as a crime against humanity, and trafficking as a crime of enslavement. The Statute provides the framework to deliver gender-inclusive justice.

In addition to these important international conventions, goals and statutes, global transnational activism is buoyant. The historical development of UNSCR 1325 is unusual because its achievement came through massive, determined lobbying by large NGOs who launched a global campaign called Women Building Peace: From the Village Council to the Negotiating Table (for background, see IANWGE n.d.; Porter 2007; Tryggestad 2009). Through the adoption of this unique resolution, the UNSC acknowledged for the first time the norm that women are vital to international peace and security. Member States no longer have an excuse to ignore women's roles in furthering peace and security.

Typically, for the sake of simplicity and accessibility, UNSCR 1325 was summarised as the 'three Ps': *prevention* of conflict, *protection* of women and girls during conflict and *participation* in peacekeeping (outside forces brought in to restore order), peacemaking (official ceasefires, mediations, roundtables and negotiations), peacebuilding (all processes that build trust, restore dignity and develop peace) and political decision-making (in law, government, police, defence and communities). Given UNSCR 1820 and then 1888, 1889 and 1960, these resolutions became conceptualised as constituting the 'four Ps', with the additional *prosecution* of gender-based war crimes.

While useful initially, the oversimplification of this message meant that the interrelationships between, say, prevention of conflict and prevention of sexual and gender-based violence (SGBV) were not fully grasped. Also, the issue of participation in peace processes cannot be adequately resolved by merely having any random woman at the table, since not all women have experience in women's rights movements. What matters is ensuring the participation of suitably experienced women who want to make a significant difference in all levels of conflict resolution and peacebuilding. The arguments made progressively throughout this book defend rights-based arguments that women should be included on an equal basis, but we also claim that women's inclusion is crucial in bringing different perspectives and 'the possibility of transformation for peace, political and social relations, and women's status' (Anderlini & Tirman 2010, p. 16). More recently, the UN documents have emphasised four central pillars to encapsulate these resolutions: prevention, participation, protection, and relief and recovery. The following chapters focus on these pillars.

These resolutions are used as a lobbying device for activists and as the basis for writing toolkits for practitioners and policy-makers (International Alert & Women Waging Peace 2004). They provide a framework to guide policies and programs to bring women to the foreground of the international security agenda. UNSCR 1325 has been translated into over 100 languages (for a list of these languages, see PeaceWomen n.d.). In fostering a regional women's media network of Fiji, Tonga, Bougainville and the Solomon Islands based around UNSCR 1325, femLINKpacific suggest that this resolution is a framework for making women and a gender perspective relevant to all aspects of peace and security. They suggest it should be used 'as a key to open doors into negotiations, as a loud hailer to have their voices heard, as a pen to inscribe their issues onto the agenda, as a mirror to hold up to governments to remind them of policy and budget commitments, and as a lens to help see security through women's eyes' (femLINKpacific 2008, p. 5). Consequently, they suggest it has started to change security thinking, particularly through increased collaboration between governments and civil society. Sanam Naraghi Anderlini (2007, p. 197) remarks that, 'in all likelihood, Council members were not fully aware of the way in which women's groups in civil society, governments, and the UN system would keep Resolution 1325 alive'.

What does this resolution say? UNSCR 1325 (UNSC 2000a) is an eighteen-paragraph resolution. It urges Member States to address the issue of furthering peace and security for women and girls, and to increase the 'representation of women at all levels of decision-making' to prevent, manage and resolve conflict (2000a, para. 1). It calls for mainstreaming of women's concerns and interests in all aspects of conflict management, peace negotiations, peace agreements, strategy documents, budgets, operational planning and all aspects of peacebuilding processes. This call is extremely expansive, encompassing all aspects of participation along the full continuum from peace processes to disarmament, demobilisation and reintegration (DDR) and the entire gamut of post-conflict reconstruction and peacebuilding work.

UNSCR 1325 seeks to rectify the systematic exclusion of women from peace negotiations and post-conflict reconstruction. It underscores that states have obligations to increase women's involvement in peace and security matters. Thus, the resolution marks an important recognition that women and gender concerns are relevant to peace and security, even if enforcement mechanisms are lacking. The preamble to the resolution expresses concern that 'civilians, particularly women and children, account for the vast majority of those adversely affected by armed conflict, including as refugees and internally displaced persons, and increasingly are targeted by combatants and armed elements' and reaffirms 'the important role of women in the prevention and resolution of conflicts and in peace-building'. As part of implementing UNSCR 1325, Elisabeth Rehn and Ellen Johnson Sirleaf were appointed by the UN to conduct an independent expert assessment on women, war and peace. They visited fourteen areas between 2001 and 2002, observing the violence that shatters lives before, during and after conflict. They write: 'In retrospect, we realise how little prepared we were for the enormity of it all, the staggering numbers of women in war who survived the brutality of rape, sexual exploitation, mutilation, torture, and displacement; the unconscionable acts of depravity; and the wholesale exclusion of women from peace processes' (Rehn & Johnson Sirleaf 2002, p. xi). They found that whether women were victims of gross atrocities, refugees, IDPs, combatants, heads of households, community leaders, activists or peacebuilders, 'women and men experience conflict differently' (2002, p. 2).

UNSCR 1820 builds on UNSCR 1325; it addresses victims of sexual violence during conflict and again emphasises the importance of having women in positions from which they can combat sexual violence.[2] The resolution stresses the necessity of taking 'effective steps to prevent and respond' to sexual violence as a way to contribute to international peace and security (UNSC 2008a, para. 1).

UNSCR 1888 builds on UNSCR 1820 by addressing the problem of SGBV as a weapon of war. It too seeks 'effective steps to prevent and respond' to acts of sexual violence as ways to contribute significantly to the maintenance of international peace and security and to bring perpetrators of sexual violence to justice and ensure that 'survivors have access to justice, are treated with dignity' and receive redress (UNSC 2009b, paras 1, 6). An emphasis is on 'criminal accountability, responsiveness to victims, and judicial capacity' (2009b, para. 8b).

UNSCR 1889 extends the earlier resolutions by emphasising the obligation to consider women as necessary agents for creating sustainable peace and security. Again, it seeks to 'increase women's participation in UN political, peacebuilding and peacekeeping missions' (UNSC 2009c, para. 4). Also, it spells out the requirement to gather information on women's needs in 'post-conflict planning, in order to improve system-wide response to those needs' (2009c, para. 6). These recommendations go some way to 'ensure gender mainstreaming in all post-conflict peacebuilding and recovery processes and sectors' (2009c, para. 8).

What wonderful resolutions! If they were fully implemented, evaluated and monitored, the situation of women and girls would be transformed. The successful implementation of these resolutions would act potentially as a deterrent to the prolonged horrors of human rights abuses and gross violations against women and girls. However, as we shall see in the following chapters, in many places, there is still remarkable ignorance of these resolutions, let alone implementation or evaluation. In the absence of enforcement mechanisms, the resolutions provide non-binding policy frameworks. The resolutions do recall binding obligations outlined earlier. Three significant impediments to the progress of these resolutions remain: 'the accountability gap, the information and analytical, and the implementation gap' (Butler, Mader & Kean 2010, p. 8).

Nevertheless, in concentrating on practical aspects of women's participation, it is worth underlining their unacknowledged informal contributions, highlighting instances of women's agency and the strength of their contributions as peacebuilders. UNSCR 1325 and its related resolutions 1820, 1888 and 1889 have been making a difference to women's lives since 2000, and we document good practices. It is true that UNSCR 1325 is widely criticised for conceptual gaps, failure of implementation and inadequate guidelines for application; however, at the first anniversary of the resolution, women from Afghanistan, Kosovo and East Timor told their stories and testified that the initiatives proposed in the resolution are meaningful. We write after the tenth anniversary, when significant progress is obvious in ways outlined in the following chapters. We argue that what is required is not more resolutions and conventions, but the full and effective implementation of UNSCR 1325 and its related resolutions.

The PeaceWomen Project of the Women's International League of Peace and Freedom traced the degree to which the UNSC internalised the thematic agenda of the resolutions over a ten-year period (Butler, Mader & Kean 2010). Specifically, the analysis assesses the language of country-specific resolutions and the extent to which they reflect the language and intent of UNSCR 1325.[3] The analysis shows that from 'the 432 resolutions monitored, 40.3 per cent have references to women and/or gender' (2010, p. 10), and that from these 174 resolutions, the most frequently addressed themes are peacekeeping, sexual exploitation and abuse, human rights and international humanitarian law and SGBV. The Project usefully documents extracts from resolutions that illustrate good practices as well as noting where there is no reference to gender.

An important qualification must be made. UNSCR 1820, adopted in 2008, recognises sexual violence as a security issue given that it affects the health and safety of women as well as the economic and social stability of nations. It urges protection and an end to impunity – the failure to bring perpetrators of human rights violations to justice. Impunity is the main reason for continuing violence against women in places like the DRC and Darfur in Sudan, and, in particular, the failure to arrest leaders who give orders and are responsible for those militias who carry out their orders. Increasingly, prosecution is seen as essential to justice, as a way to empower victims as survivors. 'Sexual violence threatens international peace and security when it constitutes a *crime of international concern*, is *commanded/condoned*, *civilians are targeted*, a *climate of impunity* prevails, it has *cross-border* implications and/or it entails a *ceasefire* violation' (Anderson 2010, p. 248).[4] We acknowledge the enormous problem of SGBV, in particular, violence against women (AusAID 2008b). However, we do not concentrate on this important area, except in Chapter 3, where attention to this type of gross women's rights abuse and human suffering is integral to improving the protection of women and girls. Rather, we provide evidence for successful examples of women's leadership and initiatives in peace and security matters, looking at both formal and informal participation in decision-making in conflict prevention, conflict resolution and peacebuilding.

National action plans

In 2004, the UNSC asked Member States to develop NAPs to demonstrate their implementation of UNSCR 1325. It is worth noting that the UNSC itself 'has not set a high standard. From 2000 to 2006, the Council referenced SCR 1325 in just 25.52 per cent of its country-specific resolutions' (Anderlini 2007, p. 192). All countries have differing strategic priorities they must consider and incorporate when developing a plan. For example, some European countries are implicated in assisting with different conflict zones, sometimes due to their post-colonial ties, and thus feel an obligation to focus on redeeming aspects of their colonialism. On the other hand, Colombia, Serbia, Israel and Fiji have integrated the mandates of UNSCR 1325 into policy and legislation. A brief summary of select NAPs highlights some striking features.[5]

At the time of writing, twenty-five NAPs have been released.[6] Denmark was the first to adopt its plan, in June 2005. This plan is focused on international PKOs and seeks to increase the balance in recruitment of staff to Danish defence forces, to protect women's and girls' rights in local areas where Danish troops are deployed and to increase the participation of women in peacebuilding and reconstruction in areas where there is a presence of Danish troops. The Danes have since revised their plan for 2008–13.

Rather than giving an outline of each NAP, we highlight Liberia's March 2009 plan as being of particular interest, given that Liberia has the first female Head of State in Africa, President Ellen Johnson Sirleaf. Liberia's plan had vast international support from UNIFEM[7] and the UNDP and donor support for implementation from Austria and Italy. Its formulation was conducted in a highly consultative, multi-stakeholder process. Liberia is in a post-conflict recovery phase and hence epitomises the principles and intent of UNSCR 1325. NAP is constructed on four pillars of protection, prevention, participation and empowerment, and the promotion of the Liberian

NAP. The Liberians highlight ten strategic issues, which reflect an equally clear approach to implementing the plan. Take, for example, a strategic issue such as the need for government provision of psychosocial trauma counselling for women and girls affected by gender-based violence committed during war. The Liberians wisely recommend the prioritisation of trauma training with outputs of trauma counselling policies developed and in practice, as well as measurable indicators of number and quality of policies, systems and procedures in place.

In the Asia-Pacific region, the Philippines launched its plan in March 2010, after it was initiated by civil society. Its NAP spells out some causes of conflict, including poverty, lack of education, discrimination of minority groups, poor governance, clan wars and injustices. It has clear indicators, timelines and actors responsible for the four goals on which it concentrates: protection against and prevention of violence; empowerment and participation; promotion of women and mainstreaming; and capacity development, monitoring and reporting.

Nepal adopted its plan in February 2011 after substantial regional consultation, including with women survivors of conflict-related violence and a push from civil society groups. Unlikely but useful partners in the process of developing the plan were the police and the Ministry of Defence. The Nepalese NAP outlines five pillars with corresponding objectives.

- Pillar 1 is 'participation' and 'aims to ensure the participation of women at all levels of decision-making, conflict transformation and peace processes'.
- Pillar 2 is 'protection and prevention' and 'focuses on ensuring the protection of women's and girls' rights and prevention of violations of these rights in conflict and post-conflict situations'.
- Pillar 3 is 'promotion', with 'the objectives to promote women and

girls' rights and mainstream gender perspectives in all aspects of conflict prevention, conflict resolution and peacebuilding'.
- Pillar 4 is 'relief and recovery' and 'addresses the specific needs of and ensures participation of women and girls in the design and implementation of all relief and recovery programs'.
- Pillar 5 is 'resource management and monitoring and evaluation', with the objective 'to institutionalise monitoring and evaluation and ensure required resources for the implementation of the NAP through collaboration and coordination of all stakeholders' (WUNRN 2011).

Each pillar and its objectives have corresponding strategic objectives, specific actions, desired results and indicators. Moreover, the NAP identifies the actors responsible for each objective and a timeframe for each action.

Critical evaluation

Many of these NAPs have come about 'largely due to the unrelenting advocacy of women's groups' (Anderlini & Tirman 2010, p. 31). The development of NAPs is important as a sign of a commitment by Member States. However, 'national action planning is delaying actual action' because 'governments claim credit for them but rarely are questioned or assessed on their implementation and impact' (2010, p. 4). Whether Member States have released a NAP, are in the process of doing so or have little intention of doing so, it is still important to try to evaluate the achievements of UNSCR 1325 and its sister resolutions. Importantly, do they really make a difference? Overall, it seems reasonable to conclude that while there has been strong support for UNSCR 1325 by knowledgeable NGOs, women's agencies in the UN and civil society groups, it has been poorly implemented. This gap between rhetoric and action has been identified by UNIFEM (2008a, p. 2) as the *accountability gap*. The resolutions have 'unleashed a bee-hive of activities mostly in the areas of operational and procedural reforms, staff training, system-wide planning and coordination and several review meetings' (Abugre 2008, p. 2). The Secretary-General has reporting obligations specified by UNSCR 1325 that keep the issue of implementation on the international agenda, but not necessarily on national agendas.

Charles Abugre (2008, pp. 3, 7) suggests three key reasons why the effect of UNSCR 1325 has been 'more words than deeds', or, as he aptly expresses it, why '1325 is at once everywhere – in countless conferences, websites, policy documents and official pronouncements – and yet nowhere substantively'.

- There are 'inadequate, inflexible and unpredictable financial resources to drive implementation. Accountability mechanisms are weak – concentrated in UN and donor-inspired talk-shops which produced it' but with few effective sanctions for non-performance (2008, p. 3). There remains a clear disconnection between what is happening on the ground and in UNSC debates. Also, in peacekeeping missions where there are violations of the resolutions, the UN is ineffective in accountability mechanisms. 'Every rape by a UN or humanitarian personnel that goes unpunished, every peace mission that has only a token presence of women, every unjust war waged on others justified by pretext, every demobilisation scheme that ignores the special needs of women undermine the long-term goals of 1325' (2008, p. 9).
- There are limitations in the resolution's wording to 'urge' and 'encourage', and only to the Secretary-General does it 'request'. Its formulation under Chapter VI of the UN Charter, which adopts noncoercive measures, means that it deals only with recommendations, and so the incentive to implement is weak.[8]
- There are external factors that impact on the effective implementation of UNSCR 1325. This resolution was 'to a large extent

a product of a then emerging new security agenda – the Human Security Agenda [– which] sought to formulate security as more than the absence of armed conflict to include the fulfillment of basic human rights', an agenda largely hijacked by the post–September 11 war on terror (2008, p. 4).

A significant shortcoming of UNSCR 1325 is that it 'does not directly address itself to the deep-seated issues at the root of gender inequality, including patriarchy, notions of masculinity and militarised power' (Olonisakin & Ikpe 2011, p. 225). Addressing structural roots of violence including gendered inequality is crucial in moving towards positive peace.

As will become clear throughout the chapters in this book, there are many weaknesses with these resolutions, in that, while the rhetoric is positive and promises much, often their implementation is weak and without adequate enforcement strategies. Without effective monitoring, actual progress is difficult to measure. The in-principle acceptance of resolutions like UNSCR 1325 does not necessarily flow to practice.

Also, many women who are involved in informal processes of peacebuilding are doing the work of the resolutions without being directly aware of it. This is significant. It shows that women with little or no knowledge of international conventions or resolutions still do much of the labour of these international commitments, albeit in informal, unacknowledged ways. It says something more. Women's work in informal peacebuilding reveals a systemic devaluing of reproductive labour, that is, the care and maintenance of families and communities, including voluntary work that ensures the well-being of communities. In not attracting an income, this type of work is not seen as productive labour in the way that men more typically are paid for their peace work as negotiators or diplomats. The resolutions make visible women's reproductive and community work and call for greater recognition of women's contributions, in monetary and symbolic ways.

Our focus in this book is specifically on assessing the efficacy of UNSCR 1325 in instigating positive change for peace and security. We are supporting Torunn Tryggestad's (2009, p. 541) claim that 'with the adoption of this resolution, a formal barrier was broken in terms of acknowledging a link between the promotion of women's rights and international peace and security – between traditionally soft sociopolitical issues and hard security'. Tryggestad (2009, p. 542) argues that new norms are emerging so that 'women, peace, and security has appeared as a normative issue that is increasingly difficult for member states to shun'. Given that women's issues traditionally are relegated to 'soft' policy not considered by the UNSC, 'the adoption of Resolution 1325 marked a change in its attitudes' (2009, p. 542). As the Secretary-General's report states, the tenth anniversary year of 2010 indicates 'that a plethora of activities ... lack a clear direction or time-bound goals and targets that could accelerate implementation and ensure accountability' (UNSC 2010a, para. 72). Evaluating the effectiveness of the implementation of UNSCR 1325 and its related sister resolutions is a fundamental goal of this book.

The *Global monitoring checklist on women, peace and security* (Onslow 2009) released by the UK organisation Gender Action for Peace and Security (GAPS)[9] highlights key achievements and challenges in Afghanistan, the DRC, Nepal, Northern Ireland and Sri Lanka. Their research reveals several cross-cutting trends.

- '[N]ational governments lack broad and deep understanding of substantive issues covered by UNSCR 1325, such as women and SSR, women and governance, women and legal reform, and women and peace negotiations' (2009, p. 147). Increasing the number of Gender Advisers is recommended in order to train

national government stakeholders, Parliamentarians, Ministers, civil servants and ambassadors.
- '[T]he impact of UNSCR 1325 implementation is difficult to establish given the lack of mechanisms to measure, monitor and evaluate progress on women, peace and security' (2009, p. 148). Clear gender-sensitive indicators are imperative.
- The absence of political leadership in advancing the women, peace and security agenda means that responsibility for UNSCR 1325 is 'being marginalised to under-funded gender Ministries, rather than being led by Ministries working on peace and security issues' (2009, p. 149). Clear lines of responsibility are warranted.
- Dedicated budget allocations are limited, and both government and donor funding should be tied specifically to the implementation of UNSCR 1325.
- Reliable data on violence against women are difficult to access, and the consolidation of such data is important. Women continue to be excluded from high-level discussions including peace negotiations, and thus GAPS recommend 'quotas of at least 33 per cent in negotiating teams, constitutional drafting committees and national and provincial parliaments' as well as financial support for female candidates for elections (2009, p. 152).
- Levels of impunity remain high, and prosecution and conviction of perpetrators are essential.

Despite this critical assessment, progress is occurring. Particularly in the lead-up to the tenth anniversary of the landmark UNSCR 1325, considerable global activity appeared. For example, during 2010, more than 1,500 women from conflict-affected countries met with senior UN leaders to participate in dialogues on conflict resolution and peacebuilding through Open Days on Women, Peace and Security.[10] The primary purpose of these days was to listen to women's views on how to improve the implementation of UNSCR 1325 and to deepen local ownership of the resolution. Despite differing contexts, three common priorities keep emerging: women talk of the need for increased political empowerment for women's engagement at all levels of decision-making; concerns with more effective justice, protection and security are paramount; and women stress the need for economic resources and aid to allocate sustainable financial resources to support women in recovery processes.

The tenth anniversary was used to press governments to make additional commitments to protect women during conflict, to increase their participation in peace processes and to demonstrate the validity of governments' commitments with policies, finances and monitoring (see PeaceWomen 2010). For example, Australia reaffirmed a commitment to ensuring protection in complex emergencies and enforcing zero tolerance for sexual abuse. Australia is also committed to promoting women to star rank in the military, and also to increasing numbers of women in the police force and ensuring that laws and national security frameworks protect women and girls in line with international obligations. A draft Australian NAP was released for consultation in August 2011; we hope this consolidates a political priority to strengthen women's roles in conflict prevention, resolution and peacebuilding as part of Australia's peace and security strategies.

As a resource in the lead-up to the UNSC debate on the tenth anniversary of UNSCR 1325, the *Cross-cutting report on women, peace and security* (UNSC 2010b) provides substantial evidence for significant progress that has been made, particularly in peace operations, the focus of Chapter 4. Also, the report of the Secretary-General at the tenth anniversary documents 'a detailed action plan aimed at changing practices among national and international actors and improving outcomes on the ground' (UNGA 2010, para. 6). This plan has seven commitments:

- promoting women's engagement in peace processes as part of conflict resolution (2010, para. 27);
- making peace agreements 'more systematically gender-responsive' (2010, para. 29);
- tracking UN funds for gender equality and women's empowerment (2010, para. 34);
- 'increasing the proportion of women civilians deployed to post-conflict environments' (2010, para. 37);
- 'increasing the proportion of women decision-makers in post-conflict governance institutions' (2010, para. 40);
- addressing the rule of law, and institutions that administer justice, determine legislative frameworks and provide security (2010, para. 45); and
- strengthening gender-responsive economic recovery (2010, para. 49).

Another significant indication of progress is the new UN Entity for Gender Equality and Empowerment of Women – known as UN Women – which began in 2011.[11] It amalgamated four agencies: UNIFEM, the UN Division for the Advancement of Women (UNDAW), the Office of the Special Adviser on Gender Issues and the UN International Research and Training Institute for the Advancement of Women (UN-INSTRAW).[12] Michelle Bachelet, former President of Chile, heads it as Under-Secretary-General. It has four main pillars of work: normative, legal and political; implementation at country level; a mainstreaming agenda; and the active involvement of women. Its tasks are to work to overcome gender discrimination, promote empowerment and achieve equality between women and men. In the peace and security area, UN Women works on three issues: strengthening women's participation in decision-making, ending sexual violence and impunity, and providing an accountability system. UNIFEM was the UN's lead agency on implementing UNSCR 1325 and had a positive track record of being innovative and collaborative in working with civil society groups. It was a small development organisation. It is the hope of many that this new UN Entity, UN Women, with an enhanced budget will prove to be highly effective.

Another indicator of progress is concrete work on indicators. The Technical Working Group on Global Indicators for UNSCR 1325 initiated a comprehensive mapping exercise that yielded more than 2,500 indicators. This initial set was reviewed and a short list developed. In April 2010, the Secretary-General released twenty-six proposed indicators. Indicators signify priorities. If results are not measured, success cannot be distinguished from failure. The indicators embody a concept typically used in project management called SMARTER, which reminds policy-makers to be focused on policies that are specific, measurable, attainable, relevant, tracked, evaluated and reassessed. Indicators are meant to drive processes towards results that are monitored and evaluated regularly and consistently. The indicators cover the four main pillars: protection, prevention, participation, and relief and recovery. In October 2010, the global indicators were endorsed.

Indicators are crucial, but they are not enough. There is a need for leadership within the UNSC to state that it will regularly address these issues. Despite ten years of policy development and research, good practices have not yet become what they should be, namely, standard practices. Indicators should be contextualised, so that tracking takes into account particular circumstances. For example, in some places, there may be few women elected to Parliament, but there may be substantial democracy training and capacity development skills workshops that prepare women to have the confidence and knowledge to stand for election.

It is pertinent to ask whether indicator reporting is realistic for countries in conflict when the priority is to meet basic needs such as obtaining food, water, shelter and security. There are many obstacles for countries in conflict to committing to monitor and evaluate these types of resolutions. When there is political instability, the support mechanisms for data collection are not clear, and institutions are weak. Member States may be perpetrators and parties to conflict and so are unlikely to give honest responses; indeed, they may use data selectively, choosing to ignore that which is deemed inconvenient. For instance, numbers of women in Parliament may be cited, but failures to prosecute government-sanctioned human rights abuses omitted. The suspicion is that less than a full picture is often presented. Moreover, target groups such as security forces and police may be unwilling to provide accurate data. Some civil society groups may not feel safe to report, knowing the likely repercussions of being targeted when they give accurate information. Indeed, access to accurate information is usually problematic given the difficulties of data collection where mobility and communications may be non-existent or cut off. Data may be collected in urban areas but not in rural regions, where the heaviest conflict often exists. We acknowledge these difficulties but argue that evaluation is important to give as clear a picture as possible of differing contexts in order to know how to address root causes of injustice, inequality and insecurity.

To conclude, there are some who argue that, ultimately, 'UNSCR 1325 is not radical enough to be used as a transformative gender mainstreaming tool' (Barrow 2009, p. 51). What Amy Barrow means by this is that gender mainstreaming can adopt an integrationist model of 'add women and stir approach', or it can be transformative, with 'the adoption of an agenda-setting mainstreaming model' (2009, p. 66). The International Civil Society Action Network and the MIT Centre for International Studies conducted a six-country field study, returning to interview women in conflict zones to see the actual impact of UNSCR 1325 in those countries (Anderlini & Tirman 2010).[13] Their key findings are pertinent. 'Many governments, UN personnel and civil society organisations are still unaware of, or misunderstand, UNSCR 1325', and this haphazard understanding 'is crippling effective implementation' (2010, p. 3). Given that 'outreach, consultation with and inclusion of women's voices is not part of the standard operating procedures of governments or mediators involved in peace processes', this means that Member States continue to fail in including 'women and their perspectives in a sustained and substantial manner' (2010, p. 3). When women are included, it is usually because of women's lobbying or the presence of Gender Advisers who encourage participation. Those who have wreaked violent havoc gain access to peace talks and 'tend to focus on ceasefires, political arrangements and conflict management' without 'seeking a comprehensive peace' (2010, p. 4). Women's active participation is crucial. 'The message of "women build peace" is transformative, empowering, and can gain traction, yet it is the least common message conveyed by many UNSCR 1325 advocates' (2010, p. 5). We proceed to develop arguments that demonstrate how women's active participation in building peace and security transforms the possibilities for sustainable peace.

CHAPTER 3

Protecting women and girls from violence, and preventing conflict

To transform eloquent commitments on protecting women and girls from violence into concrete strategies, a proactive approach to dealing with conflict is essential. Such an approach calls for holistic responses that go beyond bringing perpetrators of violence to justice, important as this is, and includes preventing conflicts and establishing a just social and political order, without which there can be no lasting peace and stability. In this chapter, we maintain that a gender-responsive framework for protection must be founded on a rights-based model that affirms the rights of women and girls (in addition to men and boys) not to be violated and to be protected from all types of violence. This model unequivocally denounces granting impunity by not prosecuting those who violate human rights and commit acts of violence against women and girls (and also against men and boys). It also underscores the desirability for a whole-of-government approach that brings relevant stakeholders to the table in designing, planning, implementing and monitoring initiatives that are aimed at preventing conflicts and protecting women and girls.

We begin by briefly examining the concept of protection and explaining how it is intrinsic to human security before moving on to focus attention on what this means for the protection of women and girls. We explore how UNSCRs 1325, 1820, 1888 and 1889 articulate the requirement to protect women and girls. Next, we highlight the tensions between precept and practice, that is, Member States' seeming commitment to the fine principles of protection and prevention rarely being matched by concerted strategies of implementation. There follows a discussion on what constitutes effective protection, where a dual focus on providing access to justice and preventing conflicts is emphasised. The chapter concludes by identifying remaining challenges. A central argument flows through each section: prevention of conflict is the most crucial dimension of protection. Thus, promoting peace and security is a long-term strategy towards strengthening protection.

Framing protection in resolutions

How protection is defined depends on how the concept of security is framed. Most often, the stark reality of violence leads the concept of protection to be framed in terms of protecting civilians (men, women and children) from genocide, war crimes, ethnic cleansing and crimes against humanity. However, there are other gender-specific threats that contribute to the vulnerability of women and girls during conflict and post-conflict reconstruction, such as forced recruitment into armed combat, forced displacement or return, restriction of movement and lack of access to land, markets, jobs, education and basic needs (Swithern & Hastie 2009). This vulnerability is compounded by many women being catapulted into traditionally male-dominated political and economic spheres in order to ensure their survival and that of their families (Anderlini 2005). A *human security approach to protection* takes into account multiple threats and frames the concept of protection in terms of a rights-based discourse. This framework affirms the 'full respect for the rights of the individual in accordance with the letter and spirit of the relevant bodies of law, that is, human rights law, international humanitarian law and refugee law' (Giossi Caverzasio 2001, p. 19). Such an approach to protection and to the respect for human rights is relevant also to men and boys.

How then is protection of women and girls from violence framed in UN conventions and resolutions? For more than a decade, the issue of protection in times of conflict and during post-conflict reconstruction has garnered national and international attention. In 1998, then Secretary-General Kofi Annan, for the first time, addressed the need to protect civilians during conflict, calling it a 'humanitarian imperative' (UNGA 1998, pp. 11–12), and acknowledged that women suffer disproportionately in such situations. This Declaration reflects years of advocacy dating back to 1969 when the Commission on the Status of Women raised the issue of special protection for women and children during armed conflict and emergencies. This was followed, in 1974, by the UN General Assembly (UNGA) adopting the Declaration on the Protection of Women and Children in Emergency and Armed Conflict. Subsequent declarations, such as the 1993 Declaration on the Elimination of Violence against Women and the 1995 BPFA (which identified women and armed conflict as one of twelve critical areas of concern), reiterated the need to address women's vulnerability during conflict. Agreed conclusions on women and armed conflict in reports of the Special Rapporteur on Violence against Women, whose mandate includes the violations of women's human rights in situations of armed conflict, and those of other Special Rapporteurs on the former Yugoslavia, Rwanda and the DRC, the Special Rapporteur on Torture and the 1998 Commission on the Status of Women,[1] have contributed to the growing understanding of the complexity of women's and girls' experiences during conflict (for a more complete chronology, see IANWGE n.d.). Subsequently, UNSCRs 1265 and 1296 repeatedly expressed their concern over 'the hardships borne by civilians during armed conflict, in particular as a result of acts of violence directed against them, especially women, children and other vulnerable groups' (UNSC 2000b, preamble). They stressed the 'importance of fully addressing their special protection and assistance needs in the mandates of peacemaking, peacekeeping and peace-building operations' (UNSC 2000b, para. 9).

Much of the work on protecting women and girls draws on the 'responsibility to protect' (R2P) framework, first articulated by the International Commission on Intervention and State Sovereignty (ICISS) in 2000.[2] In its report titled *The responsibility to protect*, the ICISS (2001, p. 67) envisioned protection as a 'continuum of intervention, which begins with preventive efforts and ends with the responsibility to rebuild'. The concept and practice of R2P was embraced formally by the UNGA at the 2005 world summit and accepted by the UNSC in 2006. Gareth Evans explains how it encompasses three elements:

- The *responsibility to prevent* addresses 'both the root causes and direct causes of internal conflict and other ... crises putting populations at risk'.
- The *responsibility to react* refers to the obligation 'to respond to situations of compelling human need with appropriate measures'.
- The *responsibility to rebuild* states presupposes the duty to provide 'full assistance with recovery, reconstruction, and reconciliation, addressing the causes of the harm the intervention was designed to halt or avert' (Evans 2008, p. 41).

Alex Bellamy (2009, p. 3) in his book *Responsibility to protect* suggests that R2P was initially conceived 'as a way of guiding policy-makers in their deliberations about whether or not to respond to ... mass atrocities with non-consensual military intervention'. R2P must be approved multilaterally through the UNSC. It must be consistent with just war theory (Walzer 1977). *Jus ad bellum*, 'the justice of war', refers to the right to use force and go to war. It includes prerequisites like just cause for military intervention, legitimate authority sanctioned by the UNSC, right intention, proportional means that respect international law, last resort and a reasonable prospect of success and eventual peace. *Jus in bello*, 'the justice in war', refers to limitations on conduct in war to spare non-combatants, and includes prerequisites like proportionality of means and non-combatant protection. The issue of non-combatant immunity is particularly important given that there tends to be ninety civilian deaths to every ten military losses, a reversal from World War I statistics (Kegley & Blanton 2010, p. 509). With the changes in battlefields to everyday living areas such as marketplaces and villages, a reason why R2P is pertinent to this chapter is that *'prevention is the single most important dimension of the responsibility to protect'* (Evans 2008, p. 41, italics in original). Too often, protection and prevention are not adequately linked. Our basic argument throughout this chapter is that protection and prevention are inherently connected.

This broad human security view of protection is embedded in the UNSCRs on 'women and peace and security' (1325, 1820, 1888 and 1889, as well as 1960). R2P's principles 'to prevent' and 'to react' are reflected in UNSCR 1325's focus on the necessity of protecting women and girls from gender-based violence by ending impunity (the assumption that SGBV will go unpunished), prosecuting perpetrators of violence and excluding the granting of amnesty for crimes against humanity. R2P's principle 'to rebuild' is reflected in the attention given by the resolution to considering a gender perspective when negotiating and implementing peace agreements, supporting local women's peace initiatives and indigenous processes, and adopting measures that respect the human rights of women and girls as they relate to the constitution, electoral system, police and judiciary.

Building on this resolution and continuing to adopt a holistic framework for protection, UNSCRs 1820 focuses on sexual violence during conflict and reiterates the requirements to exclude sexual violence crimes from amnesty provisions in conflict resolution processes and to end impunity by prosecuting persons responsible for such acts. In addition, this resolution calls for implementing zero tolerance standards towards all forms of sexual violence in UN peacekeeping missions and increasing the number of women police and peacekeepers deployed in UN missions. Recognising that prevention is as important as dealing with the immediate consequences of conflict, the resolution calls for consultations with women and women-led organisations to develop effective mechanisms to protect women in refugee camps as well as in DDR and in justice and SSR.

The more recent UNSCRs 1888 and 1889 raise concerns over obstacles that prevent the active and meaningful participation of women in conflict prevention and resolution and in participation in post-conflict public life, which, as UNSCR 1889 (UNSC 2009c, para. 8 italics in original) states, occur

> as a result of violence and intimidation, lack of security and lack of rule of law, cultural discrimination and stigmatisation, including the rise of extremist or fanatical views on women, and socio-economic factors including the lack of access to education, and in this respect, *recognising* that the marginalisation of women can delay or undermine the achievement of durable peace, security and reconciliation.

Together, these resolutions call for holistic national approaches to address sexual violence in armed conflict, through criminal accountability, responsiveness to victims, building judicial capacity and including a women's protection adviser among Gender Advisers and human rights protection units in the UN Department of Peacekeeping Operations (UNDPKOs).

Precept versus practice

While in principle an interdependent approach to human security and protection is accepted widely by UN bodies, liberal democratic governments and humanitarian aid organisations, there appears to be an unresolved tension between precept and practice. Accepting in principle the validity of these resolutions and the necessity of attending to the protection broadly envisaged is easy. In practice, there appears to be a much narrower interpretation of protection, which is largely restricted to mitigating women's and girls' experiences of violence, especially sexual violence (Anderlini 2005). Vasuki Nesiah (2006) points out that throughout the 1990s, the focus was on ending impunity for acts of violence against women by reforming local national and international judicial and legal systems. At the international level, efforts were made to ensure that the Geneva Conventions included rape as a grave breach of its provisions and to reform the Rome Statute of the ICC to recognise rape, sexual slavery, enforced prostitution, pregnancy, sterilisation and other forms of sexual violence as crimes against humanity and as war crimes (Bedont & Hall-Martinez 1999).

There are two notable international war crimes prosecutions on rape. Historically, war rape was categorised as a crime against the honour and property of men, rather than a crime of violence against women. In the International Criminal Tribunal for the former Yugoslavia, evidence of sexual violence was not being treated as seriously as other crimes. Women did not talk about rape, the shame of their abuse was so deeply felt, and many knew their rapists. Yet, it was clear that the practice of impulsive and individualised rape as a spoil of war had moved to a strategic course of action of forced abductions and systematic gang rapes, particularly of Bosnian Muslim women, for reasons of humiliation, ethnic impregnation and, consequentially, the destruction of family structures. A female member of the Trial Chamber, Judge Odio Benito, challenged the Prosecutor after submissions came from women's organisations. Her interpretation, based on a case of two Serbian women raped in the Čelebići detention camp, was instrumental in rape and other sexual assaults being considered as torture. In the Kunarac case,[3] rape was defined as a violation of sexual autonomy, an element of torture. This was the first indictment in which the crime of sexual enslavement was charged as enslavement, that is, either a war crime and a form of torture (not just an attack on the honour of women) or as a crime against humanity. It expanded the definition of rape to encompass all situations in which consent is not freely, voluntarily given. A subsequent Foča judgment set the second precedent in international criminal law, in prosecuting rape as a crime against humanity. The trial shed light on the large-scale, systematic sexualised assault on Muslim women and on the role this violence played in the war in Bosnia and Herzegovina.

In the International Criminal Tribunal for Rwanda (ICTR), 'rape formed no part of the first series of ICTR indictments' (Copelon 2000, p. 224). The international women's human rights movement mobilised to support the election of female judges and to prevent harassment of witnesses. Changes occurred when Judge Navanethem Pillay, the only female judge in the Tribunal Trial Chamber, was hearing a case and pursued her inquiry with two women who were called to testify to other crimes. A witness's testimony linked Akayesu, a politician from the Mouvement Démocratique Républicain who served as mayor of the Taba commune, where many Tutsis were killed, to rapes. The Akayesu case was a landmark in that it was 'the first international conviction for genocide, the first judgment to recognise rape and sexual violence as constitutive acts of genocide, and the first to advance a broad definition of rape as a physical invasion of a sexual nature' (2000, p. 227). This case emphasised the ethnic targeting of Tutsi women, showing that wartime rape and sexual violence can constitute acts of genocide aimed at destroying a group. The most powerful woman in the pre-genocide Rwandan government, Pauline Nyiramasuhuko, the national Minister of Family and Women's Affairs in 1994, ordered civilian death squads to rape Tutsi women. She was the first woman to be charged with rape as a crime against humanity.

UN administrative issuances, such as the Special Measures for Protection from Sexual Exploitation and Abuse[4] and the Observance by UN Forces of International Humanitarian Law, now adopt a zero tolerance policy to sexual violence. To strengthen the international community's response to sexual violence during conflict, UNSCRs 1888 and 1889 call for the appointment of a Special Representative on sexual violence and armed conflict. This call has received support from international conferences such as the International Colloquium in Liberia of March 2009, which recommended, among other things, annual reporting on UNSCR 1820 and systematic data collection on sexual violence in conflict.

At local and national levels, attention is often directed towards establishing gender-responsive judicial systems. This involves reforming legal norms and standards and the manner in which judicial proceedings are conducted to ensure greater sensitivity to women victims. While these efforts are instrumental in drawing attention to significant protection problems in times of conflict, sexual violence is only one aspect of women's experiences during conflicts (Gardam 1997). The tendency to focus on this experience to an extent that other experiences that also have a grave impact on women and girls are neglected results in inadequate responses to the complex needs of women and girls during conflict. The argument repeated in this chapter is that a commitment to precepts of protection and prevention has to translate to a commitment to provide resources and strategies, and a concerted effort to fulfil promises to protect from all types of violence and to prevent further conflict.

Ensuring effective protection and prevention of conflict

Again, we reiterate the central argument of this chapter, that the prevention of conflict is the most crucial dimension to the protection of women and girls. Judith Gardam and Hilary Charlesworth (2000) point to the complex nature of women's vulnerability during conflict and post-conflict reconstruction. There are many examples of this vulnerability. When women and girls are combatants and prisoners of war, their experiences differ from those of men and boys. Women with poor education and training face significant economic hardships resulting from assuming the role of primary income earner. Women and girls are often mistreated in refugee camps, and their reproductive role makes them vulnerable to shortages in medicine and basic hygiene products. A shortage of food, compounded by cultural factors in which preference is given to men and boys, makes women and girls vulnerable to malnutrition. Most significantly, the exclusion of women from post-conflict decision-making processes means that many of these issues remain unaddressed during the reconstruction and recovery phases.

To address these complex vulnerabilities, the ICRC has held detailed interagency discussions on protection and posits a model that highlights the different spheres of action, gravitating outwards from immediate needs to long-term prevention (Giossi Caverzasio 2001).

- The sphere of *'responsive action'* aims to stop, prevent or alleviate the worst effects of the abuses.
- The *'remedial action'* sphere focuses on helping people to recover by assisting and supporting them while they live with the subsequent effects of a particular pattern of abuse.

- *'Environment-building action'* centres around building political, social, cultural and institutional norms that are conducive to protection (Slim & Bonwick 2005, p. 42).

There are significant overlaps between the spheres, but, in simple terms, ensuring *effective protection* for women and girls involves providing access to justice and adopting a long-term approach that addresses structural inequities and prevents further conflicts.

Providing access to justice

Protection and gender justice are linked intricately in achieving peace and security (Mazurana et al. 2002). Since 'injustice is not just a *consequence* of conflict, but is also a *symptom and cause* of conflict' (Mani 2002, p. 25, italics in original), there can be no meaningful peace if attempts are not made to pursue the achievement of gender justice. An extensive view of justice 'builds recognition of difference and responsiveness to individuated needs, as well as the protection of the rights of difference into its basic conception' (Gould 1996, p. 180). Thus, injustices that occur as a result of conflict must be redressed, the rule of law reinstated and concerted attempts made to strive for distributive justice to address ongoing causes of structural and systemic injustice (Gould 1996).

Much attention is paid to transitional justice mechanisms and their potential to provide justice for human rights violations committed during conflict. 'Transitional justice refers to the short-term and often temporary judicial and non-judicial mechanisms and processes that address the legacy of human rights abuses and violence during a society's transition away from conflict' (Anderlini, Conaway & Kays 2004, p. 1). Transitional justice mechanisms are meant to serve a dual purpose of ensuring accountability for human rights violations and creating a space for reconciliation. Transitional justice confronts past violations of human rights and seeks new, just, social, political and legal arrangements. Its mechanisms include trials, truth commissions, reparations, judicial reforms, amnesty, disarmament and reconciliation (Mantilla 2006, p. 6). Each context differs in terms of the causes of violations and thus the justice that ensues. However, each different conflict-affected country shares a background of widespread violence, human rights violations, destruction and trauma. Typically, most people share the desire for sustainable peace with justice in which all citizens enjoy dignified lives that can be lived free from fear or suffering.

One significant part of a transitional justice process is a truth commission, which listens to victims' stories, uncovers injustices otherwise silenced or denied and complements formal judicial processes. Primary objectives vary in different states, as reflected, for example, in emphases on national reconciliation in Chile, criminal justice in Argentina, dignity of victims in Peru, consolidation of peace and democracy in the DRC and reconciliation between victims and perpetrators in Timor-Leste (Freeman 2006, p. 33). There have been many truth commissions, including those held in Algeria (2003), Argentina (1983), Bolivia (1982), Chad (1990), Chile (1990), the DRC (2003), Ecuador (1996 and 2007), El Salvador (1992), Germany (1992), Ghana (2003), Guatemala (1997), Haiti (1995), Kenya (2009), Liberia (2006), Morocco (2004), Nigeria (1999), Panama (2001), Paraguay (2004), Peru (2001), Rwanda (1999), Serbia and Montenegro (2002), Sierra Leone (2002), the Solomon Islands (2009), South Africa (1995), South Korea (2000), Timor-Leste (2002), Uganda (1974 and 1986) and Uruguay (2000) (US Institute of Peace 2011).

Successive truth and reconciliation commissions have made progress in adopting a gender lens to their work, moving from proceedings of the early truth commissions in Latin America, in which gender concerns were invisible, to including 'women's hearings, dedicated gender units and international technical support as well as a broader and more gendered definition of their mandate and harms covered' (Valji 2007, p. 8). As Vasuki Nesiah (2006, p. 3) maintains, 'recent commissions have taken three broad approaches'.

- Commissions like Ghana's stated that they adopted gender mainstreaming; but 'without a focal point and a designated staff to address related issues, gender can become invisible' (2006, p. 3). For gender mainstreaming to be meaningful, gender must become an active, ongoing, analytical and organisational tool.
- The Peruvian commission established a special unit tasked with a focus on gender, but this 'did not permeate the other units' everyday functioning' (2006, p. 4).
- The third approach requires broad political support and involves 'treating gender as a crosscutting theme as well as a specific-focus area' (2006, p. 4), as was the case in Timor-Leste, with a focus not simply on sexual violence but 'on a multifaceted understanding of women's experience of human rights abuse' (2006, p. 5).

The Commission for Reception, Truth and Reconciliation in Timor-Leste (CAVR) is discussed in greater detail in Chapter 7, but a brief summary is relevant here because of its special attention on redressing the lack of protection of women and girls during the Timorese conflict. It includes mechanisms to enable criminal prosecutions of perpetrators, for example, the Serious Crimes Unit and the Special Panel for Serious Crimes set up in Timor-Leste. A long-term approach to justice involves SSR aimed at transforming the military, police, judiciary and related institutions (Anderlini, Conaway & Kays 2004). CAVR (2005) demonstrates how gender and women's issues can be integrated into truth commissions. Prior to establishing the Commission, women were consulted during the design and the selection of its members, which included two women as national commissioners. Attempts were made to create gender-balanced district teams, and women-only community discussions were held in subdistricts. One of the eight national public hearings held focused discussions on women. A special six-month research project on women and conflict was funded to document the experiences of female victims. The findings of the research are mentioned in CAVR's final report. Two key women's organisations were also involved in the design and delivery of CAVR's collective reparation program. The establishment of a Victim Support Division that conducted healing workshops and an urgent reparations program put victims at the centre of the Commission's work. Despite all these efforts, in some local women's assessment, while clearly there were efforts to boost a gender balance during CAVR's processes, 'women's participation in the CAVR was moderate... in general, women's participation was better in activities coordinated by the national office that had strict quotas for women, such as the national public hearings and healing workshops' (Wandita, Campbell-Nelson & Leong Pereira 2006, p. 296).

In addition to truth commissions, ensuring ongoing access to justice necessitates reforming the security sector at the national and local levels. Such access is crucial both as means of protection and as means to prevent further conflict. In the Solomon Islands, the Regional Assistance Mission to Solomon Islands (RAMSI) Law and Justice Program (supported by AusAID) provides training and mentoring to local lawyers and supports the Public Solicitor's Office to host free legal clinics (AusAID 2009). In addition, the Solomon Islands Law Reform Commission (LRC) broadcasts a series of programs to introduce people living in villages to the work of the Commission and to themes related to criminal law, including the nature of criminal law, corruption, gender-based violence and the penal code. As part of reaching out to the community, LRC lawyers attend community outreach programs run by RAMSI to explain in Pijin the relationship between the Solomon Islands' constitution and other laws such as *mami*, or 'the mother', law (Kabui & Guthleben 2008).

Similarly, in Nepal, the National Judicial Academy adopted a resolution in 2006 to mainstream gender issues in its policy and practice, as part of ongoing legal reforms, by integrating gender issues into the standard training required for all lawyers and judges. The curriculum, developed with support from the UNDP's Mainstreaming Gender Equity Programme, focuses on gender equality and justice. It aims to build the capacity of legal workers to analyse critically the legal provisions related to gender issues and to familiarise them with international women's and human rights instruments to which Nepal is a signatory (UNDP 2006). Part of this effort includes support from the UNDP to compile reference materials for the training to help the judges and lawyers to refer to judgments relating to gender justice and women's rights.

The value of investing in efforts to reform and strengthen the formal justice sector cannot be underestimated in terms of the increased opportunity of protecting women and girls through preventing further conflict. However, access to these systems is often expensive and beyond the reach of women in rural and remote areas. Traditional justice systems, often the first port of call for many women, are usually ill equipped to cope with gender-based crimes. In a post-conflict context, these crimes are in reality often dealt with by traditional mechanisms (da Costa 2006). Nagorik Uddyog, an NGO in Bangladesh, recognising the importance of *shalish*, an indigenous mediation system, works to transform the system so that it is more sensitive to gender-based crimes. The organisation assists in the formation of *shalish* committees, in which one-third of the members are women. Intensive capacity development programs are organised for members of the committee on a range of laws that are relevant to women's rights (Wojkowska 2006). Recognising the significant role that traditional justice systems play in enabling restorative justice, PNG's National Law and Justice Policy and Plan of Action 2000 clearly articulates its commitment to 'placing restorative and community-based law and justice programs at the centre of all future law and justice reforms' (McDonald 2008, p. 23). The ability of these systems to provide gender justice depends on the extent to which their capacity is built through training, institutional support and legal reform. These efforts must be supplemented by the establishment of a referral system to the police, juvenile justice officers and the higher courts (Garap 2005).

Supporting reforms to judicial systems involve reforms to policing, especially attempts to promote women's participation in policing. Such efforts include establishing specific police units to manage sexual violence against women and girls. In Afghanistan, the UN Population Fund (UNFPA) supports the establishment of family response units within the Afghan National Police, which are staffed by Afghan policewomen trained in dealing with issues of violence against women. As part of its UNSCR 1325 NAP, the Netherlands allocated a special fund for training police officers in Afghanistan; Dutch staff within the European Police Office provided training to Afghanistan's national police on dealing with women victims of violence and women prisoners prior to withdrawing from Afghanistan (Majoor & Brown 2008). Another example of efforts to reform policing is the establishment of police stations staffed entirely by women, such as those found in Timor-Leste, India and the Philippines (Clegg, Hunt & Whetton 2000). These women-only police stations have a specific mission to deal with SGBV crime. According to Megan Bastick, Karin Grimm and Rahel Kunz (2007, p. 147), 'the inclusion of women police officers has concrete operational advantages, not least because women and girls who have suffered sexual violence often prefer to report such crimes to a female police officer, to effect broad institutional change and to challenge the dominant "masculine" environment'.

Access to justice, whether formal or traditional, often hinges on the availability of and access to affordable support services. Women and girls who suffer gender-based violence often are unwilling or unable to report the crimes committed. Shame, stigma, ignorance of options and poverty inhibit the reporting of such crimes. Where services are available, they vary from medical treatment to psychological and legal counselling and also to informal support. Other support services to women who have suffered through violent conflict are important. For instance, Women for Human Rights, an NGO in Nepal, provides temporary living spaces, psychosocial counselling, and legal and medical services, as well as microcredit loans for income generation activities, to women who are widowed as a result of the conflict between the Maoists and the military.

Adopting a more integrated approach, the National Department of Health in PNG, in addition to developing clinical and medicolegal guidelines for primary healthcare providers on dealing with rape, set up Stop Violence Centres to provide 'medical assistance, counselling, referrals and legal support to women who have experienced violence' (AusAID 2009, p. 39). The Centres are linked with the Sexual Offences Squad of the Royal PNG Constabulary to assist women in lodging complaints through the formal court system. Another aspect of PNG's efforts to provide access to support services is the establishment of the Fmali Seif, a free hotline to be used by women in crisis. A call to the hotline is responded to by sending a team to transport the vulnerable caller to a safe location (usually a police station or hospital). This innovative project is funded by AusAID as part of the Yumi Lukautim Mosbi project in partnership with Digicel and G4S Secure Solutions (PNG) Limited (AusAID 2009).

With respect to the conduct of the military, militias, paramilitaries and sometimes peacekeepers, a contentious issue remains: granting impunity for violations of human rights, specifically the rights of women and girls. Typically, either such crimes are taken for granted as part of war and therefore ignored in peace negotiations, or impunity is offered as a concession to bring combatants to the peace table. In order to deal with institutionalised attitudes towards violence against women, national governments seek to establish and revise codes of conduct for peacekeeping personnel, including a zero tolerance policy on sexual abuse and prostitution. Accordingly, many of the NAPs on UNSCR 1325 include elements such as establishing codes of conduct that foster a zero tolerance culture on sexual abuse and prostitution. For instance, in Belgium, serious violations of international humanitarian law (genocide, crimes against humanity and crimes of war) are incorporated into the country's criminal law. Another common initiative undertaken nationally by countries that provide peacekeeping forces includes training and awareness-raising for all personnel who participate in peace and humanitarian operations. The training includes instruction on the importance of the protection of women and girls and consequent disciplinary action when warranted and, if applicable, criminal proceedings in the case of violations.

Addressing structural inequities and preventing conflicts

Women's ability to participate in and acquire the power to exercise control over decision-making processes at the family, community, national and international levels is vital to achieving women's empowerment and addressing the structural gendered inequities that perpetuate marginalisation. The issue of participation as a means of addressing structural inequities is discussed in Chapter 5. Suffice to say here that existing discriminatory practices and differences in rights and entitlements that exist prior to conflict significantly impact on the manner in which men and women are affected by conflict (Aguirre & Pietropaoli 2008; Chinkin 2003a; Gardam & Charlesworth 2000). Recognising this, UNSCR 1325 (UNSC 2000a, para. 2) calls for 'an increase in the participation of women at decision-making levels in conflict resolution and peace processes' and 'measures that support local women's peace initiatives and indigenous processes for conflict resolution, and that involve women in all of the implementation mechanisms of the peace agreements'. In addition, CEDAW (1979, Article 7) provides some direction on specific measures that can be taken to reach these goals, in encouraging participation in 'all public functions at all levels of government'. Related measures include quotas and reserved seats, to ensure at least a critical mass of 30 to 35 per cent of women in political processes at national and international levels.

In addition to these measures, preventing conflicts from occurring or escalating is a proactive response to protecting women and girls. According to Rehn and Johnson Sirleaf (2002, p. 111),

> [p]reventing deadly conflict is as much about knowing the signs, as it is about acting on them. Women have much to offer but their analysis is often devalued and their solutions deemed irrelevant. Because women are disconnected from what are considered 'high politics' and the 'seats of power', there are few opportunities for information from and about them to inform preventive actions.

Gender-sensitive early warning systems can play a vital role in mitigating the circumstances that contribute to or result in violations of the rights of women and girls. The rationale for such systems is simple: if the threats and vulnerabilities faced by women and girls are not taken into account, it is unlikely that response efforts will deal with protecting women and girls. By not adopting a gendered perspective, early warning systems risk increasing women's vulnerabilities to having their human rights violated (Organisation for Security and Cooperation in Europe/Office for Democratic Institutions and Human Rights 2009). Standard early warning devices have excluded women's perceptions of threats and vulnerabilities, and, as a result, the robustness of such systems is compromised. In addition, such exclusion denies women the opportunity to participate in a meaningful way in conflict prevention and post-conflict reconstruction. UNSCR 1325 seeks to rectify this exclusion. The benefits of gender-sensitive early warning systems are twofold. On the one hand, by casting a wider net of indicators and taking into account women's perceptions of threats, they provide a more nuanced understanding of instability. On the other, they ensure that the responses to conflict do not perpetuate discriminatory policies but address the specific vulnerabilities and threats faced by women (Schmeidl & Piza-Lopez 2002).

UNIFEM's Solomon Islands Gendered Conflict Early Warning Project illustrates how gender-sensitive early warning systems may be developed. The gendered early warning indicators were developed in consultation with five local women's organisations and based on standard early warning indicators combined with gender-sensitive and context-specific indicators. Based on the data collected and analysed by the five partners and community focus groups, early warning reports were drafted and distributed to all permanent secretaries in government, NGOs, donors, churches and the five pilot communities. These reports also acted as sources for articles in the local newspaper and radio announcements on women's radio networks and the Solomon Islands Broadcasting Corporation. The reports include a 'response options matrix' developed by men and women from the community and the five partner organisations, for use across all national, international (donor) and community levels, for each of the forty-six indicators. The response options were picked up by various government departments and NGOs. The Department of National Unity, Reconciliation and Peace, Oxfam Australia and Save the Children use the matrix to provide inputs for their strategic plans, while AusAID and World Vision are using the reports as a tool to facilitate dialogue with organisations working on peacebuilding in the Solomon Islands. Locally, women candidates during the 2006 election used the reports in their campaign manifestos.

The crux of our argument is that if preventing conflicts is a proactive approach to protection, then maintaining and promoting peace is a long-term strategy geared towards protecting the rights of women and girls. This strategy involves both providing communities, especially women and girls, access to information and skills to protect their rights and also challenging attitudes that see violence as an appropriate means of conflict resolution. Innovative use of media plays an important role in making women aware of their rights and provides them with vital information on how to protect themselves. For instance, in Nepal, rural women are being trained to become community radio reporters. The radio program titled *Changing Our World* utilises the process of documenting the stories of rural women to cover issues relating to women's human rights, peacebuilding and violence against women. In Palestine, the Ashtar Theatre Company tours schools, youth centres, women's and disabled people's groups, presenting plays to raise awareness of issues such as sexual violence (International Alert & Women Waging Peace 2004).

Other organisations adopt a capacity development approach to protection and the prevention of conflict. The Fiji Women's Rights Movement (FWRM) regularly conducts feminist legal theory and practice training for NGOs and women. The sessions challenge approaches to law that are unaware of the complexities of gender and seek to address the social, cultural and political contexts that shape any legal system. In Nepal, the Centre for Development and Population Activities trains newly appointed peace and gender focal points in each of the country's national-level Ministries, to improve their ability to develop post-conflict programs sensitive to gender and social inclusivity. Taking a more community-based approach, as part of its NAP for implementing UNSCR 1325, Liberia has initiated an innovative program that seeks to engage communities in promoting peace and protecting the rights of women and girls. Communities select women and girls, men and boys to be '1325 champions' who 'lobby national, country and community structures and the security sector to strengthen prevention of violence policies' (Government of Liberia 2010). These champions are involved in developing civic education programs on topics such as 'the role of families in preventing violence against women and girls' and 'the role of women in socialising the community to peace'. They are aired on the community radio network and other Liberian radio stations (International Alert & Women Waging Peace 2004).

In recent years, there has been an increasing realisation that protecting the rights of women and girls necessitates working with men to challenge accepted notions of violence and masculinity. Primarily, the focus is on raising awareness among men of how entrenched ideas of masculinity, gender relations, male power and privilege can contribute to violence against women. For instance, the Male Advocates Program in Fiji, funded by AusAID and initiated by the Fiji Women's Crisis Centre (FWCC), works with men from all walks of life to help them become anti-violence advocates. Population Services Pilipinas Incorporated in the Philippines works specifically with male village leaders and the police force to promote their involvement in eliminating violence against women through awareness-raising workshops. Aakar, an NGO based in India, produces documentaries and uses these films and drama as means to initiate a dialogue between young men and women and to generate action on issues like violence against women. Harnessing Self-Reliant Initiatives and Knowledge Incorporated in the Philippines uses a peer-to-peer approach to establish male community educators who advocate eliminating violence against women (Esplen 2006). All of these examples demonstrate how addressing the root causes of conflict is a long-term strategy that helps to prevent conflict and build peace.

Remaining challenges

Many within the global community have taken the first steps towards recognising that, while conflicts affect everyone, men and women experience violence differently, and hence measures to protect men and women should be different as well. Although the rhetoric of protecting women and girls permeates the discussion of UNSCRs 1325, 1820, 1888 and 1889, in reality, the ability to transform discourse into action is plagued by inconsistent political commitment, the absence of any penalties or sanctions for repeated violations of women's rights and lack of adequate resources and organisational capacity.

A fundamental criticism levied against efforts to promote access to justice is the extensive focus on top-down and state-centric initiatives in which international aid assistance is given largely to government legal institutions, especially the justice sector. The best practices highlight a more balanced approach that gives equal importance to bottom-up approaches, 'legal empowerment' or 'microjustice' initiatives (Gould 1996). State-centric models tend to neglect community-based approaches to protection. Communities – women and girls, men and boys – often are seen as recipients of protection rather than active agents capable of ensuring their own protection. Community-based protection initiatives involve affected communities that identify, analyse and prioritise protection as well as reflect on existing strategies and capacities to prevent and respond to physical and other security issues, thereby offering an important (although underexplored) avenue to engage women (Berry & Reddy 2010, p. 4). These types of initiatives are not to be seen as alternatives to state-based models; rather, they are an additional level of engagement in dealing with protection (Berry & Reddy 2010).

With respect to transitional justice mechanisms, women's organisations and feminist legal scholars highlight the fact that women are often excluded from processes that discuss and settle on the design of transitional justice mechanisms. This is not surprising, because such discussions take place during peace negotiations in which women have limited opportunities to participate. These peace negotiations are critical, as they debate the issues of impunity and accountability for human rights abuses. Since these negotiations are dominated by men, women's and girls' experiences of conflict and their demands for justice do not always make it to the table. Christine Bell and Catherine O'Rourke (2007, p. 25) point out that

> [n]egotiation processes are also gendered at a deeper level in that they typically focus on ceasefires followed by complex divisions of power between divided groups through innovative electoral and governmental arrangements and/or divisions of territory. Matters that address underlying issues of discrimination, domination and improvement of physical, social and legal security, particularly with regard to gender, are often addressed as secondary, or not at all.

Further, the overwhelming tendency of transitional justice mechanisms and judicial processes in general to focus on SGBV has a reductionist effect on dealing with complex protection demands. Efforts must continue to highlight the use of SGBV as a weapon of war; tackling this terrible violence is a priority. More attention is required on addressing unequal power relations that lie at the heart of the use of violence as a means to enforce and perpetuate existing power relations. Men can play a significant role in transforming unequal power relations. 'Gender justice can only be furthered if there is a focus not just on the crime but its context, motivation, and location within a continuum violence ... [W]hat we are missing is a simultaneous focus on the inclusion of women in all processes designed to deliver redress' (Valji 2007, p. 11; see also Cockburn 2004 and Sellers 2009).

In this regard, UNSCR 1325 is path-breaking, as it unequivocally calls for greater representation of women at all levels of decision-making to prevent, manage and resolve conflict. The trouble lies in enforcing this intention. Invariably, national governments and institutions established post-conflict during a transitional justice period are tasked with ensuring greater representations of women (Ní Aoláin & Rooney 2007). Given entrenched gender stereotypes and unequal gender relations, usually there is little political will to push this agenda forwards. There are other dangers to guard against as well, namely, resorting to tokenism to fulfil mandated requirements and the 'you again, you again' syndrome.[5] Processes that seek to enable active participation must take into account intersectionality, which brings to light ways in which gender intersects with other factors, such as sexuality, social class, race, ethnicity, age, ability and disability, in mediating subjective experiences of multiple discriminations. This approach argues that while 'all women are in some ways subject to gender discrimination, other factors ... combine to determine one's social location' (Association of Women in Development 2004, p. 1). Intersectionality 'highlights the need to account for multiple grounds of identity when considering how the social world is constructed' (Crenshaw 2003, p. 176). It calls for the recognition that women are not a homogenous group. Accordingly, multiple culturally adapted and flexible strategies are necessary to ensure that this diversity is truly represented by those who are in decision-making areas that promote the prevention of conflict and protection from violence. Further, the establishment of mechanisms that support diverse women in keeping connections with local communities increases the chance of representation being meaningful.

Staying with this theme of inclusive participation and its links with protection against and the prevention of conflict, it is erroneous to assume that all women have feminist inclinations. For example, it cannot be taken for granted that female police officers are naturally more likely to be sensitive to gender issues, especially SGBV. Some women might find it difficult to work against dominant masculinity, which is so prevalent in most police forces, and may prefer to remain silent (Mangold 2003). Others may be coopted into adopting dominant masculine behaviours in order to gain acceptance as legitimate police officers, for example, being tougher on rape victims than their male counterparts (Bastick, Grimm & Kunz 2007; Clegg, Hunt & Whetton 2000). Consequently, an SSR that does not just increase the number of women police officers but also reforms the environment in which policing takes place is likely to be effective. Such reforms include more than merely ongoing gender awareness training for male and female officers. Efforts have to be put in to improving human resource policies that enable women and men to achieve a better work and life balance and enforcing codes of conduct, especially zero tolerance for sexual harassment.

Additionally, concerns have been voiced on the 'increasing "sexualisation" of interrogation methods during detainment' (Durham & O'Byrne 2010, p. 39), such as those accounts of physical, sexual and psychological abuse witnessed at Abu Ghraib and committed by women, as well as by men, towards men. Helen Durham and Katie O'Byrne (2010, p. 39) argue that 'more than other international actors, many military actors are readily able to understand gender as a constitution of power relations and . . . choose to utilise that understanding in order to violate and humiliate those they hold captive'. The issue of sexual violence against men goes unreported or is at least under-reported, often due to the stigma attached to sexual violence (an issue faced by women as well) and criminalisation of homosexuality in many countries, which results in fear of being prosecuted (Lewis 2009; Oosterhoff, Zwanikken & Ketting 2004; Stemple 2009). A gendered response to SGBV recognises that men, women, boys and girls are all vulnerable to this type of abuse. Unless a gendered lens is adopted, it is difficult to unpack dominant masculinity and femininity and to explore gendered power relations. What frequently happens is that all men are seen as potential perpetrators of violence and all women as victims, and programs are designed that continue to entrench this oversimplified understanding. As Lara Stemple (2009, p. 634) suggests, 'gender norms harm both men and women. It is possible to take sex and gender into account without setting up false divisions that pit all men against all women, villains against damsels in distress'.

Other challenges to be addressed to further the interconnected goals of protection and prevention include gender-responsive DDR programs. Many female ex-combatants find it hard to reintegrate into their communities, because they shatter existing gender stereotypes by engaging in activities considered impossible or atypical for women. As a result, 'they are treated, not like men, not like women, but something else, like monsters' (Hogg 2010, p. 100). This issue is exacerbated in the case of girl soldiers who are victims of forced marriages, forced pregnancy and domestic sex slavery. Since this highly vulnerable group is not protected by the Convention on the Rights of the Child or its Optional Protocol, Durham and O'Byrne (2010) recommend exploring the use of human rights law and international humanitarian law in conjunction with domestic child protection legislation to protect young girls during conflict and when conflict ceases, as ex-combatants in a young person's body.

The task of protecting women and girls does seem daunting in the light of the atrocities committed during conflict as well as in post-conflict situations. While it might be overly optimistic to believe that there can be a complete stop to human rights abuses, peace-builders, policy-makers, legal officers, activists and academics can gear themselves to respond more effectively to protecting women and girls. New NAPs on UNSCR 1325 (and increasingly on its sister resolutions), strategic plans of humanitarian aid organisations and bilateral and multilateral donors' development policies must clearly articulate a gender-responsive framework for protection based on a rights-based model that respects women's rights. These plans and supporting legal norms must unequivocally denounce granting impunity to those who violate human rights in general and commit acts of violence against women and girls in particular.

In addition, any plan or strategy on protection must adopt gender-sensitive language. Using broad categories such as 'civilians', 'people', 'refugees' or 'IDPs' masks gender-specific experiences of threats and vulnerabilities. The use of gendered categories and their intersections with other social determinants will result in more nuanced, targeted and therefore effective strategies that can be monitored and evaluated. In terms of implementing protection frameworks, a whole-of-government approach is recommended, because it emphasises coordination and cooperation between development policies, national women's machineries, diplomatic and, where relevant, military and justice departments. Finally, peacebuilders, donors, policy-makers and all involved in transitional justice processes ought to engage more meaningfully with local communities, and in particular with women's organisations, in promoting nonviolent civilian peacekeeping, establishing community-based protection initiatives and prioritising conflict prevention.

CHAPTER 4

Ensuring gender perspectives in peacekeeping

Gender and peacekeeping in the UN are considered in several analyses and reports (Barnes 2006; Bertolazzi 2010; Charlesworth 1994; Etchart 2005; Olsson & Tryggestad 2001; Puechguirbal 2010; Raven-Roberts 2005; UNDPKO 2009a; Vayrynen 2004) as well as in a substantial academic edited collection (Olonisakin, Barnes & Ikpe 2011). We do not aim to replicate these. Instead, this chapter clarifies what is involved in ensuring that gender perspectives are incorporated meaningfully into PKOs in line with the requirements of UNSCR 1325.[1] Three arguments are developed.

1. After explaining the broadening nature of multidimensional PKOs, we argue that women's inclusion in these operations is essential for a vast range of reasons, such as equal rights, sensitivity to gender-specific localised needs and the unique value of different responses.
2. We provide rationales as to why women and gender training should be included in PKOs and demonstrate what some UN

Member States are doing to implement UNSCR 1325 in their PKOs and training.
3. We explain some of the major obstacles to gender-responsive peacekeeping and maintain that there are good practices that show how to develop the capacity for gender-responsive peacekeeping.

A sensitive qualification is necessary. We do not want readers to think that we simplistically want more women trained as warriors or see women as innately nurturing beings in need of protection and men as always the perpetrators of violence. We are advocates for peace. We endorse Lynne Segal's (2008, pp. 21, 33) points that 'rethinking the gendered nature of warfare must also encompass the costs of war to men' and that women too 'join men in the work of objectifying and psychologically annihilating the "enemy"'. Nonetheless, given that some women choose to join militaries, in the absence of any international law that makes war illegal, and given the increasingly humanitarian and peacekeeping nature of many military missions, we support the emphasis in UNSCR 1325 on increasing the number and profile of women's roles in PKOs.[2] However, we are in agreement 'that the issues of gender and peacekeeping should never be reduced to the number of women recruited as peacekeepers. Promoting security is about providing real human security for the population, not about the militarisation of women' (Butler, Mader & Kean 2010, p. 13).

Women and peacekeeping directives under UNSCR 1325 (UNSC 2000a) are twofold: increasing women's equal participation in peacekeeping, and ensuring that peacekeepers are aware of the relationship between gender equality and sustainable peace. UNSCR 1325 also calls on the Secretary-General to incorporate a gender perspective in PKOs. In 2000, Secretary-General Kofi Annan gave a comprehensive answer to the question of what it means to have a gender perspective in peacekeeping. He called for gender to be considered in mandates for peacekeeping, needs assessment missions and policy and strategy development, and for training programs and codes of conduct for military and civilian peacekeepers, along with human rights support, humanitarian assistance, development and reconstruction activities.

Women's inclusion in multidimensional operations

The first PKO by the UNSC was supervision of the truce after the first Arab–Israeli war in 1948. Now, there are both UN-led and non-UN-led PKOs that are undertaken by regional groupings. We utilise a concept of 'peacekeeping operations' broadly understood

> as internationally mandated, uniformed presences, either under United Nations auspices or under the authority of a regional organization like the Economic Community of West African States, the African Union, and the North Atlantic Treaty Organization (NATO). Armed UN peacekeepers, unarmed UN Military Observers (UNMOs), armed and unarmed UN Police (UNPOL) and soldiers serving under their national commands by the Security Council, like the... Australian-led force in Timor-Leste, all come within the definition of "peacekeeper" (UNIFEM & UNDPKO 2010, p. 5).[3]

Dyan Mazurana, Angela Raven-Roberts, Jane Parpart and Sue Lautze (2005, p. 19) identify three types of PKOs.

- Some observer missions monitor and observe ceasefires, verify troop withdrawals and patrol borders and demilitarised zones. These are composed primarily of civilian personnel who act as electoral witnesses and observers to acts of violence and

human rights abuses, such as in the UN Mission of Observers in Tajikistan or the UNMO Group in India and Pakistan.
- Other PKOs are multinational forces of military, police and humanitarian actors deployed to protect civilian populations, enable humanitarian components of the operation to carry out their work, help parties to achieve a resolution of armed conflict and assist in political, judicial, economic and social reconstruction. Examples include the UN Peacekeeping Force in Cyprus and the UN Integrated Mission in Timor-Leste (UNMIT).
- Other peace enforcement operations take direct action against threats to peace and acts of aggression, such as the UN Interim Administration Mission in Kosovo.

Contemporary PKOs increasingly are complex, 'multidimensional' and involved in local civilian life. They include transitional civil administration experts in communications and public information who conduct elections and instigate economic reform as well as SSR. Personnel also build sustainable institutions of governance, monitor human rights, conduct humanitarian work and foster the DDR of former combatants. The change in scope to multidimensional PKOs has increased the impact of peacekeeping on locals. As Nadine Puechguirbal (2008) notes,

> [p]eacekeepers are deployed in a post-conflict environment where there is no law and order, where the local men and women live in precarious economic and political conditions, where women and girls are at risk of sexual violence. Because conflict is a profoundly gendered experience, it is of high importance that peacekeepers understand the impact of war on women, men, boys and girls so that they do not further marginalise groups of the society that have already been made vulnerable by war.

For feminist researchers and practitioners, one of the difficulties in working in the area of SSR is that it covers traditional security actors across the full range of police, defence forces, intelligence officers, lawyers and Parliamentarians as well as non-state actors like militias and rebel groups. Many of these actors have no understanding of differentiated gender needs. A chief goal of 'SSR encompasses a transformation of all actors in a security system towards accountability, transparency and democratic governance'. This goal involves 'shifts in mindsets and the transformation of a political system' (Mobekk 2010, p. 279).[4] Alex Bellamy and Paul Williams (2010, p. 363) point out 'the contradiction at the heart of most peace operations: they are conducted by soldiers trained in the art of war ... [G]ood warriors do not necessarily make good peacekeepers'. We reiterate our discomfort with advocating more military peacekeepers, so we move to a brief critique of masculinist militarism.

Overcoming essentialist views of women, masculinism and militarisation

Despite the introduction of UNSCR 1325, post-war societies continue to re-establish masculinised privilege in their political cultures (Moran 2010). Puechguirbal (2008) finds that the exclusion of women from the political reconstruction of their country is embedded in peacekeeping language, in particular, the construction of the relationship between the protector and the protected. She observes that throughout peacekeeping missions women continue to be portrayed as victims and mothers needing to be 'protected' rather than as active participants in post-conflict societies. Yet some women ex-combatants are seeking a greater role in regional peacekeeping missions throughout Africa, for example, in Rwanda. These women undoubtedly have first-hand experiences of the impact of war on civilians and thus can be active agents in shifting the mindset of SSR. With a transformative outlook, these women potentially play a crucial role in building good community relationships, an increasingly important part of peacekeeping.

Further, many male peacekeepers continue to view security merely as the cessation of hostilities, while many women understand security broadly, as encompassing safety from violence while carrying out daily activities. Puechguirbal (2008) argues that peacekeepers do not typically consult local women on local matters, because women are seen as passive victims who experience conflict and security in the same ways as men. Men and women experience conflict differently. In not responding to such differences and through working with men who previously held influential positions, peacekeeping officials, aid workers and government and private donors reinforce existing male domination and power in the host country. Yet, gender roles have changed, and senior peacekeeping officials have not kept abreast of the changes. Practices such as establishing meetings at times when women have to go home to continue their domestic chores, or not considering local patriarchal dynamics that prevent women from speaking freely in front of men, bar many women from participating in decisions on peacekeeping. The voices of diverse groups of local women, stakeholders, peacekeeping forces and representatives of development agencies must be included from the outset.

Policing is an important part of peacekeeping. In 2008, in eighty countries that contribute to UNPOL forces, fewer than thirty deployed women (UNDPKO 2008, p. 7). Member States were asked to establish a policy to increase the percentage of women in their peacekeeping contingents. In 2010, women comprised 4.14 per cent of UN military experts such as advisers, observers and liaison officers, 2.42 per cent of troops and 8.7 per cent of police (for annual statistics, see UNDPKO 2009a). Loreta Telleria Escobar (2009) notes that a focus on numbers of women in peacekeeping is not enough to challenge essentialist views of women or prevailing masculinist practices. Rather, UNSCR 1325 must be implemented in terms of the types of tasks performed by those deployed in the field. At present, most female peacekeepers are confined to nursing and administrative roles, which reproduces rather than challenges gender stereotypes, thus perpetuating inequalities. Why include women in peacekeeping field operations? This question can be answered both in terms of rights and in terms of 'usefulness' or 'value'. To take the latter first, there are several arguments put forward for the benefits of deploying women in PKOs.

One important reason to defend women's value is their engagement with local women. In this argument, women are believed to be role models for women in the host community, encouraging other women and girls to participate and lead (UNDPKO 2008, p. 10). Barbara Schoetzau (2007), in support of this argument, quotes Comfort Lamptey, a UN Gender Adviser for the UNDPKO:

> We had women from Timor-Leste and Burundi attest to the fact that the fact that we had women peacekeepers helped them galvanise their own aspirations to either join the local police, which we were helping to build in the case of Timor... Similarly, in Burundi we had the head of the UN mission who was a woman and the local Burundi women said they were very inspired that the head of the UN in the country was a woman and that strengthened their own aspirations.

It is necessary for women in PKOs to liaise with local women, because in some traditional societies it is more acceptable for women to work with women (Schoetzau 2007).

Another crucial reason for including women lies in the reporting of, and protection from, SGBV.[5] The global community is now more aware of widespread SGBV and of sexual exploitation where peacekeepers are deployed, particularly in Liberia, Sierra Leone and the DRC. Official rules to prohibit personnel from engaging in SGBV came about only in 2003. The perpetration of SGBV and exploitation by peacekeepers is an ongoing and serious issue; the inclusion of female peacekeepers is thought to lower the incidence of sexual violence and abuse, including in camps of IDPs and refugees (UNSC 2008b). Gendered stereotypes assume that women are gentle, conciliatory and able to calm aggressors. However, Olivera Simič (2010) argues that there is little evidence that the presence of women in PKOs changes the attitudes of male peacekeepers towards local women. Given that SGBV and exploitation offences are often tolerated by the top management of missions, which are overwhelmingly male, SGBV is an issue entrenched in gender hierarchies and a macho culture. Any notion that women should be the 'civilisers' reinforces gendered stereotypes. Simič claims that the problem of sexual violence in PKOs requires more than the addition of women to act as moral guardians. The elimination of SGBV needs justice systems that end the impunity of offenders. However, where abuse has been perpetrated by men in the security forces, women can provide a safe reference point for women to report such abuse, which they might not report to a man in uniform. Having female peacekeepers can build trust with the local community (UN News Service 2009). It also increases the reporting of occurrences of sexual violence (NGO Working Group on Women, Peace and Security 2008, p. 2). However, 'if the participation of women in peacekeeping forces is argued for on the basis of women's allegedly pacifying effect on men, responsibility for men's behaviour is foisted on women, and the questions concerning military culture, training and masculinity are not addressed' (Valenius 2007, p. 515). We are not supporting the mere inclusion of women, but are arguing for the transformative potential of women well versed in knowledge of equal rights who can challenge orthodox masculinised approaches and work with sympathetic men to make a difference.

Peacekeeping missions, by being inclusive, can act as role models for gender equality in transitional justice settings, where there are windows of opportunity to influence change. That is, such missions start to debunk stereotypes, which are notoriously difficult to break down in traditional cultures. Also, missions composed of both women and men are more representative of the host country's population. Including women in PKOs broadens the repertoire of skills and styles available within the mission, often with the effect of reduced conflict and confrontation. For example, Anu Pillay (2006, p. 4) argues that

> [w]omen are more likely to bring the experiences of the severe human consequences of conflict and a commitment to expose the 'underbelly' of war. They are apt to see more clearly the continuum of conflict that stretches from the beating at home to the rape on the street to the killing on the battlefield and can often relate more vividly to the links between violence, poverty and inequality in daily lives.

While arguments on the benefits women bring to PKOs are politically strategic for promoting the inclusion of women in PKOs, Carol Cohn, Helen Kinsella and Sheri Gibbings (2004, p. 137) argue that '[w]hat is potentially lost with the "use-value" approach is that women should be there because they have a right and a reason as individuals, people, as human, not simply or solely because they are somebody's vision of a peace-maker'. They make the important point that women are being represented as, for example, a check on sexual abuse by peacekeepers, in the 'use-value' discourse. This sets the terms for women to enter peacekeeping, thereby creating expectations for women that are not imposed on men and constraining what women are 'allowed' to bring to PKOs. We argue, along with Cohn, Kinsella and Gibbings, that in order for UNSCR 1325 to become a platform for transforming how peacekeeping and security are conceptualised, a shift is warranted from the exclusive focus on women as victims or as peacebuilders to a focus on the problem of militarised masculinist identity in security and war. However, to include women as agents, even in small ways, is an important step towards transforming these structures. While the following overview of including gender in PKOs works primarily within the discourse of women's value, we suggest that this is the beginning of a potentially much larger transformation.

Contributions of women to peacekeeping operations

Although pre-UNSCR 1325, the UN Observer Mission to South Africa (UNOMSA) is an exemplar for the contribution women make to PKOs (Pillay 2006). This Mission was deployed in the lead-up to the first free elections in South Africa after the dismantling of apartheid. It was all-civilian, women-led and gender-balanced. Half of the team leaders were women, even in the most volatile provinces of KwaZulu-Natal and Gauteng. The Mission was mandated to quell violence in order to allow negotiations to proceed, so it had dual peacekeeping and peacebuilding roles. Women members of UNOMSA noted that the gender balance and female Head of the Mission allowed for greater attention to the wider needs of the community, networking, sharing information and using a hands-on approach. There were no reported incidents of abuse or undisciplined behaviour. Mission observers reported that the presence of women in the team worked to defuse tension and violence, preventing explosions of anger and retribution. Angela King, the UNOMSA head, observed that the presence of women in leadership positions was a catalyst to changing the views and attitudes of many of the local women and contributed to the determination of South African women to have a voice in their new polity (Pillay 2006).

The UN Organisation Mission in the Democratic Republic of

the Congo (MONUC)⁶ was established in 2002 with a mandate to pay attention to UNSCR 1325. In this Mission, the responsibility for gender mainstreaming lay with a Senior Gender Adviser in MONUC's Office of Gender Affairs. The Office reported a number of successes. A gender unit actively contributed 'to the inclusion of gender considerations in the DRC's DDR process' through collaborating with locals 'to prepare communities for the return of ex-combatants, as well as the ex-combatants for what they might expect when they return' (Schroeder 2004, pp. 2, 14). The Office enabled the participation of women as part of civil society meetings with visiting ambassadors of the UNSC. Staff facilitated women's groups' ability to organise and prepare for peace negotiations and also assisted exchanges between women from the DRC and from other conflict regions. A conference was supported to review strategies for addressing sexual violence. The Office trained educators to teach magistrates, lawyers and legal auxiliaries (including in armed forces) in gender justice. Staff participated in the training of the Congolese National Police. They influenced electoral laws to ensure that women voted and trained Parliamentarians who started engaging with women's constituencies, which helped to advance the gender program by expanding the pool of female candidates available for political office. Comparatively, Pillay (2006, p. 8) argues that 'UNOMSA demonstrated how successful gender balances in staffing and leadership could be' and that MONUC showed 'how a gender perspective, even with limited resources, can still bring about a notable measure of change in terms of participation and access for women'.

The UN Mission in Liberia (UNMIL) was established by UNSCR 1509 in 2003 'with an explicit mandate to mainstream UNSCR 1325' (Njoki Wamai 2011, p. 52). As Emma Njoko Wamai (2011, p. 52) explains further, 'women with the political will to mainstream the resolution were appointed and elected', such as Ellen Margrethe

Løy as Special Representative of the UN Secretary-General and Africa's first elected female President, Ellen Johnson Sirleaf. Maud Edgren-Schori (2008, pp. 9–10) identifies notable characteristics of peacekeeping missions that are successfully gender-responsive; they:

- demonstrate a strong commitment by peacekeepers to applying a gender perspective and tools for monitoring progress;
- have qualified senior gender expertise;
- mainstream gender as a collective organisational responsibility;
- conduct systematic training; and
- allocate financial resources directed towards targeted actions.

Rakhi Sahi was in the first group of female commissioned officers in the Indian Paramilitary Force's Central Reserve Police Force and later trained the second all-women battalion of the force. She was Commander of the second all-women Formed Police Unit (FPU)[7] that was part of UNMIL. She tells of the significant difference the all-women Unit made.[8] An important upshot of some of the practices she highlights is that having women on foot patrol cut down domestic violence and sexual violence, and their visible presence acted as a deterrence to further violence. Women's strong mediation skills helped to defuse potentially violent situations while being respectful towards local customs. The FPU engaged in significant community liaison and community policing activities, which were not part of the UN mandate, yet they succeeded in integrating into the community, thereby building confidence and trust with local people. They taught girls aged seven to fourteen self-defence skills, taught both boys and girls Indian dance as part of a cultural exchange, which served as a way to engage positively with girls and boys, and facilitated humanitarian aid. Public information was provided on security awareness, human rights and the need for women's rights programs. A gender-sensitive camp design was created for displaced persons. The impact of having women in security reform helped to change the perception of women as being weak, which motivated some Liberian women to join the police force and to take other leadership roles. The FPU was a visual role model of empowerment. Sahi suggests the need for more incentives to encourage women to participate in such units, particularly with the offer of more return trips home to see children, partners or other significant family members.

Shubhra Tiwari is the Additional Superintendent of Police in India and the coordinator of the Gender, Child and Vulnerable Persons Protection Team for the police unit in the UN Mission in the Sudan. She is responsible for community policing activities.[9] She stresses that the presence of women in UN missions enhances their access to vulnerable populations such as women, children and the disabled. When UNPOL was given access to the IDP camps in Sudan, crime rates decreased and women demonstrated skills in building solid relationships. Tiwari's mandate in Sudan is to assist local police, so her team liaises with the local police to access the community. She stresses the importance of trust-building and breaking the ice through sport, music and art. The team works hard to integrate its mandates into community-building work. The Secretary-General is calling for 20 per cent of peacekeepers to be women by 2014, and Tiwari suggests it is currently 7.25 per cent.

As of July 2009, there were three women serving as Head of Mission, in the Central African Republic, Liberia and Nepal, and six serving as Deputy to the Head of Mission, in Burundi, Chad, the DRC, Lebanon, Liberia and Sudan. In UNDPKO missions alone in July 2009, there were five women serving at the levels of Under-Secretary-General and Assistant Secretary-General and over twenty at the level of Director (UNSC 2009a, p. 12). A snapshot of women in peacekeeping in 2010 shows the growing impact of UNSCR 1325. In that year, there were five female Heads of Mission, in the Central African

Republic, Cyprus, Liberia, Nepal and Timor-Leste, with four female Deputy Special Representatives, in Chad/the Central African Republic, the DRC, Iraq and Liberia (UNSC 2010a, p. 35). The UNDPKO has made inroads into implementing UNSCR 1325. In November 2006, it adopted a policy edict on gender equality in peacekeeping. 'An internal action plan on how to implement UNSCR 1325 has also been adopted. All peace operations established after 2000 have a Gender Adviser, Gender Unit, or gender focal point in the field headquarters' (Tryggestad 2009, p. 551). What this actually constitutes in the field varies, so, in 2010, 'of the 17 UNDPKO missions 11 have a dedicated gender adviser' (UNSC 2010a, p. 35). Having a gender unit or a Gender Adviser is important, but there is even greater impact when they are part of a broader gender-mainstreaming strategy.

Peacekeeping and gender training

UNSCR 1325 asks Member States to include UN-developed guidelines and training on gender in their national training programs for peacekeeping personnel, both military and civilian. It also calls on Member States to increase their financial, technical and logistical support for gender-sensitive training efforts on the national level and through support of relevant UN agencies. One way to try to make peacekeepers aware of links between gender equality and peace is to provide gender training, which is defined by UN-INSTRAW (in Lyytikäinen 2007, p. 8) as

> a capacity-building activity that aims to increase awareness, knowledge and practical skills on gender issues by sharing information, experiences and techniques as well as by promoting reflection and debate. The goal of gender training is to enable participants to understand the different roles and needs of both women and men in society, to challenge gender-biased and discriminatory behaviours, structures and socially-constructed

inequalities, and to apply this new knowledge to their day-to-day work.

The requirement for peacekeeping personnel to receive gender training is made in response to four factors.

- The changes in the scope of PKOs mean that operations have a significant impact on the host country, including women, and this impact should be a positive one that supports women-led changes to women's social and economic status, rather than one that consolidates patriarchal dominance.
- In reality, women and men often have distinct security needs and are affected differently by conflict. This reality requires that peacekeeping personnel strive to provide inclusive security for all members of society (2007, pp. 5–6).
- UNSCR 1325 recognises that incorporating an understanding of the impact of armed conflict on women and girls into peacekeeping practices can promote peace and security. To achieve this objective of sustainable peace, gender training is essential 'to sensitise and raise awareness among security sector personnel and improve their ability to respond to gender-specific security needs' (UN-INSTRAW 2007a, p. 1).
- There is a necessity to prevent SGBV by peacekeeping personnel (UNDPKO 2008, p. 8).

Gender training addresses the gap between the goal of gender equality and standard practices of peacekeeping. Edgren-Schori (2008) argues that this gap is caused by resistance to acknowledge women's rights, ignorance of gender analysis tools and an indifference towards learning how a gender perspective can make a difference. Gender training can reduce this resistance, ignorance and indifference. Pre-deployment gender training is effective. During the

UN-INSTRAW (2007a, p. 8) dialogue on 'Gender training and capacity building for the security sector: a discussion on good practices', it was noted that the Canadian police officers that were deployed in Haiti were better informed and prepared than other nationalities, due to good preparation before they were sent to a mission. However, a significant proportion of peacekeeping personnel arrive in the theatre of conflict with only a limited conceptual understanding of gender and its role in cementing peace (UNDPKO 2008, p. 8). Many troops receive little or no gender training before arriving at their duty stations. Abugre (2008, p. 25) suggests that this is the outcome of limited resources in the main peacekeeping-contributing countries.

Gender-sensitive training

We have begun to make the case for why gender training is needed, so it is illuminating to provide some positive examples. To begin with, we need to clarify that, in terms of gender training, 'a gender-sensitive approach implies full equality, participation and representation of women in security sector institutions, oversight and management' (Mobekk 2010, p. 281). Angela Mackay's (2005) experience with developing and trialling the first UN-developed gender training packages for peacekeeping troops reveals several important guidelines for gender training. The package was trialled in Timor-Leste and in Ethiopia. The initial trial included a session for recent graduates of the Timor Loro Sa'e Police School, and Mackay describes this as an opportunity for the trainers to learn from the East Timorese. The training of educators is vital to the effectiveness of gender-sensitive training. Many peacekeeping trainers are drawn from the military and often are unfamiliar with gender issues. Interaction with locals can be a vital part of training the trainers, but materials should be presented in simple language. Mackay found that the most successful aspect of the field trials in Ethiopia was the inclusion in the training of members of the local population, such as clergy, nuns, teachers, mayors, NGO representatives, de-mining organisations and the ICRC. The presence of local people had two advantages. First, for many peacekeepers, this represented their first opportunity to meet local people, who provided a 'gateway into the culture' (2005, p. 275). Second, the contributions of mission human rights staff made the material more digestible and relevant for military personnel. The trials also revealed that gender training needs to be context-specific, with a varied focus for different people doing different jobs. They also showed that such training affords a richer experience when there is a mixed group of participants, with at least 30 per cent being women. Since there are so few female peacekeepers, having civil society participants, such as in Ethiopia, is useful to achieve this balance.

Implementing UNSCR 1325 requires a commitment to support those countries that regularly provide troops but often lack the resources to train them in gender sensitivity. In 2010, the top ten troop- and police-contributing countries, in descending order of numbers, were Bangladesh, Pakistan, India, Nigeria, Egypt, Nepal, Jordan, Ghana, Rwanda and Uruguay. However, developing countries have limited resources and capacity to train their troops. Some maintain that most opportunities for gender training are in developed countries rather than in developing countries, from where the majority of troops originate (Lyytikäinen 2007, p. 9). However, from the mid-1980s, there was a concerted effort in the humanitarian aid sector to develop gender awareness policies in developing countries, but the tools gained have not translated to the security sector. Supporting training initiatives represents a significant opportunity for development partners of governments and donors to make a useful contribution, and there are examples of good practices in this area.

For example, prior to UNSCR 1325, the Training for Peace Project was established in 1995 with funding from the Norwegian Ministry of Foreign Affairs. As part of this Project, a partnership between the African Centre for the Constructive Resolution of Disputes (ACCORD), the Norwegian Institute for International Affairs and the Institute for Security Studies in South Africa formed with peacekeeping training workshops held in eleven countries of the South African Democratic Union. Unfortunately, despite attempts to encourage women to attend, only 10 per cent of participants were women, reflecting the masculinised nature of the military (UNSC 2008b). However, more recent gender programs in the area of civil policing in these regions, launched by Norway and Sweden, were more successful. Heidi Hudson (2005b, pp. 125–6) notes that, under Norwegian guidance, a gender perspective was integrated into the civil policing project from the beginning. Hudson suggests that this is a proactive approach that is central to obtaining positive results. The Strategy Workshop with Women's Constituencies from Troop and Police Contributing Countries (UNDPKO 2007) in South Africa noted as another good practice the provision of gender coaches to senior leadership to encourage an internalisation of gender processes. According to the participants in this workshop, who included military, police and civilian officials, representatives from twenty-two countries in Africa, Asia, Europe and Latin America, and participants from current and former peacekeeping countries, training ought to be long-term and include modules related to human rights and civil affairs.[10]

The Pearson Peacekeeping Centre (PPC) is a Canadian institution that aims to enhance the effectiveness of peace operations through training, research and capacity development. Its training is based on human rights, the rule of law, international stability, collective security and diplomatic primacy. It provides training for those in conflict zones, including civilians, military personnel and police officers, through courses, peace operation simulations, workshops and conferences. The organisation identifies four aspects of its work that are crucial for success (PPC 2009a).

- The courses are multidimensional, adapted to reflect diversity in the field and promote dialogue and cooperation.
- The organisation uses stressful simulations which compel learners to think as quickly as they would be required to do in a conflict situation.
- The PPC is supported by an extensive international network of experts, industry leaders and key organisations.
- The services are multinational, multilingual and multicultural.

The PPC has carried out a number of programs related to UNSCR 1325 in Africa under its Pan African Police Project, including the Women in Peace Operations Seminar, which includes women and men and covers gender and peace operations. A women-only workshop trains women to develop their capacity to integrate gender mainstreaming into their work (PPC 2009b). The PPC funded three female UNPOL officers who were serving in Africa and the Americas to attend the UNSC open debate on UNSCR 1820 and the consequent roundtable on implementing UNSCRs 1820 and 1325 (PPC 2009b). It also operates inside Darfur, where it has developed a training program to address SGBV (PPC 2009a). Interested stakeholders hold workshops, dialogues and conferences on best practices for gender-sensitive training for peacekeepers.

The UN-INSTRAW Virtual Discussions 'Good and bad practices in gender training for security sector personnel' in 2007 and 'Current situation in gender training' in 2008 were online dialogues that included more than 140 experts in the academic and security sectors. The dialogues focused on current issues in gender training, and three fundamental principles underlying good practices for gender training emerged.

- Institutionalisation of gender equity, rather than isolated programs, is essential. Without other forms of gender mainstreaming,

gender training is not enough on its own to change gender responsiveness.[11]
- There is great value in gender training undertaken by personnel from all ranks. Insufficient attention is paid to gender training for senior officials, and this stymies the progress of those in lower ranks. For example, the Swedish armed forces have a gender coaching program that provides senior officials with one-to-one training with gender experts.
- Training must be long-term, integrated into military education when women and men join as recruits, with mandatory refresher courses held at regular intervals.

The reports from these UN-INSTRAW dialogues reiterate that in relation to the training curriculum and materials, good practices are diverse. Active learning, such as role-plays and drama, was carried out by the ICRC in the DRC regarding the prohibition of SGBV and the obligation to provide survivors with medical and psychological care. Case studies based on real-life experiences and operations-based training are useful, particularly when they describe the lives of peacekeepers to the locals and have participants relate them to occasions in their own lives when their dignity was violated. Community meetings between security sector personnel and community activists create awareness-raising and dialogue. Materials to take into the field are good reminders of gender training. For example, in Kosovo, police officers were given notebooks that included references to gender policies and relevant phone numbers in which to record investigation details. Gender checklists also are useful. These were used in the DRC and Haiti to improve patrolling and for gathering security-related information. In Bosnia and Herzegovina, the NGO Medica Zenica gave 'evidence-finding packages' to police to help collect evidence in SGBV cases.

A crucial part of successful gender-sensitive training is to engage men in the process. The participants of the UN-INSTRAW Virtual Discussions suggested that organisations such as the White Ribbon Campaign and Men's Resources International are useful in engaging men in preventing violence against women. In Haiti and Brazil, a group of men working to end violence against women are trained as peer educators to disseminate messages against violence to other men. Having a male trainer who has an understanding of male privilege and is willing to speak out against discrimination faced by women, working with a female trainer who is well versed in gender power issues, is a good practice for engaging male participants. In Eritrea, in-mission gender training created a dialogue between peacekeeping personnel and the local men and women. In Uganda, gender training workshops were part of the disarmament of armed rebel groups such as the Lord's Resistance Army, used as a point of entry to promote gender responsiveness in the host country. In northern Uganda, civil–military liaison offices have been established to improve relations between the army and women civilians.

If training is to be effective, its impact must be evaluated. For example, ACCORD uses oral and written evaluations to measure participants' responses to the training. Engaging local civil society organisations as skilled partners is useful for conducting external evaluations and also for building healthy community links. The Kofi Annan International Peacekeeping Training Centre in Ghana contacts participants a few months after training as a way of measuring long-term impact, though the outcome of this evaluation process is not yet known. There are several possible indicators and benchmarks for evaluating whether the security of civilians improves as a result of gender training. For example, the Kosovar police measure the impact of gender training through the number of reported cases of SGBV, the number of arrests and data from shelters for victims of SGBV. Other possible indicators include the number of gender focal points and SGBV reporting mechanisms. These mechanisms permit a comparison of sex-disaggregated data collected in investigations and in interviews with female security sector personnel regarding SGBV, discrimination and harassment. Mackay (2005, p. 278) argues that what counts in evaluating training is not merely the content but the effect of the training. She makes suggestions for possible benchmarks of effectiveness that include the absence of abuse by peacekeepers, protection of vulnerable populations, establishment of clear codes of conduct and engagement with local women. Other benchmarks include numbers of women in decision-making positions, support for men affected by war to prevent domestic violence, and employment opportunities for local women. The difficulty with these kinds of measures of effectiveness, however, is that they are not clearly causally linked to a gender training course. Generic measures are not always helpful. Role-related performance-based measures that relate to clear codes of conduct are more useful. However, 'training' is an important part of the wider implementation of UNSCR 1325.

Mainstreaming gender in peacekeeping
We analyse gender mainstreaming in more detail in Chapter 6. It is possible to learn a lot from a review of best practices undertaken by UN Member States to mainstream gender into PKOs and in delivering gender-sensitive training for peacekeeping personnel. As Charles Abugre (2008, p. 25) highlights, 'the obligations are both internal – in terms of member states mainstreaming gender in their own institutions and engendering their peacekeeping, police and civilian forces provided for peacekeeping or peace enforcing missions – and external in terms of providing predictable and adequate resources'. The commitment to include women in PKOs is a threefold process involving actions to promote the recruitment, retention and promotion of women; evaluation of barriers to the participation of women in PKOs; and building political will. A nominal commitment

to pre-existing or new legislation on equal opportunities rarely translates into practice. It requires specific commitments by police, military, government and development organisations, and changes in training, equipment and other terms and conditions to make a peacekeeping career attractive to women.

In the UN survey of troop-contributing countries, Bangladesh reported formal directives to increase the intake of female officers in the armed forces and, together with Kenya and India, established separate units of women police. Nepal removed the restrictions on women entering the army and has graduated the first class of female officers from its military academy, who were posted in various units across the country, including a commander unit (UNDPKO 2006b).

In Jordan, the Public Security Directorate provided a special observer course on peacekeeping for policewomen. Since 2000, the proportion of women members of Jamaican contingents to UN peacekeeping forces has reached nearly 50 per cent, including women Contingent Commanders in both Liberia and Darfur. In Germany, women make up two-thirds of the staff of the Center for International Peace Operations, the governmental entity in charge of training and recruiting for international missions, and in 2007, 52 per cent of participants in courses were women (UNSC 2008b).

South Africa improved the conditions of women deployed in peace missions, including 'resilience programs' for families during women's absence from home. Consequently, the South African police service has reached its target of 40 per cent of staff being women, and the South African national defence force achieved its target of 30 per cent of staff deployed in PKOs being women (UNSC 2008b).

The Indian UN FPU comprises more female officers than male logistics staff. FPUs are used to bridge the gap between regular and lightly armed police and fully armed 'blue helmets', the name given to UN peacekeepers identified by the wearing of blue berets or helmets. Armed less heavily than the regular security unit, an FPU is tasked with providing general support to UN policing in Liberia, where they protect UN officials and civilian police while they perform their duties (Institute of Social Studies Trust 2007, p. 45).

In January 2007, the first all-women UN peacekeeping force of more than 100 Indian policewomen arrived in Monrovia. They were trained in combat tactics and weaponry, crowd and mob control and counter-insurgency, and their patrol of the streets was critical. Most of the officers were mothers, so they not only provided security but mentored Liberian women, particularly young mothers, in health care. They also organised self-defence classes for young women. In November 2008, India began training 200 female security officers to be deployed on the India–Pakistan border (UN-INSTRAW 2008).

Two all-women FPUs were established in Nigeria and deployed in Liberia to UNMIL. The Pacific Regional Policing Initiative, an Australian project, begun in 2003, has seen a measurable increase in female police across the Pacific region in both operational and training roles (AusAID 2007b). The advantages in having women peacekeepers are numerous: in many traditional cultures, it heightens acceptability for women to deal with women, especially on sensitive issues like violence, and it can act as an example to male counterparts in reducing sexual exploitation.

Developing capacity for gender-responsive peacekeeping

Having provided examples of why gender-sensitive training should be included in PKOs and having given some examples of what is happening on the ground, we note that obstacles to building gender-responsive peacekeeping remain. It is worth summarising the findings of a significant survey sent to female peacekeeping personnel involved in eighteen current PKOs (Bertolazzi 2010). This included military, police and civilians as well as the Gender Adviser or gender focal point in each mission. Recruitment of women is difficult. Disincentives include the fact that most missions 'are non-family duty stations... Most of the women in peacekeeping operations are unmarried, divorced or have no children' (2010, p. 14). MONUC is the largest PKO, yet it 'shows no clear mandate on female recruitment'; indeed, countries 'that have not included a single woman in their personnel are Pakistan, Bangladesh and Morocco, which form part of the largest troop contributing countries' (2010, p. 15). Military experience is a key requirement in many high-rank UN positions, which prevents many women from applying for senior peacekeeping posts. 'The overwhelming majority of respondents agreed that women peacekeepers bring different perspectives and attitudes to their work' (2010, p. 17), particularly in interacting with the local community.

The Canadian Committee on Women, Peace and Security Sub-Committee on Capacity-Building conducted a survey of civilian women on the barriers they faced in participating in peacekeeping (UN Association in Canada 2007). The research identified UN and mission-based barriers that include sexism and nepotism in UN hiring processes, with examples of limited opportunities for advancement to higher ranks as well as sexual harassment, discrimination regarding women's dependency status and length of required commitment.

For such obstacles to be overcome, political will to implement UNSCR 1325 and related resolutions requires public, as well as interdepartmental governmental, dialogue that begins the process of transforming the language of peacekeeping from a male-dominated experience to one that incorporates ideas and practices of human security and gender equality. For example, South Africa has established ongoing consultative processes on gender-responsive peacekeeping through its annual Department of Defence and Gender Conference, which assesses progress achieved and challenges experienced in the implementation of the Department's Gender Mainstreaming Strategy (African Department of Defence 2009). In March 2008, Guatemala hosted an international seminar that brought together people from training centres, Defence Ministries and civil society organisations to discuss women's participation in peace operations. Recommendations included women's participation to be a constant agenda item, support for research to underpin a policy on gender equity in the armed forces and Gender Advisers to be placed inside Ministries (Latin American Security & Defense Network 2009).

Crucial to building political will is tackling the challenges as part of developing capacity for gender-responsive peacekeeping. The number of women in PKOs remains low. While there are some instances of progress, in general, initiatives on women, peace and security continue to be silo-based (PPC 2008, p. 1). The PPC Roundtable (2008, p. 4) conducted research on barriers to women's participation in peacekeeping, including the lack of commitment to the implementation of UNSCR 1325. It found a deficiency of information about opportunities in peace and humanitarian operations as well as vague understandings of the impact of women's participation in missions. Also unclear was women's access to positions in host countries and thus a want of direct support to the development of women's capacity at local and national levels. In a similar way, the Pacific Regional Policing Initiative, established in the Pacific Islands in 2003, noted that while there has been a measurable increase in female police as a result of this initiative, family expectations, cultural taboos and lack of confidence and peer support networks continue to constrain gender equality (AusAID 2007b).

The changing nature of peacekeeping presents a further challenge. Hudson's (2005b) overview of peacekeeping in Africa highlights three trends in peacekeeping that present hurdles to increasing women's visibility in peacekeeping and implementing gender-responsive training.

- As mentioned already, there is the increasing militarisation of peacekeeping, towards an emphasis on peace enforcement.
- There is the increase in regional PKOs operating in situations characterised by limited resources and instability.
- The privatisation of peacekeeping results in an increasing reliance on mercenaries as part of regional forces.

Hudson notes that these changes mean that women, who have traditionally been better represented in civilian aspects of PKOs, are more likely to be excluded, given the masculinisation of the military. Gender concerns are unlikely to be in the foreground where there are limited resources or where mercenaries are not obliged to be part of gender-responsive training.

It is useful to conclude by looking at a longitudinal ten-year impact study assessing the implementation of UNSCR 1325 by twelve UN peacekeeping missions in eleven countries (UNDPKO 2010). This study concludes that missions have been successful in increasing women's participation in politics, both as voters and as candidates, but not in increasing the participation of women in peace negotiations and agreements, a serious concern which we explore in the next chapter. Only modest degrees of success have occurred in DDR programs, in which 'more effort is needed to sensitise and train senior UN and government leaders and DDR program staff on related gender issues (2010, p. 9). Further protection measures are needed for female IDPs and refugees, given that patrols and escorts around camps have proved successful. The presence of uniformed female peacekeepers overturns traditional gender stereotypes and encourages local women to seek out new positions. But gender-sensitive SSR is still the exception, given that most national security institutions have cultures that are 'unfriendly to women; and in which discrimination and sexual harassment of female officers are widespread', and in which SGBV remains 'a formidable challenge'. A positive impact is seen 'in the implementation of legal and judicial reforms by supporting the adoption of gender equality provisions in national constitutions and relevant national laws', though capacity across the judicial system in most transitional justice settings remains weak (2010, p. 10). Practical recommendations and illustrative examples on the implementation of UNSCR 1325 in peacekeeping contexts are available. For example, if there are predictable risks of rape when women or girls collect firewood or water, then a systematic patrol and escorts to those areas can explicitly address the protection of civilians (UNIFEM & UNDPKO 2010).

Beyond the UN, NAPs around UNSCR 1325 should include a review of all national policies and regulations that inform peacekeeping to ensure that they are aligned with global charters on women's rights and gender equality, and that they do not have a discriminatory effect that impacts negatively on female recruitment and deployment. These plans should include the establishment of gender units or gender champions at senior levels within defence forces, police departments, aid agencies and foreign affairs departments, to support the recruitment and deployment of women and to be held accountable for compliance with UNSCR 1325. The collection of sex-disaggregated data and gender statistics relevant to peacekeeping is part of monitoring and accountability mechanisms ensuring the implementation of NAPs. Adequate human and financial resources assist the implementation of these policies. Any national policy on the recruitment and deployment of women ought to include numerical targets. The establishment of specialised units within military and police personnel offices can oversee the recruitment and deployment of women. Research on factors that enhance the recruitment, retention and deployment of women helps to build a bigger picture, including the need to promote women in leadership positions in national forces and peacekeeping.

Pre-deployment training plans must be based on a fundamental review of existing training approaches to ensure the incorporation of complementary training to address language barriers, cultural sensitivity, civic responsibility, human rights and gender awareness. These should engage nationally available gender expertise. They should also help to integrate gender awareness into the curricula that shape the long-term education of military and police personnel, and provide foundation skills to female military and police officers to enhance their selection for peacekeeping. Regular reviews of gender training outcomes, including post-mission debriefs, can identify and remedy gaps in training and other support needs. Specific modules for personnel working at different levels are important.

National-level research, including exit surveys of returning female peacekeepers, on factors affecting the working environment for women in PKOs will assist future planning. National policies guiding participation in peacekeeping should include clear and transparent codes of conduct and guidelines on conduct and discipline matters, including appropriate training for all personnel. Appropriate briefings for senior military and police officials nominated to serve in peacekeeping missions ought to enable them to establish and maintain a management regime in which women as well as men can perform optimally. The nominal commitment to selecting women to serve in leadership positions in peacekeeping has to translate practically. Incentive structures can take into account women's family circumstances.

'The increased attention paid to gender and SSR following the adoption of UNSCR 1325 has been predominantly in policy statements and documents on SSR tools. The gap between policy and practice persists and gender issues are still treated as an afterthought' (Mobekk 2010, p. 288). We would agree that 'would-be peacekeepers need to be educated in the arts of peacebuilding' as well as in the taken for granted war-fighting (Bellamy & Williams 2010, p. 376). Increasing the involvement of civilian personnel is one approach.

Indeed, we endorse Sandra Whitworth's (2004, p. 186) vision that this might involve deploying 'contingents of doctors, feminists, linguists, and engineers; regiments of construction workers and carpenters; armies of midwives, cultural critics, anthropologists, and social workers; battalions of artists, musicians, poets, writers, and social critics'.[12]

CHAPTER 5

Increasing participation of women in decision-making and peace processes

This chapter addresses UNSCR 1325's call 'to ensure increased representation of women at all decision-making levels' (UNSC 2000a, paras 1, 2) and the call, 'when negotiating and implementing peace agreements, to adopt a gender perspective' (2000a, para. 8). Women's leadership and participation in decision-making are integral to nation-building. Why? There are three main reasons.

First, equality-based arguments emphasise that equal participation of men and women in decision-making both demonstrates an ethical commitment to inclusivity and is a fundamental pillar of good governance. Interestingly, 'equality' is not mentioned in any of the operative paragraphs of UNSCR 1325, although the preamble stresses the importance of women's 'equal participation and full involvement in all efforts for the maintenance and promotion of peace and security'.

Second, rights-based frameworks highlight the necessity of changing structures and relationships of power in order to create a just society. They emphasise that women have the right to a voice in decision-making and must exercise this right if they are to challenge and transform oppressive gendered power relations. The right to participate meaningfully in rebuilding a polity includes the right to build gender-equitable policies and laws. Enshrining the principle of equality in constitutional, electoral, legislative and judicial reforms is a first stage of overcoming gender inequalities. As Charlotte Bunch (2004, pp. 30, 31) argues, 'peace, security, equality, human rights and development' are interrelated. She suggests a direct link between human security and human rights; thus, 'human rights constitute an ethical vision of how people should be treated and of one's basic entitlements simply by virtue of being human'.

Third, women experience conflict in different ways from men and thus often have different priorities from men in resolving, preventing and addressing conflict. Sometimes these differences are expressed simply, as having greater success with consensus-based approaches, accommodating others' needs, using collaborative approaches or establishing relations of trust. Distinct perspectives on conflict, peace and security must be included in peace processes to sustain long-term stability. Through promoting women's participation in international peace and security, the adoption of UNSCR 1325 broke stiff barriers between traditionally perceived hard security issues and so-called soft issues of human security.

Principles and priorities

This chapter underscores that all three reasons – equality, rights and different contributions – are important motives for increasing women's participation in decision-making and peace processes. Equal participation of women supports collective bargaining to challenge oppressive power structures and demand the inclusion of their perspectives and concerns into peace processes, negotiated agreements and new legislations being drafted as societies transition to stability. Increasing women's participation in decision-making and peace processes is fundamentally about breaking down institutional barriers. Doing so will not only increase the critical mass of women in decision-making, but will also create an enabling environment for their effective and sustained participation, resulting in more gender-inclusive peace and development outcomes. 'The argument for representation is not just aimed at the inclusion of women, but at transformative feminist engagement with international politics' (Bell & O'Rourke 2007, p. 30), an argument we extend strongly later in the chapter.

Building on these three main interrelated reasons for increasing the participation of women in decision-making and in peace processes, we make four main points in this chapter.

1. We explore women's involvement in formal peace processes[1] and, in doing so, shift the emphases from and supplement the examples of women's informal activities given in other chapters. We offer examples that show how women's participation in peace and security often challenges orthodox modes of operating.
2. We trace how women find a place at the peace table and note that while few women succeed in this, when they do, many make a significant contribution.
3. We stress that building a case for the importance of women's participation in decision-making on peace and security in all stages of the peace process is more than merely playing a numbers game. As we argue, the reasons for making this case include the three underlying rationales outlined above, namely, equality measures, enjoyment of inclusive rights and the opportunity to demonstrate distinctive contributions.
4. We summarise the remaining challenges that will have to be overcome in order to address the low number of women participating in peace processes.

Before pursuing these four thematic points, there are a few further qualifiers needed. Participation means lots of different things. It can include women as mediators or members of mediation teams, delegates of negotiating parties, all-women negotiating parties, signatories, witnesses, representatives of civil society groups, Gender Advisers and members of technical committees devoted to gender issues (UNIFEM 2010, pp. 5–9). Participation in decision-making and participation in peace processes rarely can be neatly divided; however, we focus on women's participation in formal negotiations and, to a lesser degree, as elected Members of Parliament. Also, we reiterate that inequity in participation persists despite a consensus on the importance of women's participation in decision-making, evidenced by successive international conventions, declarations and resolutions, such as CEDAW of 1979, the UNGA's Declaration on the Participation of Women in Promoting International Peace and Cooperation of 1982, the BPFA of 1995 and UNSCR 1325 of 2000.

CEDAW's (1979) Articles 7 (political and public life) and 4 (special measures and the CEDAW Committee's general comment no. 25, which elaborates Article 4) point to a range of strategies that can be adopted to promote women's active participation in decision-making, including legislative amendments (electoral procedures and quota systems), setting numerical goals and targets, and capacity-building, to name a few. The UNGA's (1982) Declaration on the Participation of Women in Promoting International Peace and Cooperation's Article 12 builds on CEDAW with its call for appropriate measures to be taken at the national and international levels. This requests equitable representation in governmental and non-governmental functions, equal opportunity to enter the diplomatic service, appointing and nominating women as members of delegations to national, regional and international meetings and supporting women's employment in the Secretariats of the UN and specialised agencies. Highlighting persistent inequalities between men and women in the sharing of power and participation in decision-making at all levels, the BPFA strategic objective E.1. reiterates provisions mentioned in CEDAW, with a special focus on 'women and conflict' emphasising women's participation in all matters related to peacekeeping, preventive diplomacy, peace mediation and negotiations (UN 1996).

Finally, UNSCR 1325 (UNSC 2000a) brings all these recommendations together with a dual focus on women's participation in institutions and field-based operations and the inclusion of women's organisations in peace processes. Specifically, the resolution urges Member States to support local women's peace initiatives and indigenous processes for conflict resolution, to involve women in the implementation mechanisms of peace agreements and to provide lists of female candidates to the UN Secretary-General for inclusion in a centralised roster. The resolution also urges the Secretary-General to appoint more women as special envoys and representatives and to expand the role of women in UN field-based operations. Individually and together, these conventions, declarations and resolutions provide a powerful framework for enabling equitable and substantive participation in decision-making and peace processes.

Where are the women and why involve them?

Women's participation in formal 'track 1' peace processes, comprising bilateral or multilateral negotiations, is limited. The numbers speak for themselves. There has been no involvement of women in track 1 peace processes in Angola (2002), Bosnia (1995), Cambodia (1991), Ethiopia (2000), Guinea (2002), Nepal (2003 and 2006) or Tajikistan (1997), and most of the peace agreements in these countries were rejected by various political parties (Caprioli, Nielsen & Hudson 2010, p. 98).[2] This absence of women from peace tables is of profound concern. According to a recent study commissioned by UNIFEM (2010), women's participation in formal track 1 processes remains ad hoc, averaging at 8 per cent, with fewer than 3 per cent of signatories in the peace processes being women. Women are also conspicuously absent in chief mediating roles in UN-led peace talks.[3] Yet women have engaged with formal processes and have served on mediating teams in Cyprus, Kenya and Uganda, as Gender Advisers to mediators and delegates in Darfur, and sometimes as members of technical committees, such as in Sri Lanka. They have participated as delegates of negotiating parties in Kenya, Guatemala and the DRC, and, as in the case of Northern Ireland, have formed an all-women negotiating party. On rare occasions, for instance in Afghanistan, El Salvador and Somalia, they have been signatories to peace agreements, though women and their organisations are more likely to have played observer roles when peace agreements are signed.

This poor state of affairs is indefensible, as women are at the forefront of activity, initiating and maintaining peace, primarily through their participation in informal peace processes. Termed 'track 2', these processes run parallel to track 1 and are led by civil society organisations, comprising activities ranging from peace marches to initiating peace dialogues and discussion platforms to end hostilities and work towards reconciliation. From resisting militarisation to promoting dialogue between warring parties, at the community level women have used a range of strategies to build and maintain peace (Alton 2002; Anderlini 2000; Sorensen 1998). There are numerous examples of women working at the grassroots to build peace. For instance, in the Solomon Islands, women played an important role in bringing an end to the conflict between the local people on Guadalcanal claiming to be represented by the Isatabu Freedom Movement, and migrants from the neighbouring island of Malaita, where the Malaita Eagle Force claimed to uphold Malaitan interests.

In May 2000, women in Honiara, the capital of the Solomon Islands, held a roundtable resulting in the Women's Communiqué on Peace, which set out a range of activities that women would participate in and organise to bring about peace. When tensions escalated in June 2000, the Women for Peace, a group comprising women of all ages and religions and from all provinces, was formed to support women's peacebuilding initiatives. Through various activities, such as weekly prayer meetings, meeting with militants, government and police, organising forums and conferences, and visiting displaced families, Women for Peace sought to convince the two militant groups to end violent conflict (Paina 2000). They actively mobilised 'women, chiefs, elders, village leaders, parliamentarians, provincial members, church leaders, and foreign governments to unite and speak with one voice – the voice of peace and reconciliation' (Pollard 2000, p. 44). This example of participation pre-dates UNSCR 1325 but provides a useful example of how many women are engaged without the official sanctions of UN resolutions.

As victims, survivors, peacebuilders and in some cases ex-combatants, women have a big stake in resolving conflicts and being involved in post-conflict reconstruction and future political and socioeconomic development. With women making up at least 50 per cent of the population in most countries, without their participation it will be difficult to establish a broad-based legitimate peace mandate owned by the community (Bouta, Frerks & Bannon 2005). Thus, arguments based on equality emphasise the need for a critical mass of women to access the peace and reconstruction process to ensure that their voices and concerns are inscribed into peace negotiations. 'It is only when women are present in significant strengths, and are able to participate effectively, that they are likely to start ringing up the changes' (Morna 2004, p. 31). The significance of a critical mass of women is premised on the belief that they will be harder to marginalise, as the possibility exists for them to form a strong coalition to advocate women's concerns.

Throughout this book, we emphasise how equality-based arguments can be strengthened by closely aligning them with rights-based frameworks that stress that people have an equal right to a voice in the decisions that shape their lives (VeneKlasen & Miller 2002). Rights-based approaches are inherently political, as they recognise that, without substantial changes to power relations, oppression and subordination will continue. In a peace and conflict scenario, this means that changes to who is involved in making decisions about peace are paramount: 'allowing men who plan wars to plan peace is a bad habit' (Hunt & Posa 2001, p. 38). Both equality-based and rights-based defences of women's participation ask questions like whose voices are being heard and what issues are being considered legitimate? Unless women are part of decision-making processes that value justice, equity, equality, dignity, respect and inclusion, sustainable peace remains a pipe dream. An exclusionary, limited and fragile state is the more likely outcome of women's absence from such processes.

The rights-based approach's emphasis on access to a voice in the decisions that shape people's lives ties in with the underlying argument of this chapter, that is, the view that women bring a unique perspective on peace and security to the negotiating table. As Rachel Mayanja (2010, p. 18), the Special Adviser to the UN Secretary-General on Gender Issues and Advancement of Women, points out, '[w]omen's participation enriches the process, as women are likely to put gender issues on the agenda, set different priorities and possibly bridge the political divide more effectively'. In a sample of twenty-four major peace processes since 1992, UNIFEM (2010, p. 3) found that, while data are not always easy to collect accurately in war zones, 'only 2.5 per cent of signatories, 3.2 per cent of mediators, 5.5 per cent of witnesses and 7.6 per cent of negotiators are women'. As mentioned already, where no women were involved, most of the agreements were rejected by various political parties. This provides a significant reason for adopting a gender perspective as a requirement in all stages of peace processes. Antonia Potter

(2011, p. 3) defines a gendered peace agreement as 'one which has taken into account the perspectives, rights and needs of all people affected by it from the particular standpoint of their sex and how that is interpreted within the culture they inhabit'. Gender perspectives are relevant in SGBV, DDR, land access and ownership, cabinet portfolios, quotas and employment.

It is true that 'typically peace agreements are framed in gender-neutral language', given the assumption that the contents are 'equally applicable to, and equally appropriate for, the needs of both women and men'.[4] We have gloomy reminders that 'there is no peace agreement that provides an overall model for appropriate provisions for ensuring that the needs of women within the conflict zone are served alongside those of the men' (Chinkin 2003b, p. 2). But there are recurring key proposals that women's groups want to have incorporated into peace agreements, namely, 'statutory guarantee of women's rights and equal treatment', a minimum 30 per cent quota of women in decision-making processes, special measures that ensure the safe return and reintegration of displaced women, women's rights to property ownership and inheritance, and the end of impunity (Nakaya 2004, p. 144).

The equality, rights and difference arguments are about improving the quality of sustainable peace.[5] Caprioli, Nielsen and Hudson (2010) suggest that when women are included in peace processes, prospects for more durable peace agreements improve. They cite formal or robust informal involvement of women in agreements still mostly in force in Afghanistan (2002), Burundi (2000–03), the DRC (2002–03), East Timor (1999), El Salvador (1992), Indonesia (2005), Kenya (2008), Liberia (1996–2003), Mozambique (1992), Northern Ireland (1998), the Philippines (1996), Rwanda (2002), Sierra Leone (1999–2000), South Africa (1991–96) and Uganda (2002). What this reveals is 'that the higher its level of gender inequality, the greater the likelihood that a state will experience intrastate conflict' and also that 'peace agreements are more durable when women formally participate in their negotiation' (UNIFEM 2010, p. 25).

The authors of this UNIFEM report (2010) emphasise the added value of women's demands in peace processes. For example, on security and protection, when women demand that SGBV be understood as a violation of the ceasefire, a range of security issues are introduced, such as the need for gender-sensitive SSR and special measures to protect women refugees and IDPs. When women demand both a seat at the peace table and increased political participation post-accord, it is more likely that attention to quotas, affirmative action measures, non-discrimination guarantees and gender machineries at ministerial levels will be introduced. When women are involved in peace processes, their attention to socio-economic empowerment and recovery is likely to emphasise land and inheritance rights, access to credit and education, investment in skills training and capacity development, and the special needs of ex-combatants and women-headed households. Involvement of women in peace processes generally means that attention to justice and reparations seeks accountability for crimes of sexual violence and the payment of reparations that are practically meaningful to victims.

The UNIFEM (2010, p. 3) authors suggest that 'there is a correlation between more inclusive and open models of negotiations and a higher likelihood that the outcome agreements will hold and conflict will not return'. Prospects for successful peacebuilding 'are generally better in societies where women have greater levels of empowerment. Women's status in society reflects the existence of multiple social networks and domestic capacity' (Gizelis 2009, p. 505), such as women in Sierra Leone mobilising resources to rebuild schools and Rwandan women forming networks from both Hutu and Tutsi communities to reconstruct local services. Shadia Marhaban (2010, p. 1), writing on the marginalisation of women in Aceh, says that 'the practice of democracy cannot be "given"; one has to embrace it'. Equality and visibility are crucial, but it cannot simplistically be assumed that the inclusion of women will always make a substantive difference. Indeed, simply unreflectively adding a gender perspective can undermine meaningful participation. For example, Marhaban was the only Acehnese woman in the nine-member negotiating team for the Helsinki Memorandum of Understanding that ended three decades of war between the government of Indonesia and the Free Aceh Movement.[6] She writes that 'women are given token seats in official bodies such as the Parliament, in order to adhere to the Indonesian electoral regulation that calls for, but does not oblige political parties participating in elections to include at least 30 per cent of women candidates' (2010, p. 1).

There are many different ways to participate in politics and in peace processes. In Nepal, while not achieving their goal of being represented in the peace room, women use 'different means to exercise influence and gain access to decision-making bodies' (Baechler 2010, p. 5) through participating in pre-talks, consultative meetings, capacity development activities, and being part of the 'peace task force' (2010, p. 5). What difference does this make? Women are active as agents of change in many areas. Their focus on human rights violations, impunity and human security helps 'to create a nation-wide women's movement across sectors, professional groups, parties, and identity groups' (2010, p. 5), which gives them space 'to raise their voices in the streets of Kathmandu and district headquarters, as well as in the political sphere of the state institutions' (2010, p. 5). Women who were party members have been elected to committees.[7] 'Because of their focus on human security' (2010, p. 5), women's facilitative roles across party lines and sectors in the complex Nepali society are valued; their 'solidarity with both the victims of the civil war and Nepal's systematic forms of exclusion helped to overcome ideological, social, ethnic, and caste boundaries' (2010, p. 5).

Finding seats at peace tables and in Parliaments

According to Anderlini (2000, p. 5), 'the peace table is not a single event. It spans the entire process of negotiations, often beginning in the midst of war, and continuing through the various phases of the transition to peace'. Discussions at the peace table cover a range of issues, from drafting new constitutions that will enshrine the rights of all citizens, to how power will be shared and to economic and social reconstruction. For example, in South Africa, women across all parties agreed that all parties should have a one-third female representation in each negotiating team for the constitution process. 'Accordingly, the South African Constitution includes a comprehensive Bill of Rights with relevant gains for women on matters of reproduction, property rights, healthcare, education and culture' (Porter 2003, p. 250). These issues have a significant impact on the lives of men and women and make a strong case for enabling women's participation in peace processes in addition to men's contribution. Helping women and their local organisations to find a foothold in peace, reconstruction and reconciliation processes, and ensuring their sustained participation in times of peace, require procedural and structural reforms to peace negotiations and post-conflict legislative arrangements as well as ongoing capacity development.

Before looking at some examples of women's participation in peace processes, it is useful to examine an important longitudinal study conducted by Christine Bell and Catherine O'Rourke (2010). Their database (Bell & O'Rourke n.d.) included 585 peace agreements in 102 peace processes. They analysed explicit references to women, gender, widows, girls, sexual violence or rape in peace agreements, in addition to international legal instruments addressing women, such as CEDAW and the Convention on the Nationality of Married Women, dating from 1999–2010, to ascertain 'whether the "gender perspective" mandated by the resolution has been adopted'. They found 'that only 16 per cent of peace agreements contain specific references to women. However, quantitatively peace agreement references to women have increased post Resolution 1325, with the rise being more marked among agreements in which the UN had a third party role' (Bell & O'Rourke 2010, p. 942). Since UNSCR 1325, references to women have increased 'from 11 per cent to 27 per cent of agreements' (2010, p. 954). These researchers suggest that a qualitative review of the agreements indicates that 'many of these references are unsubstantial. There is little evidence of systematic inclusion of women in peace agreement texts, or systematic treatment of issues across peace agreements within conflicts', with prevalent imagery of women as 'the good woman/victim/mother' (2010, p. 968). Progress is slow.

Several factors combine to make it challenging for women to find a firm foothold in the peace process. Peace negotiations are framed largely as a means to bring those at war to a common platform to end violence. This means that the process is dominated by male leaders of the parties in conflict. Women demanding a place at the peace table are questioned about their lack of a constituency (Anderlini & Tirman 2010). Prevailing discriminatory attitudes that exclude women from participating in politics and decision-making before a conflict often spill over during peace negotiations, with peace processes not being regarded as 'women's business' (Anderlini 2000). The tendency to see women only as victims contributes to an essentialised understanding of their vulnerability, which often is used as a reason to keep them away from the peace table. Women's organisations that are effective in enabling peace at the grassroots level usually lack the funds, resources, networks and capacity required to participate in formal peace talks.

The attempts in Afghanistan to include women in the peace process highlight the importance of providing opportunities for informal peace processes to intersect and feed into formal peace processes. Pressure from women's groups in the country forced the UN Special Representative for Afghanistan to change his multistage political plan, which noted the importance of women's participation in all negotiation stages except the first. Finally, three women participated in the Bonn Agreement of 2001 as delegates, with an additional three as observers. As the Bonn Agreement deliberations were underway, the Afghan Women's Summit was held in Brussels, and the women attending the Bonn deliberations were allowed to travel to Brussels and share information on the negotiations. The Brussels Proclamation, which resulted from the Summit, called for, among other things, the inclusion of women in the Loya Jirgah (Grand Assembly) and in all peace and reconstruction processes, and the participation of female Afghani lawyers in the drafting of the new constitution and other legal provisions. The significance of this Summit and the Proclamation is evinced by the Members of the European Parliament declaring that international aid for reconstruction will be 'conditional on the participation of women in decision-making and in use of such aid' (Neuwirth 2002, p. 257).

The Afghan Women's Summit draws attention to the need to fund women to attend events linked to peacebuilding. Issues relating to financial costs of participation often are neglected. Most peace agreements negotiated by a third party take place away from conflict zones, in neutral territory. Women's organisations are often required to cover these expenses, while the expenses of negotiating parties are met by a designated fund. Women suffer an additional burden as well: participating in extended negotiations results in a loss of income and increased expenses, such as providing for child care. Thus, financial support for female leaders and their organisations is critical to facilitate their participation in peace processes.

To address the issue of legitimacy, women's organisations working for peace have come together in some instances to establish a formal constituency. Northern Ireland is a case in point. The attempt to end the conflict in Northern Ireland and establish peace between Ulster unionists and the British government on one side and Irish republicans on the other took the form of establishing multiparty talks, initially in the hope of a Northern Ireland Forum for Political Dialogue, which was set up in 1996. Parties elected to the Forum participated in all-party talks aimed at negotiating a peace agreement. A two-track electoral system was put forward to ensure broad-based representation, whereby ninety representatives were elected from the eighteen territorial constituencies (five from each constituency). From the ten parties that secured the most number of votes, two representatives (from each of the ten parties) joined the ninety representatives to form 110 delegates at the peace table (Fearon 2002). Women's organisations lobbied political parties to include women in their candidate lists. However, since their demands were largely ignored, some women's groups that had been advocating for peace at the community level came together to form the Northern Ireland Women's Coalition (NIWC). The Coalition met weekly to debate positions which were informed by the core principles of equality, human rights and inclusion.[8] Their strategy was to organise women through their various networks and contacts to gain the necessary votes. As the ninth party to secure the required number of votes, the NIWC successfully secured two seats at the negotiation table.

'At the commencement of the peace talks, the NIWC was the only party with women delegates at the table' (Kilmurray & McWilliams 2011, p. 2). The final team of ten (including those at the negotiating table and those providing advice) was evenly balanced between Protestant unionist and Catholic nationalist women (Fearon 2002). As a result of the NIWC's place at the peace table, victims' rights, integrated education, housing, child care, youth employment and a civic forum became touchstones in the referendum campaign. Kate Fearon, a founding member of the Coalition, suggests that if the agreement had not addressed these concerns, many people might have voted against it, which would have jeopardised the peace process. The NIWC argued for the initiation of a civic forum as part of the Northern Ireland Assembly, so as to institutionalise opportunities for broader public participation in politics. This proposal was incorporated into the final Belfast (Good Friday) Agreement in 1998.

Women's political participation in electoral politics was put in the foreground by the work of the NIWC. Female delegates from other political parties began to attain higher profiles within their parties. When the Northern Ireland Assembly appointed Ministers, two of the ten were women (Fearon 2002). Co-founder of the NIWC Avila Kilmurray and the leader of the NIWC, Monica McWilliams (2011, p. 2), write that 'the inclusion of women in such negotiations is not merely a question of gender equity but also contributes to an improved negotiating process and the creation of a more durable peace agreement'. They stress the importance of relationship-building with leading protagonists who have suffered and inflicted pain, staff in the international mediators' team, parties outside Northern Ireland, the British Secretary of State, external experts, community-based groups and political prisoners, and with the international media. They stress also 'that one of the contributions it could make was to create a space for compromise' (2011, p. 10).

But what if forming a political party is not feasible? Equally, there are no guarantees that participation in peace processes will translate into long-term gains of place in post-conflict political and decision-making mechanisms. According to UNIFEM (2008a, p. 21), 'constitutional or electoral law quotas are the strongest means of increasing women's engagement in political competition regardless of political system'. In Nepal, for instance, following the 2006

Comprehensive Peace Agreement, which ended a decade-long conflict between the Maoists, the government and the monarchy, the work to draft a new constitution began. Women's groups actively rallied to demand at least 33 per cent representation by women in the Constituent Assembly (an assembly of representatives chosen by the people for the formation of a new constitution). Elections for the Constituent Assembly involved two systems: one of proportional representation and the other of direct representation.[9] Women's activism resulted in changes to the electoral law that required that, for the proportional representation elections, political parties had to ensure that 50 per cent of candidates on the party list were women. In addition, if the submitted lists of candidates failed to meet the quota requirement, they would be deemed invalid. The Electoral Commission reserved the right to remove candidates in order to ensure that quota provision was fulfilled and the candidate lists validated (Government of Nepal 2007). The success of these reforms is evinced by the fact that of the 601 Members of the Constituent Assembly elected to draft a new constitution, 197 (32.7 per cent) were women. With the numbers in place, women were able to call for the establishment of the Women's Caucus of the Constituent Assembly in 2009 to ensure that women's rights were included in the new constitution, as well as in existing acts and laws.

Another example of successful affirmative action measures such as quotas is Rwanda. The 48.8 per cent of seats won by women in the country's lower house of Parliament in the October 2003 elections was the result of 'specific mechanisms used to increase women's political participation, among them a constitutional guarantee, a quota system, and innovative electoral structures' (Powley 2005, p. 154). In the Constitutional Commission charged in 2000 with drafting a new constitution, 25 per cent of members (three out of twelve) were women. The process for drafting the constitution involved a series of consultations with Rwandans to solicit their inputs as well as to raise awareness of the principles on which the new constitution would be based. The women members of the Constitutional Commission worked closely with women's organisations and the newly established Ministry of Gender and Women in Development to ensure significant input by women's organisations. The result was that Rwanda's new constitution, adopted in 2003, enshrines a commitment to gender equality (Powley 2005). In the upper house (Senate), the constitution mandates 30 per cent representation by women. In the lower house (Chamber of Deputies), fifty-three members are elected by a proportional representation system; twenty-four seats (30 per cent) are reserved for women, to be contested in women-only elections, that is, 'only women can stand for election and only women can vote. The election for the women's seats is coordinated by the national system of women's councils' (2005, p. 156).[10] Finally, two are elected by the National Youth Council and one by the Federation of the Associations of the Disabled, making a total of eighty members.

Statistics from the Inter-Parliamentary Union (2010) on women in national Parliaments show that in 2010 the world average in both lower and upper houses combined was 19.2 per cent. Rwanda had the highest, with 53.6 per cent. Timor-Leste had 29.2 per cent, ahead of Australia's 27.3 per cent. Countries affected by conflict with less than 10 per cent in the lower house included Algeria, the Central African Republic, Côte d'Ivoire, the DRC, Lebanon, Nigeria, Somalia and Sri Lanka. There were no women in some lower houses in the Pacific islands, including the Federated States of Micronesia, Nauru, the Solomon Islands and Tuvalu.[11]

The advantage of affirmative action measures like those evident in Nepal and Rwanda is that they shift the burden of responsibility from individual women to institutional mechanisms, such as the process by which candidates are recruited. In order to be effective, affirmative action measures require women candidates to be elected into office, and this necessitates concerted efforts to remove barriers that impede women from exercising their rights to citizenship and active engagement in political parties. In the case of Nepal, for instance, in the direct representation system, in which 240 seats were contested in 2008, only twenty-nine women (12 per cent) won. This, Dahlerup (2005, p. 144) suggests, is not surprising, as none of the political parties fielded an adequate number of women candidates, and 'most women candidates were placed in constituencies where they had little chance of being elected'. Thus, increasing the number of women in Parliaments also requires a focus on improving women's access to political parties. Women rarely benefit from resources set aside for campaigning. Often, selection and nomination processes are biased or use gender-neutral criteria, which results in skewed selections. Systems of patronage tend to exclude women, making it difficult for them to integrate into the work of their political party; this 'impacts on the perception of women as viable candidates' (Shvedova 2005, p. 37).

Recognising that, historically, women have had limited opportunities to participate in the political process, many initiatives have focused on building women's leadership capacity. For example, since 1994, the Cambodian non-profit organisation Women for Prosperity (WFP) has been running workshops for women and civil society organisations on understanding the Cambodian constitution, CEDAW, the right to education and health care, marriage, family and anti-trafficking laws as well as leadership and organisational management. These initiatives were taken one step further during the 2002 first ever commune-level elections to be held after the fall of the Khmer Rouge regime. With support from the Asia Foundation, the US Agency for International Development and the National Democratic Institute (NDI), WFP ran several workshops on public speaking, speech-writing and campaigning to train women as candidates for the elections. Women secured 951 out of

11,257 commune council seats (8.4 per cent), increasing the number of women commune chiefs by nearly tenfold. Of the total number of women elected, more than 64 per cent had participated in WFP's training workshops (McGrew, Frieson & Chan 2004).

Affirmative action policies should be complemented by efforts geared towards enabling women to secure the votes required to be elected. Women's organisations like EMILY's List in Australia and the United States (supporting progressive women candidates) play an important role in helping candidates to raise money for campaigning. They have expanded the scope of their work to include capacity development on winning elections and holding office once elected, mentoring programs that link new candidates to former women Parliamentarians and facilitating access to polling and research data to help secure more votes (Sawer 2004).

Winning votes also necessitates a focus on voter registration and education. Voter registration requires proof of identity, which might be difficult for women to demonstrate, especially if they are internally displaced or lost documentation as they fled from violent conflicts (Powley & Anderlini 2004). In order to deal with this issue in Afghanistan, special measures were instituted that included creating women-only registration teams for the registration of women, offering alternative identification methods of a photograph or fingerprint and targeted civic education campaigns for women and religious leaders. This effort was complemented by women's organisations such as the Movement of Afghan Sisters, which provided voter education ahead of the 2009 Presidential elections (Sudhakar & Wolden 2010). Women-only polling stations are used in countries like Afghanistan to provide women with a safe place to vote. Voter education programs in general and those that target women in particular play a pivotal role in informing the public about registering to vote, the voting process, and voting rights and responsibilities, as well as giving details on the candidates and their platforms. Some education programs go a step further, in advocating women's right to make an independent decision on whom to vote for. For instance, during the 2004 elections in Indonesia, the Asia Foundation supported a local NGO called Hapsari to develop and broadcast programs on the rights of women voters in northern Sumatra. Similarly, in Aceh, the Foundation supported Flower Aceh, a women's rights organisation, disseminating posters, brochures and stickers with messages such as 'don't tell women how to vote'.

The jury is still out on the effectiveness of affirmative action measures in enabling a gender-inclusive peace and security agenda. Some studies have found that the presence of women during peace negotiations is linked to more gender-inclusive peace agreements (Babcock & Lashever 2007); others show that a critical mass of women in decision-making positions is more likely to result in women-friendly policies (Carroll 2001; Schwindt-Bayer & Mishler 2005; UNIFEM 2005; Wängnerud 2000); and still others fail to note any significant connection between the two (Devlin & Elgie 2008; Franceschet & Piscopo 2008; Grey 2002). Some studies show that even when only a small number of women representatives are present, they are able to significantly influence legislative agendas (Ayata & Tütüncü 2008; Towns 2003; Vega & Firestone 1995; Wolbrecht 2000). Some academics, like Jane Mansbridge (2005), argue that quotas inadvertently bolster essentialist stereotypes, that is, the assumption that only women can represent women's issues on issues faced by *all* women and, by extension, that women cannot represent men's issues or be represented by men. This is not the position we adopt. Taken together, these mixed results seem to suggest that while there is a need to increase the numerical presence of women in decision-making and peace processes, much more can be done to enable women's effective and substantive participation.

Participation is more than a numbers game

Why should women be included in formal processes in order to establish meaningful gender equality (Porter 2003; 2005)? Women are affected by conflict and thus by the consequences of peace agreements, which are intended not simply to end war but to set the basis for a new society. Inclusion of both women and men affirms rights, equality and justice. As so many examples provided throughout this book demonstrate, where women are present, they typically make a difference to the sorts of human security concerns prioritised. 'For example, the participation of women in the Guatemalan process resulted in specific commitments to women on housing, credit and land, health, attempts to locate children and orphans, penalising sexual harassment, and the creation of the national women's forum' (Porter 2003, p. 250).

Institutional barriers abound. Political party structures, rules and norms can constrain women's opportunities to advocate effectively. A case in point is the demand to follow party discipline, which discourages the development of cross-party platforms (Celis 2008; Franceschet & Piscopo 2008). Women usually are not nominated to significant cabinet portfolios or high-ranking positions in legislative committees (Sawers 2002a; Whip 1991). Marian Sawer (2004) calls attention to the lack of accountability of some women's representatives to their constituent base. Too little attention is paid to developing and supporting women's networks or caucuses that can serve as bases for women's representatives to draw upon (Reingold 2000; Thomas 1991). Some scholars suggest that other actors, such as women's movements and national women's machineries, might be more proactive in promoting women as a group rather than women Members of Parliament (Weldon 2002). Therefore, Karen Celis, Sarah Childs, Johanna Kantola and Mona Lena Krook (2007) suggest that the focus needs to be on identifying critical actors, whether as individuals or agencies, that can play a role in initiating policy changes.

Women's organisations and the international community are gradually beginning to turn their attention to addressing some of these institutional barriers.

Recognising that political parties play an important role in enabling women's access to the NDI – a nonpartisan organisation working to strengthen democratic institutions – the NDI supports women's organisations to engage with political parties. The goal is to examine potential gender inequities in the constitution of governing bodies, party manifestos and platforms, women's wings or voting rights at party conferences or conventions, and campaign financing. The call for at least a minimum of 33 per cent representation by women across all party structures and governing bodies is complemented by efforts to provide opportunities for the women's wing of a party to influence the party's platform. These include developing mentoring programs for less experienced female party members and women-friendly policies such as monetary supports for female candidates and party activists to cover childcare costs.

Equally important, legislative bodies and political parties are encouraged to support ongoing capacity development programs for elected and potential women's representatives. Azza Karam and Joni Lovenduski (2005, p. 190) suggest that in order to be effective Members of Parliament, women must learn the rules, use the rules and change the rules. By rules, they mean 'the customs, conventions, informal practices and specific regulations that govern the way a legislature functions. These include law-making processes, the division of labour in the assembly, hierarchy structures, ceremonies, disciplines, traditions, habits and the norms of the assembly including its internal functioning and its relationship to other parts of the government'. Based on its work with women's organisations in Asia and Africa, the NDI (2010, p. 80) recommends that capacity development programs should, in addition to emphasising women's rights, address potential 'gaps in women's formal or political education, while seeking to maximise or translate their existing skill sets (such as service delivery, advocacy, household business and management skills) into the political realm'. This means, on the one hand, covering information on the core responsibilities and duties of legislators, legislative systems and how they work. On the other hand, it also means paying special attention to areas like foreign affairs, defence, security and finance, so that women are able to make valuable contributions and influence these types of Parliamentary committees that traditionally tend to be dominated by men.

Study tours and exchange programs are other invaluable means to foster women's leadership. The Canadian roundtable on peacekeeping notes that lack of networks was one of the biggest barriers for women in the traditionally male areas of decision-making and peace processes (UN Association in Canada 2007). Meeting other women leaders engenders a sense of solidarity and guards against feelings of isolation and powerlessness. Conferences, workshops, forums and web networks are also ways of sharing information, including knowledge of international instruments that support women's local activism (Rehn & Johnson Sirleaf 2002). For instance, the Conflict Resolution Unit of the Department of Foreign Affairs, Ireland, has partnered with men's and women's organisations in Ireland, Northern Ireland, Liberia and Timor-Leste in a cross-learning process on UNSCR 1325. Through a series of conferences, workshops and panel discussions focusing on a specific aspect of the resolution, representatives and delegates build a collective understanding of how best to promote and protect women's leadership and interests in conflict resolution and peacebuilding, which can then be translated into action within their national contexts.

Isis-Women's International Cross-Cultural Exchange supports African women's peacebuilding efforts in a similar manner through its international exchange program, which brings together a diverse group of women leaders to exchange ideas, learn cross-cultural strategies and participate in solidarity actions to address women's issues from a human rights perspective. The new skills that women acquire enhance their capacities to facilitate change in their own country, including documenting specific experiences of women in situations of armed conflict, fact-finding and peace missions, presentation of position papers, conducting solidarity actions, sensitisation seminars, performing theatre for development and engaging in advocacy events. Exchange programs and study tours do not always need to be international in their scope. For instance, the NDI organised a tour to Uganda for female Somali leaders, including Members of Parliament as well as civil society representatives, to focus on the role women played in drafting the Ugandan constitution. A range of issues were discussed between the women, from the establishment and operations of the Uganda Women's Parliamentary Association to the importance of including women's caucuses and their links with Parliamentary women's or gender committees. The tour helped female Somali leaders to develop a legislative advocacy agenda that led to the formation of a Somali women's caucus (NDI 2010).

Promoting the establishment and maintenance of women's caucuses is another strategy used to build solidarity and to amplify women's voices. Women's caucuses model collaborative policy-making, thereby offering an alternative to partisan politics as well as opportunities to develop critical skills in policy-making and negotiations. In Rwanda, for instance, in 1996 (pre-UNSCR 1325), a cross-party caucus called the Forum of Women Parliamentarians was formed, comprising female Members from both houses of Parliament, women working in political parties and women elected through the women's council's election process. According to Connie Bwiza Sekamana, Member of Parliament, '[w]hen it comes to the Forum, we unite as women, irrespective of political parties. So we don't think of our parties, [we think of] the challenges that surround us as women' (in Powley 2007, p. 6). Similarly, in Uganda, a women's caucus, the largest organised caucus in the national assembly, was created, which included 'representatives of workers, the disabled, and a category of men labelled "Gender Sensitive Males" by women's caucus members' (Goetz 1998, p. 249). While Anne-Marie Goetz suggests its influence has been limited, the caucus is successful in bringing women across party lines together to work on issues such as violence against women and women's rights to land ownership.

Establishing and maintaining a cross-party women's caucus is challenging, because poor financing and staffing make it difficult to develop well-articulated policy positions. In addition, the pull to toe the party line or face disciplinary action places women politicians in a difficult position. There is an expectation that *all* women must necessarily agree on *all* issues for the caucus to work. However, such a high level of expectation is not placed on other cross-party working committees. A constructive step towards building a caucus might require an initial focus on non-partisan issues, such as in Sri Lanka, where the Women Parliamentarians' Caucus has come together in its call to address the low participation of women in politics resulting from the absence of affirmative action strategies and from violence against women in politics (NDI 2010).

Creating opportunities for women's caucus representatives to participate in all Parliamentary sub-committees, not just those labelled as 'women's issues' (for example, maternity benefits, violence against women and reproductive health), is more effective in integrating gender issues across a range of policy platforms. This approach is important to ensure that women's caucuses are not marginalised. Rwanda has adopted a system of creating a level playing field in Parliamentary committees by introducing a structure whereby, if the committee is chaired by a woman, the deputy chair is a male, and vice versa (NDI 2010). The work of a women's caucus can be supported by strong links to existing women's organisations.

Such links grant legitimacy to policy proposals put forward by women Parliamentarians and keep them in touch with changing and varying concerns of women.

To summarise, increasing the participation of women in decision-making on peace and security issues and fostering women's involvement in peace processes involve far more than simplistically providing access to a political party or to a seat at a negotiating table. It is more than a numbers game. As we shall see in the next chapter, gender mainstreaming has to mean more than this. It has to allow for the fact that women's participation in all aspects of conflict prevention and resolution and in peacebuilding improves the quality of sustainable peace.

Remaining challenges

A recent assessment of the extent to which national governments and international organisations promote women's participation in decision-making and peace processes highlights significant barriers that are yet to be addressed. Despite the existence of international protocols, conventions and resolutions, reaching women and their organisations has been erratic, as these protocols are not built in to the standard operating procedures of organisations. Even when they are, poor monitoring mechanisms and lack of accountability mean that little attention is paid to them. For instance, RAMSI was severely criticised by some Australian women for not having a gender unit as part of its original mission, despite the fact that the framework lists promoting equality between men and women as part of the mandate. Pressure from women's organisations resulted in the appointment of a women's adviser to oversee the adoption of UNSCR 1325 (Whittington 2006).

When there are opportunities to participate, these appear to be conditional on women proving their legitimacy. Women seem to qualify only 'if they are simultaneously prominent leaders with experience in high level negotiations and grassroots activists with a large constituency ... Meanwhile, the qualification for armed actors is their capacity to wreak violence' (Anderlini & Tirman 2010, p. 4). As Bell and O'Rourke (2007, p. 34) suggest, some women are uneasy about 'the terms on which inclusion is offered ... with women being included in preset processes in which there is little scope to reconsider and reshape the end goals'. They have developed this suggestion more recently to say that 'the difficulties of inclusion are not just technical ... [A]ttempts by women to promote gender equality through formal inclusion in legal instruments tends to result in uneven gains and even costs' (Bell and O'Rourke 2010, p. 978). The exclusive focus on ceasefires, political arrangements and conflict management leaves little room for women to voice their broader security concerns. In addition, representation in decision-making and peace processes appears to be contingent on outcomes benefiting all women, while no such demands are placed on men (Ní Aoláin & Rooney 2007). This leads to gender equity being framed as women's work as opposed to being a collective enterprise involving men and women, and indeed benefiting both. 'The difficulties of navigating the boundary between using gender as a category disruptive of traditional military and political assumptions, and "essentialising" women as bringing a "different voice", a different set of priorities, and a form of "transcendent" identity politics, is particularly acute in the peace negotiation context' (Bell & O'Rourke 2010, p. 978).

Women's poor participation continues to be framed in terms of a lack of capacity – but the question of what capacity needs to be developed is rarely addressed adequately. Rather than focusing on building skills that will enable women to participate more effectively in peace processes, typically, the focus is on generic leadership training or content-based training on women's rights and international protocols. While these types of training are useful, they should be linked more closely to building skills in undertaking gender analysis of peace and conflict issues, coalition-building and developing a common agenda. More importantly, greater attention ought to be paid to linking women's grassroots experience in peacebuilding to specific agenda items during negotiations, such as DDR, SSR governance and justice structure reforms. Unless women understand the rules of the game, there is little they can do to either leverage or change them. Sanam Naraghi Anderlini and John Tirman (2010) point to the need for capacity development programs to focus on the structure and procedures of peace processes and the mandates of international missions (such as mediation teams or peacekeeping missions). Working with women's groups to find entry points into such processes is vital to ensure that women's voices are heard.

Greater awareness of international conventions and resolutions such as CEDAW and UNSCR 1325 can provide a platform on which to ground demands for inclusion in peace processes. Rather than focusing on the content of these international mandates only in isolation, we can distinguish synergies between them. One of the biggest challenges that women's organisations face is translating the goals of UNSCR 1235 into strategic actions in ways that truly advance women's involvement in peace and security issues. While UNSCR 1325 lays out what needs to be done, it provides little guidance on how things should be done. CEDAW, with its specific recommendations for actions, provides substantive guidance on how the goals of UNSCR 1325 can be achieved. The resolution broadens the scope of CEDAW in two ways: it can be used to argue for the adoption of women's rights frameworks in conflict zones where countries are not parties to CEDAW, and it can draw in non-state actors and international organisations under the purview of the Convention. Sustaining participation can be a stiff test, especially during post-conflict reconstruction in which women's organisations are overburdened in terms of having to engage in debates at the national level as well as provide essential services.

Women are demanding more than just a seat at the peace table. Quite rightly, they want the opportunity to reframe peace negotiations and post-conflict reconstruction to include a more inclusive human security agenda. This means creating an enabling environment to foster participation. Practical considerations (such as childcare provisions or alternatives, such as funding an extended family member to attend the peace talks, covering the costs of travel and incidental costs and ensuring protection) go a long way in supporting women's participation. Additionally, women's participation extends beyond involvement in peace talks to include a pivotal role in the implementation of agreements. In terms of sustaining women's participation, it is important that peace negotiations make specific references to international declarations, conventions and resolutions that underpin women's rights rather than generic human rights. Pointed references to the BPFA, UNSCR 1325 and CEDAW provide important leverage for women's organisations, granting greater credibility and validity to their demands.

Finally, to reiterate, our argument is that peace negotiations ought to adopt a broader definition of women's participation that combines equality, a defence of rights and an understanding that women can make a difference in their approach to peace and security. Participation includes not just representation in political decision-making but also women's effective participation in civil society organisations.

CHAPTER 6

Gender-inclusive relief and recovery

Within the resolutions on 'women and peace and security', references to relief and recovery are diverse and broad-ranging. For example, UNSCR 1325 (UNSC 2000a, para. 8) calls on actors involved in 'negotiating and implementing peace agreements, to adopt a gender perspective' that responds to 'the special needs of women and girls during repatriation and resettlement and for rehabilitation, reintegration and post-conflict reconstruction'. The same paragraph refers to the need to take 'measures that support local women's peace initiatives and indigenous processes for conflict resolution, and that involve women in all of the implementation mechanisms of the peace agreements'. It also confirms the necessity to take 'measures that ensure the protection of and respect for human rights of women and girls, particularly as they relate to the constitution, the electoral system, the police and the judiciary'. These are comprehensive calls.

In terms of relief and recovery, UNSCR 1820 (UNSC 2008a, para. 13) addresses the requirement 'to support the development and strengthening of the capacities of national institutions' like judicial and health systems and local civil society networks, 'to provide sustainable assistance'. UNSCR 1888 (UNSC 2009b, para. 8) calls upon the Secretary-General to 'deploy rapidly a team of experts to situations of particular concern with respect to sexual violence in armed conflict' in order to strengthen 'the rule of law, civilian and military judicial systems, mediation, criminal investigation, SSR, witness protection, fair trial standards, and public outreach'. The key point of UNSCR 1888 is 'to address impunity...and encourage a holistic national approach to address sexual violence in armed conflict, including by enhancing criminal accountability, responsiveness to victims, and judicial capacity' (2009b, para. 8). The Secretary-General is requested to direct UN agencies 'to ensure systematic mainstreaming of gender issues' (2009b, para. 22). The resolution asks Member States, UN entities and civil society 'to build national capacity in the judicial and law enforcement systems in situations of particular concern with respect to sexual violence in armed conflict' (2009b, para. 9). It also seeks to 'increase access to health care, psychosocial support, legal assistance and socio-economic reintegration services' (2009b, para. 13).

UNSCR 1889 (UNSC 2009c, para. 10) 'encourages Member States in post-conflict situations, in consultation with civil society, including women's organizations, to specify in detail women and girls' needs and priorities and design concrete strategies, in accordance with their legal systems, to address those needs and priorities'. The resolution requests that attention be paid to

> greater physical security and better socio-economic conditions, through education, income generating activities, access to basic services, in particular health services, including sexual and reproductive health and reproductive rights and mental health, gender-responsive law enforcement and access to justice, as well as enhancing capacity to engage in public decision-making at all levels (2009c, para. 10).

It is clear that we cannot cover all dimensions of relief and recovery in this chapter, and, indeed, many aspects outlined in the resolutions above have already been touched on in the preceding chapters. In this chapter, we concentrate on four aspects of relief and recovery.

1. We examine what it means to connect women's rights and development with gender-inclusive security. We maintain that building peace in the context of economic development requires attention to gender disparities.
2. We briefly explain gender mainstreaming with its goal of gender equality, highlighting that successful mainstreaming requires a three-pronged approach, namely, an equal treatment perspective, a gender perspective and a women's perspective, where the third warrants, at times, women-specific recovery and relief programs.
3. We explain the importance of indicators in monitoring and evaluating progress on gender-inclusive relief and recovery. To do this, we show some of the advantages and also some of the drawbacks in the Secretary-General's indicators of progress.
4. We look at the enormous issue of how to go about rethinking the concept of empowerment so that it is meaningful cross-culturally.

We argue that a rights-based commitment to gender equality is the foundation on which culturally adaptable strategies of empowerment and of relief and recovery can be based. A rights-based approach to development affirms that every individual has rights that are universal and inalienable, and that every right comes with obligations to protect and respect that right. None of these strategies is easy. Over a ten-year period of examining country-specific resolutions that include language on women and/or gender since 2000, only 'seven per cent of total resolutions monitored and analysed' refer to women in a context of reconstruction in peacebuilding. This means there are stark absences in 'references to women's economic empowerment as a component of reconstruction and peacebuilding, or the impact that equitable, inclusive reconstruction and peacebuilding can have on the prevention of conflict' (Butler, Mader & Kean 2010, p. 37). Less than 8 per cent of recovery budgets in post-conflict needs assessments 'identify spending priorities addressing women's needs, and just 5.7 per cent of actual budgetary outlays of multi-donor trust funds in post-conflict countries finance gender equality or women's empowerment projects' (UNDPKO et al. 2010, p. 7). The difficulties in meeting gender equality in the relief and recovery stage of post-conflict societies are immense.

Connecting women's rights and development with gender-inclusive security

The move towards adopting a human security approach to peacebuilding helps to make explicit the links between security and economic and social development. Rooted in a rights-based framework, the human security approach underscores the right to freedom for men and women, not just from fear, but also from poverty and deprivation. In doing so, the approach recognises and values the importance of socioeconomic development in building sustainable peace. It is overly optimistic to say that the adoption of a human security approach necessarily means that the connections between women's rights, development and security are highlighted. Given this caution, Simone Wisotzki (2003) stresses that 'underlying gender hierarchies and their relevance for shaping societal practice must be made visible, and alternatives to overcoming insecurities have to be developed'.

For instance, following a conflict, women have very few opportunities for securing an income, and the inability to do so places a heavy burden on them to ensure survival of their families, particularly when left solely responsible for family maintenance. The damage to health services and the lack of access to reproductive health services, particularly ante- and post-natal care, jeopardise the health of women and girls, and result in high rates of infant and maternal mortality. Despite the fact that women and children (girls and boys) account for the majority of IDPs and refugees, their protection, access to food, health services, education, training and income-generation opportunities are often overlooked. Moreover, gender-stereotypical views, such as that men are more violent than women, result in neglect of the discrimination and deprivation suffered by female combatants. DDR programs are particularly remiss, following a very narrow interpretation of who constitutes a combatant. The absence of gender-sensitive frameworks means that DDR programs fail to recognise that while some women do indeed take an active part in armed conflict, negative stigmatisation, association with sexual violence and killing lead many women to conceal their identity. Further, women who are forced to marry soldiers use the opportunity presented by peace negotiations to flee from oppressive relationships and return to their families. These women slip under the radar, not receiving any benefits or social reintegration assistance from DDR programs.

Relief and recovery programs must fall in line with the Paris Declaration on Aid Effectiveness (2005), which outlines five guiding principles around ownership, alignment, harmonisation, managing results and mutual accountability. These principles offer opportunities to integrate strategies for advancing gender equality. Yet, still, in most countries, women's inequality and low level of education hamper development progress. Within development discourse and development practice, a change from a simplistic 'women in development' (WID) approach to a 'gender and development' (GAD) approach came about primarily for two reasons. First, there was a clear need to challenge essentialist, universal categories of women implicit in a WID approach; and second, there was increasing recognition that inequitable gender power relations that can influence and structure women's subordination must be addressed. While 'poverty is on the decline for much of the world ... for every three years that a country is affected by major violence, poverty reduction lags behind 2.7 percentage points' (World Bank 2011, p. 60). GAD approaches to peace and security emphasise the need to construct rather than *re*construct social, economic and political institutions in post-conflict communities that support gender equality (Greenberg & Zuckerman 2009). The focus in development discourse and practice therefore shifts to achieving gender balance in policy-making and resource allocation. It moves towards an equitable distribution of the benefits of development and works proactively to engage men in promoting gender equality.

In this chapter and in the following case studies, we utilise a concept of development that does not refer merely to economic growth or to capitalist market economics but to an alternative vision that fosters human capabilities, social capital and socially sustainable livelihoods. This vision overlaps with many core principles underlying liberal peace theory (Richmond 2010). These include freedoms of expression, human rights and the importance of law. But we raise objections to the familiar association of state-building practices with economic liberalisation and neoliberal versions of development. We are critical of the practices attending this association, not least because they tend to create new elites and increase global inequalities.

As John Paul Lederach (1997) has argued, the conflict resolution community, in its search for sustainable solutions that avoid an imposition of western development practices, understands the importance of drawing on local wisdom to grasp root causes of conflict in specific, historical, cultural and linguistic contexts.

Timothy Donais (2009, p. 11) also suggests that 'an acknowledgement of the importance of local agency in peacebuilding processes requires thinking through not only the meanings of *ownership* but also the characteristics of *the locals*'. Deciding which locals matter has to take into account the enormous diversity and division within local groups, so that relationships between insiders and outsiders often end in 'negotiated hybridity' (2009, p. 14) involving relevant local actors, civil society groups, national governments and diverse groups in the international community. Donais's point here is to argue for the importance of strong foundations of development that are adjusted to local conditions and developed through collaborative partnerships. The Weapons Free Village Campaign in the Solomon Islands, which followed the three years of civil unrest, is an example of valuing local wisdom. The Peace Monitoring Council set up as part of the Townsville Peace Agreement of 2000 launched this campaign in 2002 in Guadalcanal and Malaita, two islands that were most affected by the conflict. Women from the villages were 'integrally involved in the campaign and were particularly effective as peace monitors, encouraging villages to join the campaign' (Nelson 2006). They were able to draw on their traditional roles and knowledge to stigmatise weapons ownership through using peer pressure and awareness-raising among men. An evaluation of the Campaign by Carol Nelson and Robert Muggah (2004) found that the Campaign played a positive role in facilitating weapons surrender from both militant and non-militant citizens.

Establishing security is an imperative in post-conflict societies, because little development work can begin where people are homeless, traumatised, starving and distrustful of rapid change. As alluded to in earlier chapters, the idea of 'post-conflict reconstruction' is not always useful, because to 'reconstruct' socioeconomic conditions for women is, in the main, merely to reintroduce entrenched inequalities. Injustice, disparities and exclusion often generate conflict;

hence, we endorse Marcia Greenberg and Elaine Zuckerman's (2009, p. 3) view that 'a "gender lens" may sharpen understanding' of development and security. Developing a rights-based approach to gender-inclusive security is 'founded on women's rights to: participate *meaningfully* in policymaking and resource allocation; benefit *substantially* from public and private resources and services; and partner *collaboratively* with men in constructing the new peace and prosperity'. This approach articulates understandings of women-focused activities 'where purposeful investment in women's capabilities may contribute to the post-conflict agenda' (2009, pp. 3, 4). By way of example, Greenberg and Zuckerman highlight a project in Peshawar to train exiled Afghan women to teach Afghan girls, and, while this seems like a WID approach, in fact, it is a GAD approach because it targets gender equalities.

In a similar vein, Naomi Cahn, Dina Haynes and Fionnuala Ní Aoláin (2010, p. 357) support 'social services justice' which 'requires a multi-sectoral approach that involves the community as well as health, legal, security, and the social services actors'; they suggest that 'social services justice is a necessary component of post-conflict reconstruction'. This is because a response to immediate requirements 'makes gender central by grounding post-conflict needs in lived experiences [that respond] to the daily realities of life in a post-conflict country' (2010, pp. 341–2). These authors argue that 'perhaps the most significant forms of justice for women include not just criminal and civil accountability (rights-based justice), but assistance of the kind traditionally associated with development ... because it focuses on providing critical social services to facilitate all aspects of post-conflict reconstruction' (2010, pp. 354, 355). The cook-stove project in Darfur is an apt example of such a service; engineers visited refugee camps and consulted with women on the need for alternative stoves because women and girls are often sexually assaulted when travelling to collect wood and so increasingly are reluctant to venture out. In developing a more fuel-efficient stove, a lesson is learned 'that only by deep and practical engagement with the needs of the communities on the ground', which can come about only through listening to the voices of women as well as men, 'will societies advance sufficiently to ensure development agendas that are sustainable and transformative' (2010, p. 349).

It is useful to note that in the ten-year study monitoring country-specific resolutions that include language on women and/or gender since 2000, only 4 per cent 'refer to needs and rights of refugee and IDP women. This is two per cent of total resolutions monitored and analysed'. This

> analysis illuminates gaps in addressing gender-sensitive aid distribution, which would prevent the exploitation of women who are recipients of assistance. Additionally, there is seldom mention of training humanitarian actors on how to protect and promote women's rights and concerns in the provision of humanitarian assistance (Butler, Mader & Kean 2010, p. 48).

The tasks for post-conflict relief and recovery are enormous. It does mean that reforms should be introduced systematically but gradually. Involving women leaders in long-term change programs in security, justice and economic empowerment can shift intransigent attitudes to gender. For example, when women are involved in peace agreements, in terms of reconstruction and socioeconomic recovery they 'generally emphasise land and inheritance rights, access to credit, access to education ... a strong investment in skills-training and capacity-building, and special attention to the needs of female-headed households' (UNIFEM 2010, p. 15). The involvement of male leaders in development programs is also crucial, to shift entrenched gender stereotypes.

Mainstreaming gender

Having begun to make connections between women's rights and development, we turn now to examine how gender mainstreaming can contribute to gender-inclusive security. The ultimate goal of gender mainstreaming is to achieve gender equality. The term 'gender' draws attention to socially determined identities, roles and responsibilities attributed to the biological sexes and the differing expectations and values placed upon men's and women's identities, roles and relations. The term 'mainstream' refers to the dominant set of values, ideas, beliefs and attitudes, relationships and practices in a society. It includes all of society's main institutions and organisations that influence who and what is valued, how resources are allocated, who can do what and who gets what in society. The aim of gender mainstreaming is to transform the 'mainstream' in which stereotypically inscribed roles, identities and responsibilities lead to the dominance of one sex (male/masculinity) over the other. Such a transformation seeks to bring about a balance in gender relations such that differences between gender roles, responsibilities and relations are valued equally.

In 1995, the UN Fouth World Conference on Women in Beijing institutionalised gender mainstreaming as the agreed overall strategy to achieve the goal of gender equality. Despite this international level of consensus to pursue the strategy, the meaning and practice of gender mainstreaming are 'contested terrain' (March, Smyth & Mukhopadhyay 1999, p. 10). There is no single definition of gender mainstreaming; however, most definitions point to common principles.

- Gender mainstreaming is a *process* for 'making women's as well as men's concerns and experiences an integral dimension of the design, implementation, monitoring and evaluation of policies and programs in all political, economic and societal spheres so

that women and men benefit equally and inequality is not perpetuated' (UN Economic and Social Council 1998, p. 28).
- As a process, it involves assessing the implications of any action, legislation, policy or program for women and men. Its strategies seek to make men's and women's concerns and experiences integral to the design, implementation, monitoring and evaluation of, in this case, relief and recovery programs, so that inequality is not perpetuated and so that women and men benefit from such programs. 'Mainstreaming gender requires a holistic understanding of gender dynamics which does not reduce gender to the prevailing essentialist assumptions about men's and women's roles in war and peace' (Willett 2010, p. 143).
- Gender mainstreaming does not simply mean making programs or resources more accessible to women, but rather it invites the 'simultaneous mobilisation of legal instruments, financial resources, analytical and organisational capacities in order to introduce in all areas the desire to build balanced relationships between women and men' (Commission of the European Communities 1996, p. 5). In order to do this, the Council of Europe (1998, p. 4) suggests that this involves '(re)organisation, improvement, development and evaluation of policy processes . . . thus making it possible to challenge the male bias that characterises society and the structural character of gender inequality'.

Too often, 'gender mainstreaming is being developed in a context where gender is understood as a difference between men and women and not as a system of femininities and masculinities and power hierarchies between them' (Valenius 2007, p. 513). Attention given to differences heeds all gendered roles, power relations and access to resources in the aftermath of conflict and in working towards new beginnings.

'Although the language of "mainstreaming" is by no means unproblematic, the significance of asking that "the actions and operations" of the UN Security Council be undertaken with a gendered sensitivity is great' (Shepherd 2008, p. 389). This is important to note, despite the fact that 'existing attempts to mainstream gender within the UN rarely go to the heart of the institutional inequities and power relations that structure gender relations within the organisation. Rather, gender mainstreaming has been grafted onto existing power structures that are circumscribed by the essentialist nature of binary opposites in which gender has been interpreted as woman, and women remain differentiated from men' (Willett 2010, p. 143). In trying to understand the nature of this binary further, it is helpful to consider the opinion of Anne-Marie Goetz and Joanne Sandler (2007, p. 163), who write as gender equality advocates who worked in UNIFEM.[1] They suggest that there are significant deficiencies within UN structures. 'The first is fragmentation, and the lack of emphasis on building on the strengths of women's organising and women's entities.' As one example of this, civil society women's rights leaders often promote women being elected into Parliament, but then the organisation feels abandoned 'once their representatives enter the political mainstream with lost opportunities for alliance building' (2007, p. 167).

A second deficit of the gender mainstreaming strategy is more complex, in that the abuse of or lack of women's rights is not seen by many bureaucrats as urgent in the same way that humanitarian emergencies obviously are. 'Women's suffering is too routine, too normalised to generate shame and outrage.' In development discourse, the idea that gender equality is a cross-cutting issue is dominant. However, Goetz and Sandler (2007, p. 167) suggest that in addition to bureaucratic logic not readily tolerating change agents who keep referring to gender as a cross-cutting issue, a further danger with gender mainstreaming is that everyone sees themself as a gender expert, whereas it really does need specialised expertise to build gender equality.

> Instead of systemic change, we have therefore had to rely on palliatives: normative frameworks and rights agreements rather than a massive increase in prosecutions for perpetrators of gender-based violence; micro-finance instead of employment and property rights; quotas for women candidates for public office rather than campaign finance reform and democratised political parties.

Normative frameworks, microcredit and quotas are all important strategies for change but do not necessarily permeate deep structures of patriarchal inequality. As Goetz and Sandler (2007, p. 169) write further, '[g]ender mainstreaming is not a sales strategy; but it has been coopted, just like rights-based approaches and participatory development has been in some instances. It is insidious when it creates a window dressing to make it look as if there is real engagement with gender equality'. An apt example is peace agreements. While more of these do address gender issues, 'only 16 per cent of peace agreements contain specific provisions on women's rights and needs' (UNDPKO et al. 2010, p. 12).

When Angela Raven-Roberts was a UN program officer responsible for implementing principles of gender mainstreaming, she identified three main reasons for its lack of success in PKOs.

1. There was 'a lack of conceptual coherence among the humanitarian, human rights, political, and development approaches that the United Nations is expected to balance in its responses to armed conflict' (Raven-Roberts 2005, pp. 43–4), so organisational responses to gender mainstreaming often are off the cuff. For instance, gender equality is not mentioned as one of the

'essential complements' to effective peacebuilding in the *Agenda for peace* (Boutros-Ghali 1995) or the Brahimi report (Brahimi 2000), despite efforts through the 1990s to support the integration of women's rights using the WID and GAD approaches (Barnes 2006). Thus, efforts to integrate gender into relief and recovery remained informal and lacked legitimacy until UNSCR 1325, which makes gender concerns part of mainstream understandings of peacebuilding.

2. There was 'the bias against gender equality within the United Nations system' itself (Raven-Roberts 2005, p. 44). Sex-disaggregated statistics by the UNDPKO show that in 2010, women made up only 4.14 per cent of UN military experts on missions (including UNMOs, military liaison officers and military advisers), 2.42 per cent of troops (including staff officers) and 8.7 per cent of police (including individual police and FPUs) (UNDPKO 2010).

3. Related to the preceding reason, the evaluation and accountability structures were ineffective. Johnston (2004) points out that in spite of the UNDPKO's commitment to establishing gender units in all missions as part of its UNCSR 1325 implementation strategy, such units are incorporated on an improvised basis and often only as a result of intense lobbying by civil society organisations and UN agencies such as UN Women. When gender units are established, they are often under-resourced and located within a hierarchical structure in which they have little opportunity to influence change. For instance, in the 2002 UN operation in Afghanistan, the post of Senior Gender Adviser was only temporarily filled for two months and then downgraded to Gender Adviser.

Hilary Standing (2007, p. 104) maintains that gender mainstreaming is often 'a paradoxical affair', in that 'it becomes over-politicised when linked to resources to be competed for. It becomes depoliticised as the demand for "industrial" or mass production models of gender mainstreaming in the form of toolkits and checklists grows'. As she explains, easy caricatures can arise with a 'tick box' management of gender requirements. Standing (2007, p. 105) argues that it is a powerful myth 'that the empowerment language of politics and advocacy can be transferred into bureaucratic mainstreaming without its meaning being changed'. We elaborate on empowerment shortly. While there is undoubtedly a tricky link between policy and implementation, we suggest that policy can be instrumental in instigating significant change when it is self-conscious about questioning gendered, structural issues, and also when it is highly gender-sensitive to culturally diverse needs of women and men.

From a feminist perspective, an important aspect of gender mainstreaming is involving the state as a driving force for transformative change. 'The agenda for influencing the "mainstream" includes altering public policies, improving implementation and delivery of policies', and such changes in administrative systems indirectly benefit women and men (Subrahmanian 2007, p. 113). Like others, Ramya Subrahmanian (2007, p. 119) criticises the constrictions of mainstreaming when they are caught up in bureaucratic institutions. To liberate gender mainstreaming, she suggests breaking it up into its component parts, namely, 'policy reform, administrative reform, analytical and conceptual strengthening, political advocacy'. This recognises the broader political contexts in which these component parts operate.

For example, Liberia's NAP on UNSCR 1325 (Government of Liberia 2010) identifies ten strategic issues. In order to address these issues, the action plan outlines policy, advocacy, capacity development, monitoring and evaluation, and administrative reforms. For instance, in addressing the NAP's strategic issue 2, to '[p]rotect rights and strengthen security for women and girls', the policy actions call for developing and reviewing policy security frameworks with the involvement of security sector institutions, the Women's Legislative Caucus, the relevant Parliamentary committee and women's security groups. Administrative reforms focus on revising gender-blind codes of conduct and standard operating procedures of security sector institutions to ensure compliance with UNSCR 1325 and 1820 and the national gender policy. Advocacy efforts centre on the launch of an hour-long countrywide community radio program called *Women in Security Hour*.

In 2004, the UNDPKO published its *Gender resource package for peacekeeping operations* as an attempt to provide concrete guidance of what it means to mainstream gender and improve numbers of women as troops, UNMOs and UNPOL. Yet, in his 2004 report, then Secretary-General Kofi Annan (UNSC 2004, p. 24) said that 'in no area of peace and security work are gender perspectives systematically incorporated in planning, implementation, monitoring and reporting'. By 2007, Secretary-General Ban Ki-moon (UNSC 2007, p. 17) was more positive and referred to 'significant advances' in 'many substantive areas', with a 'zero tolerance to sexual exploitation and abuse' and the allocation of Gender Advisers in eleven of eighteen ongoing missions.

In response to some of these outlined deficits in gender mainstreaming strategies, it is useful to note that Australia supports a Gender Standby Capacity Project (GenCap). 'GenCap aims to ensure that humanitarian action takes into consideration the different needs and capacities of women, girls, boys and men equally' (AusAID 2010a, p. 23). It deploys Gender Advisers in early stages of sudden emergencies as well as in protracted or recurring humanitarian situations. They work alongside UN agencies, NGOs and governments. GenCap seeks to build capacities of people and organisations to prioritise gender issues in their responses, such as health requirements of pregnant women, adequate lighting in temporary shelters or access to food assistance for women-headed households.

While there is broad-based acceptance that achieving gender equality is a desirable goal explicit in gender mainstreaming, there is little consensus on how to go about it. There are significant tensions between gender mainstreaming and women-specific provisions. A women-specific approach aims at counterbalancing 'the unequal starting positions of men and women in most societies' (Verloo 2001, p. 3) by focusing on empowering women as a group through targeted programs and policies. Some fear mainstreaming will result in a dilution of responsibility – the risk that promoting gender equality could become 'everyone's responsibility but no-one's job' (Gregory 1999). Others call for a more mainstream approach that changes decision-making structures and procedures so that gender is prioritised. In such an approach, 'women not only become part of the mainstream, they also reorient the nature of the mainstream' (Jahan 1995, p. 13). There is a fundamental misunderstanding that these two approaches are mutually exclusive. We argue that both approaches are needed in the pursuit of gender equality.

We strongly support Booth and Bennet's (2002) three-pronged approach to gender mainstreaming: the equal treatment perspective, the gender perspective and the women's perspective. The equal treatment perspective focuses attention on ensuring formal equality through making certain that legal instruments grant women and men the same rights and responsibilities (such as anti-discrimination legislation). The gender perspective acknowledges the relevance of men's lives and masculinities to the equality debate. It recognises that a fairer distribution of human responsibilities must aim to transform men's roles as well as those of women (Mackay & Bilton 2003; Rees 1998). The perspective also directs attention to gender relations and the distribution of power between men and women as well as dealing with other social relationships such as social class and cultural background. The women's perspective recognises that in most communities women as a group suffer institutionalised marginalisation and discrimination. To address this issue, special attention needs to be focused on women through targeted programs (such as mandatory quotas to increase women's participation in decision-making), to 'rectify their past experience of discrimination' (Booth & Bennet 2002, p. 434). Booth and Bennet encourage us to visualise these three perspectives as a three-legged stool for which each perspective is a critical support in building and achieving sustainable gender equality. The question to ask is which leg(s) must be reinforced and which leg(s) are weak and must be strengthened?

Indicators in monitoring and evaluating progress

Having outlined the importance of both women's rights and gender mainstreaming in achieving gender-inclusive relief and recovery, we now emphasise the importance of collecting reliable data, and monitoring and evaluating progress. Systematic, meaningful collection of data on relief and recovery takes into account different contexts, actors, sexes, ages, needs and risks. Monitoring evaluates whether initiatives undertaken are having the desired impact. For example, an SSR assessment aims 'to gain knowledge of the local, regional and international stakeholder, specific security and justice providers, as well as the specific security and justice needs of the population. The data collected from assessments can feed into legislation, planning processes, budgets, reports, and existing policies and services' (Popovic 2008, p. 2). Different stakeholders respond differently to gender-related questions about rates of SGBV, equal access to security and justice mechanisms, and what reforms are prioritised.

In the ten-year study since 2000 of the monitored resolutions that included references to women and/or gender, only 5 per cent 'refer to women and justice and SSR . . . [T]hese references focus predominantly on ending impunity for crimes of sexual violence, and SGBV training for domestic security forces to strengthen their response to the needs of women' (Butler, Mader & Kean 2010, p. 40). Insufficient attention is paid to women's roles in relief and recovery work. Take, for example, the role of police. 'Studies on policing have found that female police officers use less force, are better at defusing potentially violent situations, and facilitate community policing well'. Examples of this are in Nicaragua, where gender reforms of the police sector in the 1990s led to it being described as 'the most "women-friendly" force in the region' (World Bank 2011, pp. 151–2). The all-female Indian police unit in Liberia, the Woman and Child Protection Unit in the police force in Namibia and a Family Support Unit in the Sierra Leone UN mission are further examples of responding specifically to the requirements of women and girls. Without indicators to assess progress, the urgency of specific responses is not always obvious.

Indicators of progress are measurable, quantifiable, comparative statistics. Figures alone do not tell much. Contextual narrative is essential. Nicola Popovic (2008, p. 12) distinguishes between different types of indicators, so 'input indicators measure the extent to which resources have been allocated to ensure that a project or policy can actually be implemented', while 'performance/process indicators measure the activities during implementation to track progress towards the intended results' and 'progress/outcome indicators measure the long-term results of the program or policy'. Examples of indicators in justice reform and gender can be given (in 2008, p. 21).[2] If the goal is 'an effective and accountable justice system and strengthened rule of law', then examples of gender equality include the 'promotion and protection of the human rights of women and girls, men and boys'. The data could be collected through surveys, and gender-sensitive outcome indicators for justice include 'an increase in the percentage of women and men who have confidence in the legal system to treat them fairly – by ethnicity, socio-economic group and other categories'. A similar process of goals, gender equality results, methods of data collection and examples of gender-sensitive indicators can be made for law reform, institutional reform, SGBV, gender equity, reduced discrimination or public awareness of human rights.

Karen Barnes (2009, p. 7) rightly states that while there is a significant body of literature concerning gender indicators in development interventions, there is little attention paid to developing 'indicators to capture the range of issues relevant to peacebuilding initiatives'. Consequently, there is little official monitoring of the resolutions on 'women and peace and security'. Barnes (2009, p. 9) points to 'the link between monitoring and reporting and accountability'. While she endorses a SMART approach, that is, one that makes indicators specific, measurable, achievable, realistic and time-bound, she advocates a response that is not too technical to 'maintain flexibility when defining and using indicators' (2009, p. 11).

GAPS provides country-specific information on Afghanistan, the DRC, Nepal, Northern Ireland and Sri Lanka on identifiable achievements, good practices and obstacles to the implementation of UNSCR 1325 (Onslow 2009).[3] It uses a checklist around key UNSCR 1325 actors in-country, national policy frameworks, national-level activities related to UNSCR 1325, national government financial resources, peace negotiations and agreements, governance and institution-building, SSR and DDR, transitional justice and judicial reform, SGBV prevention and response, international law and UN in-country achievements. From its research, seven findings, called 'cross-cutting trends' are highlighted (2009, p. 146). For the purpose of this section, one of the trends – the measurement of impact recommendation – is pertinent, in which policy-makers must 'ensure that clear gender-sensitive benchmarks, indicators and lines of responsibility are integrated into all policies and action plans on peace and security, development, gender equality, women's human rights and UNSCR 1325' (2009, p. 148).

UNSCR 1889 (UNSC 2009c) calls for indicators to monitor this resolution as a step towards developing a monitoring system for UNSCR 1325. As we saw in Chapter 2, only a small proportion of Member States actually have a NAP in place, let alone clear indicators and monitoring strategies. Australia released its draft plan in August 2011 for public consultation. We are hoping that clear indicators will be outlined in the final release. Again, civil society groups in Member States are advocating global accountability processes.[4] A set of twenty-six indicators has resulted from civil society organisation lobbying (UNSC 2010a). Each indicator states what is to be assessed and who has responsibility for overseeing the implementation, and lists descriptors to measure or understand what is being assessed.

One indicator in the relief and recovery area attends to the needs of women and girls from vulnerable groups such as IDPs, victims of SGBV, ex-combatants, refugees and returnees, with assistance from UN entities such as UN Women and the Peacebuilding Support Office. This indicator addresses the 'proportion of budget related to indicators that address gender equality issues in strategic planning frameworks' (UNSC 2010a). Specific groups have variable needs at different times, and resources should adjust accordingly. Disaggregated data, targets and content analysis should improve budget allocations and involve thoughtful responses that address gender equality to needy groups. For example, funding might be channelled to civil society groups with expertise in dealing with vulnerable women who are encouraged to apply for funding.

Rethinking empowerment

An important aspect of development work in relief and recovery is geared towards increasing empowerment. The term 'women's empowerment' is used frequently, but often uncritically. In particular, critics of the extent to which empowerment programs actually do transform development goals argue 'that neoliberal norms such as individualism, responsibility and economic order have shaped empowerment initiatives to a far greater extent than considerations of local input, marginalised groups, or representation' (MacKenzie 2009, p. 200). Economic independence usually is the stated objective of empowerment programs. Rosalind Eyben and Rebecca Napier-Moore (2009, p. 285) maintain that 'a privileging of instrumentalist meanings of empowerment associated with efficiency and growth are crowding out more socially transformative meanings associated with rights and collective action'. These authors remind us that associated concepts include participation, power, equality and social justice. Instead, in places like India, 'empowerment' increasingly becomes a neoliberal tool, 'a technical magic bullet of micro-credit programs and political quotas for women' (2009, p. 287). The consequence of this is stark: '[g]rowth, efficiency and effectiveness are getting stronger, while moral, justice and political arguments are weakening' (2009, p. 295). Consistent with a feminist notion of empowerment that separates itself from neoliberal interpretations of development, we emphasise versions of self-realisation, autonomy and opportunities to demand change. Empowerment should enable people to develop their full potential so that they can participate in decision-making in those areas that are crucial to their own sense of fulfilment.

From the outset, we should say that when questioning grassroots women in Timor-Leste, Fiji and Sri Lanka on their understandings of empowerment, we found a lot of vagueness. It is perhaps a term used loosely in the west that is not always meaningful in many places. A UN official in Timor-Leste defined it at a simple level as meaning *'to be able to make an informed choice and to be able to exercise or realise that choice'*. Again in Timor-Leste, an Australian researcher suggested that empowerment is very much a development concept, but the concept is richer. She said, *'I think it applies to transformation of social relations*'. It is, of course, the transformative potential of women's empowerment and inclusion in all peace and security matters that underlies this book's fundamental arguments.

Particularly since September 11, 2001, a case can be made that the rise of political Islam has disempowered many Islamic women who live in countries where radical Islamists link culture, religion and patriarchal concepts of the 'good Islamic woman'. The Research Programme Consortium on Women's Empowerment in Muslim Contexts[5] seeks to overturn patriarchal structures that undermine gender-equitable Muslim practices. Its focus is in Asia, given that 'almost half of the world's Muslims live in China, Indonesia, Iran, and Pakistan under diverse circumstances that differ not only between countries but also within each country' (Wee & Shaheed 2008, p. 9). The Consortium adopts a definition of 'women's empowerment' as 'an increased ability to question, challenge and eventually transform unfavourable gendered power relations, often legitimised in the name of "culture"' (2008, p. 16). This definition builds on the basic premise that 'women can be empowered only through their own agency – that is, through decision and actions undertaken as subjects of their own empowerment' (2008, p. 18). It contradicts typical development uses of terms like 'economic empowerment' or 'political empowerment', which imply that simply by introducing external interventions of aid into areas such as education, health care, access to health and law women will become empowered. Access to 'the economic, health, education sectors – along with religion and culture – merely constitute the arenas where power contestations take place' (2008, p. 24) and through which empowerment is manifest.

Longwe's (1991) 'women's empowerment framework' is a useful conceptual tool to unpack what empowerment means. She argues that there are five hierarchical levels of equality, which are linked to increasing levels of empowerment.

- At the lowest level, the focus is on women's material welfare, that is, access to food, health, income and so forth.
- The next level is women's access to factors of production, such as land, labour, credit, training and marketing facilities, on an equal basis with men.
- At the third level, conscientisation, there is an increased awareness of the cultural underpinnings of gender roles and responsibilities, and programs, policies and projects make a conscious effort to change the imbalance that results in the economic or political domination of one sex by the other.
- The fourth level is concerned with women's equal participation in the decision-making processes of policy-making, planning, implementation, monitoring and evaluation (March, Smyth & Mukhopadhyay 1999).
- The highest level of empowerment is control, which reflects women's agency in decision-making 'so that women have achieved direct control over their access to resources, and are no longer "given" resources merely at the discretion of men, or by the whim of patriarchal authority' (Longwe 2002, p. 10).

If policies, programs and projects focus on the higher levels of empowerment, namely, conscientisation, participation and control, there is a greater likelihood that women's empowerment will be increased, rather than if the focus is on the lower levels of welfare and access. Thus, any focus on welfare alone means that women are unlikely to find the project empowering. Equal participation in decision-making processes is more important for achieving women's empowerment than equal access to resources, important though this is, and neither participation nor access is as important as equal control.

Nani Zuminarni heads an Indonesian organisation called PEKKA, which works to empower women-headed households, given that in Indonesia this constitutes almost 14 per cent of households.

She suggests that 'empowerment is when women who are powerless, marginalised and excluded from the system are able to build their power individually and collectively' (in AusAID 2011, p. 11). Humanitarian Assistance for Women of Afghanistan is a good example of an organisation that has broadened the scope of its work from providing basic relief at the welfare level, in terms of food aid and health services to women, particularly widows, to supporting widows in five districts in Kabul to form 'solidarity groups'; these groups work towards building a collective voice for women's needs, aspirations and rights (CARE International 2010, p. 14). According to CARE, an Australian international humanitarian organisation with a special focus on empowering women and girls, these groups are still in the early stages of establishing themselves. However, they were effective in challenging warlords for their rights to land and intervening to stop forced marriages. CARE is exploring different ways to support these groups to form an independent widows' association to work at a national level.

Another example is Athwaas, which demonstrates the links between relief and recovery and empowerment. Conceptualised at a roundtable titled Breaking the Silence: Women and Kashmir, and facilitated by Women in Security, Conflict Management and Peace in December 2000, Athwaas brings Muslim, Hindu and Sikh women together to develop inclusive approaches to conflict transformation in Kashmir. Starting with a transformation of individual values and attitudes, Athwaas began by encouraging Muslim, Hindu and Sikh women in Kashmir to engage in inter-faith dialogues, to understand their contrasting realities and divergent political perspectives. Today, its work has moved to including a range of activities from trauma counselling, peace education and trust-building to socioeconomic empowerment and reconciliation (Basu 2004). Centres for learning and sharing called *samanbals* (spaces for reconciliation) have been set up by Athwaas. In addition to offering opportunities for income generation, capacity development, trauma counselling and literacy, they provide a safe space to reflect on peace and reconciliation. According to Lisa Schirch and Manjrika Sewak (2005, p. 11), the centre seeks to 'erase the artificial boundaries that demarcate the private and the public lives of women in Jammu and Kashmir. In so doing, the women have connected the violence, which takes place within the home, to the visible and invisible forms of public violence that the armed conflict has perpetuated'.

In this chapter, four main arguments have been developed.

- Connections have been made between improving women's rights, enjoying the benefits of development and building a gender-inclusive security.
- We have suggested that gender mainstreaming can further gender equality when it strategically tackles gendered inequalities, but an over-bureaucratisation that leads simplistically to a gender 'tick box' mentality undermines real achievements. Further, in addition to gender mainstreaming, there is often a legitimate case for women-only strategies in relief and recovery work.
- A case has been built for the importance of indicators that are well thought through and that can hold UN entities, states, NGOs and civil society groups to account.
- We have argued that empowerment as the strength, autonomy and opportunity to make meaningful decisions is of extreme importance to relief and recovery work in the context of transitional justice. While there are different levels of empowerment, equal control is the chief goal. However, we have warned that donor materials and programs should ensure that all expressions of empowerment are culturally literate and are adaptable to different vulnerable groups.

CHAPTER 7

Timor-Leste

I wish I knew more about 1325 in Timor.
Interviewee, 2009

So far in this book, we have set out some of the groundwork for looking specifically at three case studies. Our interpretation of the four key foundational pillars has been examined: protecting women and girls from violence and also preventing conflict; ways of ensuring gender perspectives are included in multidimensional peacekeeping; the importance of increasing the participation of women in decision-making in all peace and security matters; and some of the essential ingredients in relief and recovery work. The next three chapters differ, being in-depth case studies of Timor-Leste, Fiji and Sri Lanka. Each chapter examines similar issues:

- conflict and gendered experiences of insecurity;
- implementation of UNSCR 1325;
- protection and prevention;
- ensuring gender perspectives in peacekeeping;
- increasing participation of women in decision-making; and
- relief and recovery.

Overlaps between these issues are inevitable, since the issues are highly interdependent. Attention is paid to key actions that governments, donor agencies and NGOs should attend to in order for noticeable changes to occur.

The central argument made in this chapter is that integrating gender into a UN peacekeeping mission mandate and working closely with local Timorese women who have a history of grassroots activism mean that gender, equality and rights are central considerations in the transitional justice process. Timor-Leste provides a creditable example of attempts to incorporate gender-inclusive practices into its new state and society.

Conflict and insecurity

East Timor[1] was a Portuguese colony for more than 400 years. The last governor of Portuguese Timor, Mário Lemos Pires, set in motion the move towards decolonisation by legalising political parties. Three large parties were formed, namely, the Timorese Democratic Union (UDT), the Timorese Social Democratic Association, which later changed its name to the Revolutionary Front of Independent East Timor (Fretilin), and the Timorese Popular Democratic Association (Apodeti). Fretilin and UDT formed an alliance to campaign for independence, and, at the elections held in March 1975, they emerged as the largest parties. The alliance did not last long. In November 1975, Fretilin made a unilateral declaration of independence not recognised by Indonesia, Australia or Portugal. Indonesia's response was to have UDT, Apodeti and some of the smaller political parties sign the Balibo Declaration, calling for integration with Indonesia. Criticism levelled against the declaration by Fretilin was used by Indonesia as a partial justification for annexation, and in July 1976 the Indonesian Parliament declared East Timor its twenty-seventh province.[2]

The fight for independence, which lasted for twenty-four years, saw great suffering, with violations committed primarily by state agents in a climate of impunity in which there was a failure to bring perpetrators of human rights abuses to justice. During the brutal military occupation, many women and men were deprived of food, displaced, detained, tortured, denied self-determination, killed, or simply disappeared. Women who were part of resistance movements against the Indonesian occupation or were attached to men who were activists suffered incarceration, harassment or were left as sole carers of families. Women were vulnerable to being sexually assaulted, raped or taken as sexual slaves. Forced sexual slavery with soldiers was frequent, with threats to harm family members if women did not submit. Gang rape was used as a tool of war. Trafficking of girls and women occurred in West Timor camps, and some forced sterilisation was undertaken (UNIFEM 2004, pp. 3–5).

With Indonesian President Soeharto's fall from power in 1998, change was possible. From June to September 1999, the UN Mission in East Timor (UNAMET) organised a referendum, referred to as the Popular Consultation, and supervised the ballot on 30 August 1999. The people voted for independence. Immediately after the referendum, heavily armed militia groups sympathetic to the integration of East Timor into Indonesia and provoked by factions within the armed forces of Indonesia conducted a 'scorched earth campaign' in which villages were burned and looted, and people were attacked, forcibly evacuated, kidnapped, raped or killed. The destruction of property was enormous, with most of the entire business district in Dili, the capital, completely destroyed. Internal displacement of more than 300,000 people occurred, with an additional 250,000 to 300,000 who voluntarily fled or were forcibly taken to West Timor (CAVR 2005, 9.1.2.7).

After the post-referendum violence, the International Force for East Timor (INTERFET), an Australian-led multinational stabilisation force, attempted to restore peace and security, from September

1999 to February 2000. From October 1999 to May 2002, the mandate of the UN Transitional Administration in East Timor (UNTAET) was to provide transitional administration of the territory, including legislative and executive authority, the administration of justice and independence preparations. The nation gained independence on 20 May 2002. From May 2002 to May 2005, the UN Mission of Support in East Timor (UNMISET) provided backing to Timor-Leste's attempt to attain self-sufficiency, with the UN Office in Timor-Leste (UNOTIL) running from May 2005 to August 2006. UNSCR 1410 of 2002, which established UNMISET, 'was the first resolution to recognise the importance of a gender perspective in peacekeeping operations and mandated a focal point for gender to be included within its civilian component' (UNSC 2010b, p. 13).[3] In the first four years after Timor-Leste's independence as a sovereign state, all the major institutions of state were established. The resurgence of violence in 2006 between defence forces and rebel militia groups and the disintegration of the system of government led to further displacement of persons. Much of the 'success story' of post-conflict Timor was abruptly undone. With concern over the fragility of democratic governance and public security, the International Stabilisation Force has been there since May 2006, and UNMIT has provided support since August 2006.[4] The mandate of UNMIT, established in 2006 through UNSCR 1704, is the first time the UNSC has 'called upon an operation to develop a gender equality strategy in cooperation with national authorities' (UNSC 2010b, p. 13).

Timor-Leste is one of the world's poorest nations, ranking 162 out of 182 countries in the UN Human Development Index (UNDP 2009), and it 'ranks as the "worst performer" in East Asia and the Pacific in terms of human development' (Wandita, Campbell-Nelson & Leong Pereira 2006, p. 286).[5] While information on gender-related indices such as the GDI and gender empowerment measure is unavailable, according to AusAID's (2008b, p. 191) analysis of

Timor-Leste in 2007, '[m]aternal mortality is estimated to be 800 per 100,000 live births, among the highest in the world'. Women have lower levels of education and literacy than men, participate less in the formal workforce and usually are in lower paid, less secure work, which exposes them to the risk of sexual harassment. Until recently, women were poorly represented in decision-making bodies at all levels, but efforts are being made to change this through the continuing nation-building process (AusAID 2008b). As the least developed country in Asia, Timor-Leste faces challenges that affect men and women, but there are particular cultural, patriarchal norms that affect women specifically, such as early marriages, often at fifteen, and thus early pregnancies, a cultural acceptance of domestic violence as normal and dowries that give men's families the full right to control women.

Implementation of UNSCR 1325

In such a harsh developmental context, how have women fared? Specifically, what is the degree of implementation of UNSCR 1325 in Timor-Leste? Sherrill Whittington (2006), who headed the Gender Affairs Office,[6] acknowledges that post-conflict circumstances provide a distinctive prospect to introduce an inclusive political framework to advance women's participation. The authority of UNTAET was based on a respect for CEDAW. In adhering to the BPFA (UN 1996), the first UN document to call for a political commitment to work towards gender equality through gender mainstreaming, Whittington worked with Timorese women to advocate gender equality. At the first post-conflict gathering of women in June 2000, the First Congress of Women of Timor Loro Sa'e developed its platform for action, which emphasised the need for transparency and accountability in government, a consultative process in constitution-building and resources to empower women in public decision-making (Whittington 2006). In doing so, the

Congress set the stage for promoting women's empowerment in the country.[7]

The establishment of the Women's Electoral Caucus to provide training and follow-up support to female candidates during the 2001 elections was an early initiative that reflects the spirit of UNSCR 1325. The efforts of the Working Group on Women and the Constitution and the development of a Women's Charter of Rights in East Timor[8] were presented to the Members of the Constituent Assembly, who were given the task of drafting the first constitution. Consequently, Article 17 of the constitution recognises the principles of gender equality as fundamental rights and entitlements of citizenship, and Article 62 states that equal participation of women and men is fundamental to democracy. The *NGOs alternative report* to CEDAW states that '[e]ven though the Constitution guarantees women's rights and equality, the State has not yet developed a law on gender equality and has not taken actions to eliminate discrimination against women in laws and policies' (NGOs Working Group 2009).[9] Notwithstanding this reminder, the constitutional affirmation of gender equality is significant.

The passing of the electoral law in 2003, which provides two seats on each village council specifically for women, is another step forwards in enabling women's participation in decision-making, a central pillar of UNSCR 1325. Other critical milestones include the ratification of CEDAW and its Optional Protocol (16 April 2003) and additional international conventions.[10] A specialised Committee on Poverty Reduction, Rural and Regional Development and Gender Equality, with a Sub-Committee on Gender Equality, was formed in July 2007, an important group, given the extensive poverty. Unless poverty is addressed directly, participation in activities outside mere survival becomes less possible. Other significant achievements linked indirectly to the demands of UNSCR 1325 include the declaration of an annual National Women's Day on

3 November. In September 2008, at the National Women's Congress, held every four years, UNSCR 1325 was identified as important in progressing women's issues. Additionally, lobbying by the Women Parliamentarians' Caucus resulted in the establishment of a Gender Resource Centre in the national Parliament, which was launched in partnership with the UNDP and UNIFEM in October 2008 (da Costa 2009).

UNSCR 1325 received another boost with the Second International Women for Peace Conference, held in Dili in 2009,[11] at which the Prime Minister in his opening remarks acknowledged the role of women in the resistance movement in the struggle for independence. Implicit in this recognition is that women 'were also the main caretakers of communities while Fretilin members were engaged in guerrilla warfare, although their rights – political, economic and special – were never fully recognised in customary or Indonesian legal frameworks' (Nakaya 2011, p. 158). The conference resulted in the Dili Declaration on Women, Peace and Security, which confirms the nature of past suffering and recommends that all institutions engaged in peace processes should implement UNSCR 1325 and 1820. In July 2010, Open Days to reflect on UNSCR 1325 were held with UNMIT Gender Affairs, UNIFEM, the UNDP and civil society groups. In addition to Dili, Open Days were held in Suai and Covalima, a district on the border with West Timor. Local NGOs such as the Foundation for Rights, FOKUPERS (Women's Communication Forum Timor) – a local NGO working for women's empowerment[12] – the Association of Men against Violence and the Democracy Foundation showcased their efforts. A joint project between these organisations working with UNIFEM provides massive practical community-based support of the recommendations of UNSCR 1325 through radio, pamphlets, visits to churches, and training for women's groups, community leaders, local NGOs and the police.

Despite these positive achievements, our fieldwork in Timor-Leste, albeit for only a short period in 2009, seemed to indicate a general lack of understanding of UNSCR 1325 at a community level and even within UN agencies. Indeed, even a Senior Gender Adviser at UNMIT reported that it has been a difficult task *'trying to mobilise everyone on 1325 for the last two years'*. She attributed this to *'a lack of knowledge and awareness'*.[13] Yet the necessity of developing a gender equality strategy in cooperation with national authorities is built in to the mandate of UNMIT. An Australian academic researcher who has lived in Timor-Leste and knows the culture and people well suggested another possibility for the lack of understanding. She pointed to the fact that people have not made the connection between women's participation in decision-making processes and the resolution. There is a tendency to compartmentalise peacebuilding and women's participation in decision-making, rather than viewing them as connected. Her view was that *'one of the strengths of 1325 is arguing for women's participation in the decision-making process – I don't really see that's happening at all'*. She suggested that the reason for this is that *'conventional understandings and policy and decision-making around security is running full steam ahead here, it's not being challenged at all by this other discourse around women's security'*. It is possible to draw a curious conclusion from this: many women are doing the work of UNSCR 1325 without knowing it.

A cross-learning project is worth highlighting. This initiative brought together representatives from three post-conflict societies – Northern Ireland, Timor-Leste and Liberia – to share models and experiences that might inform NAP processes. The initiative reflects a strong partnership model in which the initial scoping exercises explored what each country was doing around UNSCR 1325. The first meeting, held in Belfast in 2009, discussed participation in the political process. There were open sessions at the start with high-level officials, academics and those with expertise. The second meeting, in Dili later in 2009, focused on prevention of violence, with a third meeting, in Liberia in 2010, considering gender perspectives in peacemaking, peacekeeping and peacebuilding, with particular attention to protection. These encounters did not merely amount to the global north preaching to the south; rather, they were mutual learning experiences.

Protection and prevention

CAVR was established in 2001 to investigate the violation of human rights during the political conflict from 1974 to 1999 (Charlesworth & Wood 2002). Its three core programs were truth-seeking, community reconciliation and victim support. The final report of CAVR (2005, 7.7.1.1, 7.7.1.9) presents a disturbing picture of the extent to which women's human rights were violated during the political conflict and notes the continuing impact of those violations:

> Although women were the victims of the same range of human rights violations as men, almost all cases of sexual violence – rape, sexual slavery and other forms of sexual violence – were committed against women ... By any standards, the contents of this chapter portray a shameful and disgraceful account of the abuse of power. It became clear that the physically weakest and most vulnerable members of communities were targeted for reasons that have no legitimate connection to either military or political objectives.

This culture of violence continues. After the referendum, 'domestic violence became the country's most prevalent crime, comprising 40 per cent of all reported criminal cases in the year 2000' (Fairlie 2003, p. 1081). According to an Australian academic researcher living in Timor-Leste, '[o]ne big factor behind domestic violence is the stress around economic livelihoods within the family unit. Those *activities that are done successfully, a lot of women will say anecdotally, that they [the activities] have the effect of reducing that stress and therefore, reducing the incidents of domestic violence when women are also able to bring in income to their families'.* While supporting this view, an Australian international mentor from Psychosocial Recovery and Discovery in East Timor (PRADET) cautioned that economic empowerment does not imply that because a woman brings in some money she will not be violated, *'but what happens is that the woman has more of a sense of her own power and more choices'.* As the researcher above suggested, the most successful interventions are *'driven by small Timorese NGOs that know how to negotiate these things'.* She went on to explain that a lot of her colleagues *'have chosen to work in civil society rather than the state, because they feel like that is where they can be the most active'.* Given this, donor funding for women's participation in small businesses is advisable, with the specific intent of encouraging economic capacity to increase empowerment and resist violence.

While progress on protection against and prevention of violence is significant, there are two remaining major obstacles: access to justice and impunity. The NGOs Working Group's (2009) *NGOs alternative report* on the implementation of CEDAW in Timor-Leste suggests that the lack of access to justice is exacerbated by laws written in Portuguese, the language of the minority elite in which male Portuguese speakers outnumber female speakers 'by five to one' (Corcoran-Nantes 2009, p. 168); the limited number of district courts (there are only four); and women being discouraged from pursuing a lawsuit in order to preserve family pride. The report indicates that the state has not incorporated CEDAW provisions into national legislation or tackled the problems of human rights violations against women. It also points out that the Judicial Training Centre, set up to build the capacity of judges, lawyers, prosecutors and public defenders, does not include information on implementing CEDAW as part of its training package (NGOs Working Group 2009, p. 23). The report makes useful recommendations, including the need to advocate and develop capacity for the inclusion of UNSCRs 1325, 1820, 1888 and 1889 in the eventual Timor-Leste NAP. It reiterates the importance of supporting the Judicial Training Centre to develop training curricula that incorporate gender, women's rights, CEDAW and UNSCR 1325. It also suggests the necessity of supporting and funding programs that translate laws into Tetun.

The Dili Declaration on Women, Peace and Security (Women for Peace 2009) is significant in its recognition that 'gender justice' is the basis for protection from fear of violence. This Declaration states the need to collect and record information on SGBV committed during and after the conflict. 'Legal pluralism, common in many post-conflict states' (Nakaya 2011, p. 159), means there is a combination of Indonesian laws, UNTAET regulations and international laws. A crucial milestone in protecting the rights of women is the enactment of the new criminal code, with legislation passed in May 2010, which criminalises domestic violence and sexual crimes as violations of women's rights and of physical integrity and security. In 2009, women formed 18 per cent of staff in Timor-Leste's police force (Myrttinen 2009, p. 32); in 2010, women made up 20 per cent of the force, which included the first female District Commander (UNSC 2010b, p. 18).[14] However, a senior UN official underscored the need for extensive training on the criminal code, particularly in treating domestic violence as a crime and designing appropriate responses to it. This includes intensifying training to the Policia Nacional de Timor-Leste (PNTL) on the criminal code, specifically on domestic violence as a crime. It appears that neither the police nor the public knows exactly what safeguards the law provides on violence. At a workshop conducted in 2009, both the UN Civilian Police Force (CIVPOL) and the PNTL recommended more confidence-building measures between the public and the PNTL, with particular reference to domestic and gender-based violence cases and also legal literacy and socialisation of the laws (UNMIT, personal correspondence, 21 August 2009). In addition to deficient understanding of multiple legal frameworks, 'language barriers, lack of competence and professional misconduct have also undermined CIVPOL's efficacy' (Nakaya 2011, p. 160). For example, deferring rape charges to traditional law means that cases of sexual or domestic violence would never be charged under UNTAET rules.

The second remaining obstacle to dealing with protection and prevention of violence involves ending impunity given to those who perpetrate violence against women. As the *NGOs alternative report* points out, Presidential amnesty to prisoners, some of whom committed acts of gender-based violence, has 'promoted a climate of impunity' (NGOs Working Group 2009, p. 8). The challenge of transitional justice is immense, in working with local, informal, indigenous justice systems and with new, formal procedures that revolve around the slow acceptance of international law on human rights. In a culture in which violence has been accepted as the norm, surprisingly, in CAVR (2005, 10.3.2.134), 'women spoke openly of the sexual violence committed against them, challenging the widely-held view that East Timorese culture forbade discussion of this subject'. Of the statements collected by CAVR, only 21.4 per cent were from women, whereas, 'in comparison, 28 per cent of deponents to the Sierra Leone truth commission were women, and 54.8 per cent of deponents to the South African truth commission were women' (Harris Rimmer 2010, p. 113). A current challenge seems to be that domestic violence is generally seen as a family concern to be resolved at the family or village level and not as a crime to be dealt with by the state:

> The police often encourage victims of domestic violence to take their case to local leaders or traditional systems despite

the fact that these systems discriminate against women and do not provide adequate remedies. Less than a quarter of cases of gender-based violence reported to the police are sent to prosecution in the formal legal system. Some members of the police force have even referred complaints of police mistreatment to local customary mechanisms (Grenfell 2009, p. 228).

The challenge of balancing traditional and formal justice systems in protecting the rights of women and girls is immense.

Perhaps the biggest advantage in going through traditional *adat* justice systems to settle family disputes, land disputes and domestic violence matters is that they can be dealt with expeditiously. *Adat* law 'binds community members together as well as to their common history and their ancestors ... generating a sense of belonging by emphasising historical and familial connections' (Grenfell et al. 2009, p. 101). This sense of community leadership means that conflicts can be resolved in ways that maintain community balance. There are, however, two significant concerns with these processes. First, traditional justice systems, in virtue of being steeped in patriarchy, can discriminate against women. Second, traditional justice systems often are contrary to international human rights standards, particularly those bearing on the rights of women and children. Accordingly, there are instances of confusion for these women, who sometimes are caught between conflicting systems of customary law and state law. Moreover, 'when the traditional justice mechanisms reflect traditional views of the role of women' there are additional problems; 'for example, even if the victim involves the police in the first instance, and most cases still go unreported, she will often relent, as the imprisonment/humiliation of her bread-winner is not in her long-term interests' (Harris Rimmer 2010, p. 130). Under the circumstances, and without forfeiting international human rights standards, it is important to strive for a model that recognises the potential of traditional justice systems to serve a complementary and mutually supportive role, especially given their recognition in the constitution. A Senior Gender Adviser suggested that

> [w]e have to deal with the traditional courts system and my view, which is supported by a gender legal expert from UNDP, is that we take on the traditional courts. We give the traditional leaders/judges training on international human rights standards and the standards expected. Those who have been trained, we give them certificates, and only those can serve on these traditional courts, and then we also 'genderise' those traditional courts, with women sitting as adjudicators as well. However, acts of violence are criminal acts and need to be dealt with under the formal criminal legal system.

It remains the case that 'ongoing monitoring of women's experiences with tradition-based and restorative justice systems is essential to ensure women's rights are being appropriately addressed' (AusAID 2008b, p. 39).

However, little progress on this seems to have been made, despite the Judicial System Monitoring Programme (JSMP), which was founded in 2001 to scrutinise legal processes established to deal with perpetrators of human rights abuses committed during the Indonesian military occupation. The JSMP extended its mission to undertake training and case monitoring. The Women's Justice Unit within the JSMP was formed in 2004 to monitor the treatment of women in the formal justice sector and to conduct advocacy and training on gender issues. A backlog of legal cases in the JSMP means that many cases do not make it to court, and there are very few Timorese legal officers in the Women's Justice Unit. A Justice Sector Support Facility has been created by a bilateral agreement between the governments of Timor-Leste and Australia to support institutional and civil society initiatives to improve access to justice for men, women and children in Timor-Leste.[15] Civil society grants to this Facility can directly promote gender justice outcomes and increase measures to respond to and prevent violence against women (AusAID 2009).

To improve women's access to justice and to avoid impunity, it is important to support local female lawyers who respect traditional justice processes and who advocate women's rights through the formal system. Judges should be given gender-sensitive training. Female judges should be given a high level of support. The gender composition of the legal sector is a concern. As Susan Harris Rimmer (2010, p. 86) explains, '[i]n August 2004, the tiny legal and judicial sector in East Timor had only a smattering of women, but there was considerable success in securing judicial positions for women ... Justice Perreira, appointed to the Court age 31, had lost her home to arson, was threatened with death by armed men and was deported, with her five children, into a militia-controlled camp in West Timor'. She has considerable insight into suffering. Statistical figures on the number of judges and lawyers date quickly. There are female judges in the Dili District Court and Bacau District Court, as well as prosecutors, public defenders and private lawyers, but 'at present there appears to be no formal Government or United Nations program to encourage women entering into the legal sector' (2010, p. 87). Legal interns from Australia and New Zealand could be sent to mentor female Timorese lawyers and legal officers and women working in the judicial arena. It is important to ensure that women understand laws on rights and equality. Importantly, there is need for more awareness of women's rights to equality in the rural districts.

Peacekeeping
Today's peacekeepers carry out a wide variety of complex tasks. The nation-building missions like that undertaken by the UN in Timor-Leste are a relatively new development, particularly given that the UN Mission had the combined function of peacekeeping and civil

administration (Suhrke 2001). As mentioned, UNTAET was the first UN peacekeeping mission to integrate gender into its mandate and include a Gender Affairs Unit. There were three aspects to the mandate: mainstreaming a gender perspective throughout UNMIT's policies, ensuring compliance with a zero tolerance policy on sexual exploitation and abuse, and supporting the development of a national strategy to promote gender equality and empowerment of women. The Unit undertook several initiatives to lay the foundation for mainstreaming gender in the UN Mission with the proviso that this could be built on in the future. There were numerous innovative initiatives (Whittington 2000). Gender mainstreaming and sensitisation workshops were held for a range of stakeholders, including UNTAET departments, peacekeeping forces, civilian police and the Timor Loro S'ae police service. Policy analysis attempted to incorporate ideas around gender justice into the Transitional Rules of Criminal Procedure. Mechanisms were established to share information with the gender focal point network and bi-monthly meetings with the East Timorese Women's Network. There was work by UNTAET to establish a Vulnerable Persons Unit (VPU) within the UN CIVPOL in district police stations, to deal with victims of rape and domestic violence, as well as any other gender-related crimes.

UNMIT continues the work of UNTAET's Gender Affairs Unit in raising awareness on SGBV among representatives from IDP camps, communities, the police, local chiefs (*suco*), women's organisations and youth groups, and in making presentations on gender mainstreaming at induction courses for all new staff members to the Mission (UNMIT 2007). In 2010, UNMIT was requested by the UNSC 'to fully take into account gender considerations ... as a cross-cutting issue throughout its mandate, stressing the importance of strengthening the responsiveness of the security sector to specific needs of women' (in Butler, Mader & Kean 2010, p. 14).

Other significant initiatives are leading the way in engendering peacekeeping. The Office of the Secretary of State for the Promotion of Equality (SEPI), UNIFEM and the UNFPA provide training for the Timorese police service on SGBV and human rights. UN Women gives training on CEDAW principles to the peacekeeping Mission. UNPOL's reclassification of rape offences as sexual offences, and the creation of two new categories of 'assault/domestic' and 'dispute/domestic' instead of bundling everything into the 'domestic violence' basket, provide a better understanding of the nature of cases. The new classifications are aimed at improving gender responsiveness in UNPOL (UNMIT 2008).

There are substantial remaining hurdles. According to UNMIT (2008), the UNDPKO police assessment mission in March 2008 highlighted the need for improvement in a range of areas. There is the task of deploying additional officers to UNMIT with training and experience dealing with gender-based crimes, particularly given the critical role in protecting women and girls. All levels of PNTL and UNPOL officers require training on the special needs of women and investigative techniques for gender-based crimes. Victims demand greater access to judicial recourse and require an effective witness protection program. In addition, Maria Agnes Bere (2005, p. 56) from the JSMP writes that the VPU was created in police stations to address victims' needs on 'attempted rape, domestic violence, sexual assault and sexual harassment', but the lack of resources and staff rotation leave many gaps in fulfilling the mandates of these units. UNICEF's independent evaluation of units also suggests that 'staffing levels and skills within the VPU are inadequate to address the cases falling within their mandate' (Styles-Power, Hamilton & Hall 2008). While the VPU in Dili has female officers and translators and the women's group FOKUPERS can provide shelter and psychosocial support, in other districts, 'women rarely knew of VPU, and often a single CIVPOL officer was simply appointed as a VPU focal point' (Nakaya 2011, p. 160).

In March 2011, UNMIT handed over policing responsibility to the PNTL, with UNPOL only in supporting roles. Ongoing support will be valuable. The development of standard training packages should include instruction on human rights, the Convention on the Rights of the Child, CEDAW and the UNSCRs on 'women and peace and security' to be integrated into basic police training. Development of gender-sensitive interviewing techniques and recording of evidence is a priority for officers within the VPU.

Participation of women in decision-making

In the first legislative Parliament of Timor-Leste, from 2001 to 2007, which created the constitution of the Democratic Republic of Timor-Leste, women formed 26.4 per cent of the total number elected. In the second Parliament, from 2007 to 2012, women form 27.7 per cent (NGOs Working Group 2009, p. 33). The post-independence period 'served to radicalise gender politics through the consolidation of the resources of women's organisations and NGOs to promote and defend women's rights and the principles of gender equality in the Constitution and in national politics' (Corcoran-Nantes 2009, p. 183). The present mandate of UNMIT is grounded in UNSCR 1325 and includes supporting the Office of SEPI in mainstreaming gender.[16] The Head of SEPI sits on the Council of Ministers. SEPI works with multiple sectors, and its achievements include legal changes to increase women's participation in decision-making bodies, legislation on domestic violence, a network of basic services for survivors and advocacy for school curricula to include the right of women to live free from violence (AusAID 2008b, p. 25). To this end, UNMIT, SEPI, UNIFEM and the UNDP have recorded significant success in fostering a greater role for women in decision-making. However, as a UNIFEM and SEPI GAD specialist explained to us, '[o]ne of the difficulties of SEPI is that it is a new body, it's a small body, so it's not always easy to influence the decision-making in other

Ministries or at the Council of Ministers level'. She suggested the need for further capacity development to influence legislation and policy and to strengthen gender mainstreaming mechanisms, especially in the districts. In this regard, the partnership between SEPI and the Centre for Asia-Pacific Women in Politics stands out. The partnership cultivates effective skills in advocacy, communications, sharing of information, managing agendas, running meetings and prioritising issues. Further possibilities are overseas study tours to open people's minds to alternative options. We were told by a UN official how one male Parliamentarian who was constantly making sexist remarks was sent to the Philippines to meet with women's groups. '*He came back completely transformed . . . The movers and shakers have been abroad and also, well of course, it's also the group that fought for independence . . . We need to take the ordinary people, members of the civil society out and give them more exposure.*'

In the Presidential and Parliamentary elections held in April and June 2007, out of the sixty-five Members of Parliament elected, eighteen were women, including women heading key Ministries for Finance (Emilia Pires), Justice (Lucia Maria Brandão Freitas Lobato) and Social Solidarity (Maria Domingas Fernandez Alves). Additionally, women are Vice-Minister of Health (Madalena Fernandes Melo Hanjan Costa Soares) and Secretary of State of Equality (Idelta Maria Rodrigues). It was difficult to find out how many successful women were educated in the diaspora and thus were exposed to democratic values, particularly in Australia, Portugal or Mozambique. The record number of women voting in these elections can be attributed to a systematic voter education program targeting potential female voters (UNMIT 2007). UN agencies took lead roles in this program, which included Timorese women's NGOs monitoring political party manifestos to assess commitments to women's rights and gender equality, supporting women in political parties and raising awareness about women's rights. Workshops were held for potential and actual candidates. The rules and procedures governing the 2007 elections gave priority in the polling lines to pregnant women and sick, physically challenged and elderly persons. Given the high fertility rate in Timor-Leste, this priority facilitated the polling process for many women, so that 47 per cent of voters were women in an 81 per cent turnout of registered voters.

Support for female Parliamentarians is ongoing. In October 2007, the Women Parliamentarians' Caucus was formed. It works across parties to further gender equality, approve the government's gender budget statements and initiate capacity development activities. For instance, UNIFEM, the Women Parliamentarians' Caucus and UNMIT's Gender Affairs Unit provide assistance on gender budgeting tools. On participation, a UN Gender Adviser suggested that '[t]here is a lot of support for women in terms of capacity-building, information, support organisations, study tours, strategic planning. There is a gender adviser in Parliament funded by UNDP under the UNDP Parliamentary program to support the work of the women in Parliament. UNDP and UNIFEM support the Gender Resource Centre which provides capacity-building opportunities for the women in Parliament'.

All strategic opportunities to enhance women's participation in post-conflict nation-building at the local level are crucial. As of 2004, local authority councils comprise the *chefe de suco* (village head) and *chefes de aldeias* (neighbourhood heads) as well as two women, two youths – one of each sex – and an elder (Ospina 2006, p. 51).[17] UNIFEM, the women's caucus and the Office for the Promotion of Equality (now SEPI) worked to support women as potential candidates through training campaigns on transformative leadership in politics. A few years on, the *NGOs alternative report* states that there are no women as sub-district administrators, but seven women are *suco* chiefs (from 442 in the country) (NGO Working Group 2009, p. 34).[18] At the neighbourhood head level, fourteen are women; and there are 1,100 women in village councils in which three of five people must be women (Ospina 2006). In 2009, the UN Democracy Fund, UNIFEM and Redefeto (Women's Network of East Timor)[19] used village council elections to enhance the proportion and quality of women's representation. Their strategy was to give 'advocacy for gender responsive electoral law, capacity-building support to potential candidates and sensitisation activities for voters, as well as promotion of a gender-responsive policy platform in campaigns' (UNSC 2009a, p. 11). After the elections, there was a follow-up project that supported a gender-responsive local development agenda by improving the knowledge and skills of those women who were elected councillors.

There are remaining difficulties in increasing the participation of women. Commenting on the first CEDAW report submitted by Timor-Leste, in August 2009, the CEDAW committee acknowledged positive progress but expressed concern over the small number of women in leadership positions, women's lack of information about their rights, the shortage of training for women who serve in the public administration, and 'the prevalence of a patriarchal ideology in the State party' (CEDAW 2009). The NGOs Working Group (2009) report on CEDAW's implementation points out that while law no. 6/2006, regarding the Parliamentary elections, 'guarantees a temporary special measure for women, requiring political parties to include one woman in each group of four candidates', there are issues with this implementation. Political parties limit the number of female candidates to one out of four, 'instead of seeing one out of four as a minimum number of women; listing the women candidates in the last position on the list of four'. The report recommends training programs for women interested in public administration. It also suggests the need for leadership and capacity development programs for elected women on how governments work and public education campaigns to promote women's leadership. There are several factors that persist in impeding women's active involvement in decision-making: patriarchy, poverty, and lack of recognition, communications and capacity.

The persistence of the patriarchal traditional power structure remains a major obstacle and impedes women's leadership. A senior UNIMET official noted that '*[w]omen have always regarded men as leaders and decision-makers and they were the followers. It is difficult for them to break out of that pattern. The social fabric is a very strongly knit community/family and extended community/family. The responsibilities and obligations are all so interwoven that it is very difficult for anyone to break out of that*'. Extreme cases of poverty, high levels of illiteracy and low health conditions hold up progress.[20] There is also a lack of recognition of the varieties of peacebuilding, including informal reconciliation work such as that undertaken by Catholic nuns as well as small groups. As an Australian academic working in Timor observed, '*1325 has yet to make a huge impact here, except for one particular reading of that, as women as natural peacebuilders – that's been a line of discourse... particularly since the advent of the crisis in 2006*'. Problems with communication and limited access to media and information technology leave many women ill informed. In many areas, there is no television or radio, a lack of communication infrastructure and poor rural road access. Diesel and maintenance of vehicles are expensive, particularly since the arrival of the UN. This issue was reiterated by a volunteer from PRADET: '*Donors should understand how expensive it is for us to go to the districts. People put the prices up – everything has gone up. I think there really has to be a generous understanding and funding to enable us to go to particularly remote areas*'.

The importance of women's leadership for the development of democratic governance, sustainable peace and development cannot be underestimated. Women's confidence that they are capable of playing an active role in politics and decision-making processes can be strengthened. As an Australian researcher told us, '*I think a lot are sort of saying it [1325] puts women in name only in these positions and so forth. I don't think it has really made an impact on decision-making processes regarding security*'. In this regard, a senior Australian Development Minister asked a pertinent question: '*So capacity for what? And often the "what" is how you build the capacity*'. Working with local women and men to answer this question will determine the success of projects, such as UN Women's Integrated Programme for Women in Politics and Decision-Making, which supports the development of a political vision of women as citizens and decision-makers (AusAID 2009, p. 24).

A major challenge to increasing the participation of women lies with gender equality. Equality sits uncomfortably with male-dominated community traditions, despite final recommendations in CAVR 'that ensure that the fruits of development are enjoyed equitably' (CAVR 2005, 11.3.2.6). Specific recommendations in the Commission are directed toward developing a culture of equality under the category 'Women' in addressing individual needs of women victims; social needs to counter prejudice against victims of SGBV; security needs to ensure gender-sensitive practices in SSR; and support of women's initiatives in the prevention and resolution of conflicts and peacebuilding. CAVR commits to 'mainstreaming gender equality and the full participation of women in the economic, social, cultural and political life of Timor-Leste' (CAVR n.d.; 2005, 11.4.1.11) as recognised in the constitution. However, increasing numbers of activists, educated Timorese and diasporic Timorese recognise that 'notions of human rights and of gender equality are perhaps the most contentious, confusing and challenging for customary approaches' in terms of differing interpretations and practices of justice (Brown 2009, pp. 154–5). As a senior activist in a large women's network put it, '*Timor-Leste has the goodwill to promote women's rights, but in fact, in the implementation, it's quite different*'. A Portuguese GAD specialist explained: '*When we start talking about gender equality, using the Portuguese words, people are not familiar with the concept, anyway. They understand the words, but they don't understand the concept*'. Instead, she suggested that it is more meaningful to '*talk about equality between women and men*'.

An advocate for men's participation in anti-violence initiatives told us that '*some of the men realised that the problem of gender is not male only but woman and man, we have to work with each other*'. Mario de Araujo is a founding member of the Men's Association against Violence. He states that traditionally 'gender' is viewed as a 'concept that foreigners are imposing on people ... along with terms such as "human rights" and "democracy", the term "gender" sits on a bookshelf with a donor logo plastered on the front'. He reminds us also that many criticise a concept such as the empowerment of women as 'merely breaking Timorese culture and causing men to be more violent and angry as women defy them' (in Grenfell & Trembath 2007, p. 14). The test is to bring such concepts into forums in which people can see the value of gender equality in communities.

In an extensive evaluation of the impact of gender programs in national NGOs in local communities, Anna Trembath, Damian Grenfell and Carmenesa Moniz Noronha (2010, p. 7) found that discursively '"gender" is coming to be increasingly used in communities'. However, there is contestation over whether it is a foreign concept, a negative concept that benefits women more than men or a positive concept. Interestingly, these researchers found that 'female community members have demonstrated significant agency in their ability to use such discursive frameworks to either negotiate a new consensus in their respective familial domains, or to find strength in their own paths where there is continued resistance within families and communities to them as change-agents' (2010, p. 8). Yet, overall, in all four communities where they conducted research, they 'encountered significant informal resistance to "gender" as a foreign and modern imposition with destructive impacts upon communities' and families' integration' (2010, p. 9). Indeed,

> thinking about the productive tension between the customary, traditional and modern may allow new ways into thinking about practical and powerful ways of creating gender change suitable to the East Timorese context ... if it can be shown that gender equality does not need to exist as part of the modern alone and mean the destruction of the customary-traditional (2010, p. 15).

With regard to equality, Idelta Rodrigues, SEPI, in commenting on her Office's strategic plan for 2010–15, confirms her desire to 'advocate for rights-based and gender-responsive policies and legislation in government. We have raised [issues] about how to implement policy on gender mainstreaming ... we also need to raise the level of gender awareness among stakeholders and the general public at the national and local levels' (in Crook 2009). Similarly, a senior member of SEPI told us that '*[h]uman rights means that we give what is the right of men and women ... So, it means we open the opportunity – we give the opportunity to women, to have a good access for their right – not take another right – not take the men's right*'. This makes an important point: that empowerment 'must be done in the context of human rights for all, equality for men and women' (Ospina 2006, p. 85). There is a strong Catholic basis to the culture and to understandings of gender roles. One way to address the need for women's rights to be accepted as part of human rights is to open dialogue between religious leaders and representatives of civil society and the state.[21] Catholic human rights activists from the diaspora, particularly Australia, can play a key role in opening Timorese religious leaders to the idea that patriarchy is wrong and that women's rights are human rights and consistent with a strong faith.

Relief and recovery

While UNSCR 1325 provides a policy framework for peacebuilding, it does not directly address challenges of state-building, such as 'the lack of consolidation with national and local judicial structures' or protection for women when 'instituting political and economic liberalisation' (Nakaya 2011, p. 165). A statement in the Dili Declaration on Women, Peace and Security (Women for Peace 2009) acknowledges a broad understanding of what constitutes security and includes truth and reconciliation, security, health, economic and social development, democratic governance and the flourishing of art and culture. This broad notion of human security was reiterated by many women and men we spoke with. An UNMIT Senior Gender Adviser acknowledged the

> [i]nter-connectedness between security, violence, economic development and domestic violence, you can't separate them. All of them are inter-woven and impact on each other. You can even interpret the non-provision of medical and health facilities, access to justice as a form of violence against women. It is a subtle sort of form of violence against women. Food security and economic opportunities, these are all not only overt elements of discrimination against women, but they are some form of violence against women as well.

The UN Missions to Timor have had an unequivocal component of a nation-building agenda that encompasses broad notions of security and development, relief and recovery. In 2002, PRADET established a 'safe space' in the Dili hospital to treat victims of domestic violence, sexual assault and child abuse. While remaining in the hospital grounds, in 2006, it transferred to a purpose-built facility. We saw how well designed the facility is, with private interview rooms and trained female staff. According to a key worker at

PRADET, '[s]ecurity for my understanding is – no violence, no war, no conflict. Security is peace. Peace in the family, in the community, in the country'.

When human security needs are so extensive, relief and recovery work for women is complex, requiring an integration of policies on gender equality and strategies for implementing UNSCRs 1325, 1820, 1888 and 1889. In this vein, Henri Myrttinen (2009, p. 37) recommends reforms within the security sector itself if it is to respond to human security needs in ways that ensure that security forces do not become private fiefdoms of patronage-based networks. Such changes are required in order to shift the understanding of SGBV from a 'merely private' problem to a grave societal threat to security, and, politically, to back the reforms by giving clear guidelines delineating the various tasks of the security forces as well as transparent, accountable and gender-sensitive oversight mechanisms.

The lack of monitoring and assessment of gender-sensitive SSR and relief and recovery work hinders attempts to evaluate progress on engendering peaceful security. Reporting indicators often are ad hoc. Donor collaboration is not always robust. Sustained core funding for salaries and resources to travel to rural regions is scarce. Much donor funding is for specific projects. The message from PRADET was clear: *'You can't do a project if you don't have a core service... We need core – a constant five year minimum – a constant core support for the services to function... and then we can do projects'.*[22] Core support should be given over a sustained period to groups working against violence who have demonstrated their ability to make a major contribution (Trembath & Grenfell 2007).[23]

Progress in a new nation is ongoing. Issues of weak capacity around state-building allied with corruption in the state bureaucracy do not auger well. In many ways, there has been a 'top down process of nation-building' in terms of establishing a democratic political system and developing legal institutions 'at the expense of a more inclusive and consultative program of Timorese social and political development' (Corcoran-Nantes 2009, p. 168). There are substantial differences between resources and services available in Dili and in the rural districts. What this means is that local communities continue to feel marginalised. This is particularly important in a state where local communities remain vital in affirming people's attachments and sense of belonging.

Nonetheless, Timor-Leste presents a valid effort to put gender concerns at the heart of transitional justice processes. This chapter shows commendable gender-inclusive processes in seeking the truth about the violations women experience and ways to include women in decision-making processes. Some of the shortcomings of the processes indicate the tremendous nature of the mission of nation-building, the exertion of a capacity to learn new skills of democratic governance and difficulties in developing institutional aspects of state-building. In Timor-Leste, gender justice involves ideals of human rights law and legal accountability, as well as practical offerings of compensation for trauma suffered and provision of assistance to offset ongoing material hardships. This broadening of understandings of justice illuminates the need for holistic approaches to transitional justice strategies that are culturally sensitive and attentive to people's needs. The women's networks and grassroots groups are active in responding to these approaches but must be resourced adequately by the government of the Democratic Republic of Timor-Leste and by the international donor community. We argue that there are grounds to be hopeful that the historic work begun by the UN Gender Affairs Unit is continuing with robust local activism.[24]

CHAPTER 8
Fiji

We would like a broad sense of security so that we are all covered, we are protected.
Weavers member, 2009

In this chapter, we draw on field-based interviews to examine the progress made in implementing UNSCR 1325 with respect to protecting women and girls and preventing conflict, enabling gender-sensitive peacekeeping, promoting women's participation in decision-making and ensuring gender-responsive relief and recovery. Three central arguments are made:

1. In order to address the complex issues faced by Fiji, it is necessary to enable women's organisations to engage with national and regional governance mechanisms to mainstream gender into peace and security debates.
2. We show how important dialogue, at multiple levels, is in Fiji as a crucial part of peacebuilding.
3. Examples of ways to bridge gaps between bottom-up and top-down approaches by adopting a programmatic rather than a project-based approach are offered, as means of supporting the country's transition from instability to sustained peace.

Conflict and insecurity

Fiji, a former British colony, gained its independence in 1970. The country's social landscape underwent a significant change during colonisation, with the British bringing ethnic Indians as indentured labourers to work on sugarcane plantations in the late 1800s. Today, Fiji's population of approximately 847,800 comprises 57 per cent Indigenous Fijians and 37 per cent ethnic Indians (US Department of State n.d.). Politics in Fiji has been divided along racial lines, and more so since 1987, following several coups. Political parties tend to be supported by either Indigenous Fijians (such as the Alliance Party, which later became Soqosoqo ni Vakevulewa ni Taukei, and then split to form the Fijian Association Party) or by ethnic Indians (such as the National Federation Party). The Fiji Labour Party is the only one that claims to be multicultural (Lodhia 2003). Such a division along racial lines has contributed to four coups in the last two decades, as the two groups have vied for political power (Laracy 2008).

Instability and insecurity resulting from the coups impact on the lives of women in Fiji in many ways: sexual abuse, economic insecurity and resultant poverty arising from declining tourism and other industries, violations of human rights and increased vulnerability to domestic violence and suicide (Alexander 2006). This impact is reflected in Fiji's falling GDI rank[1] from forty-eight in 1995 (when this ranking was first introduced) to fifty-nine in 2000 and eighty-two in 2007/08 (UNDP 1995, 2000, 2007).

Implementation of UNSCR 1325

While Fiji does not have a NAP on UNSCR 1325, some aspects of the resolution are incorporated into the national context through links to policy commitments on gender equality. These are manifest in the National Women's Plan of Action and the establishment of the Women, Peace and Security Coordinating Committee (WPS Fiji CC). The WPS Fiji CC comprises government and NGO participants and emerged from UNIFEM Pacific's Women, Peace and Security Project for Melanesia. The Committee has four main goals:

- to improve the availability of data and thus the ability to analyse root causes of conflicts and the impact of conflict on women;
- to strengthen the capacity of women and women's groups to play a role in conflict prevention and resolution, and post-conflict peacebuilding at national and regional levels;
- to advocate a gender perspective in conflict resolution and peacebuilding initiatives of governments, regional organisations and mainstream agencies; and
- to promote peace, tolerance and reconciliation, linked to economic security, through advocacy in the community and with the general public (Bhagwan-Rolls 2006a).

More recently, the framework on which Fiji, like many countries in the Pacific, draws to guide its response to peace and security has been the Pacific Plan (PIFS 2005). The Plan adopts a broad understanding of human security as a priority goal for the region and includes gender equality as a cross-cutting strategic objective. UNSCR 1325 is referenced specifically as strategic objective 12.5. Further developments in recent years that have helped to shape Fiji's response include the 2006 Pacific Regional Workshop on 'gender, peace and security', which led to a final outcomes document outlining recommendations for national- and regional-level initiatives (femLINKpacific 2009). In the same year, the UNDP's Pacific Centre, in response to the 2006 coup in Fiji, supported women's organisations to submit and speak to a position paper presented to a UN fact-finding Mission. This paper highlights critical concerns 'which women believed were vital not only to return Fiji Islands to Parliamentary democracy but also address the root causes of political conflicts' (Shanahan 2010).

In the following year, the regional Women, Peace and Human Security consultations provided the platform for developing presentations on regional security priorities to the Forum Regional Security Committee (FRSC), which is part of the Pacific Island Forum Secretariat (PIFS). There is now the inclusion of women's organisations in the bi-annual PIFS with civil society organisation dialogues on regional security priorities. In 2009, the FRSC recognised SGBV as a security threat as expressed in the Cairns Communiqué (Shanahan 2010). As we write, work is being undertaken, with support from the UNDP's Pacific Centre, to present three proposals to the FRSC.

- There is development of a regional action plan on women, peace and security launched in October 2010. It provides a broad framework to assist Forum member countries to develop relevant national programs to accelerate their implementation of UNSCRs 1325 and 1820.
- A women, peace and security interactive dialogue with the PIFS Secretary-General is mooted to inform the design and approval of the regional action plan.
- Efforts are being made to ensure the inclusion of women, peace and security as a separate standing agenda item for session 1 of the annual FRSC. This enables Forum member countries and key women's organisations to provide regular updates on the national context and priorities, lessons learned and good practices on the implementation of UNSCRs 1325 and 1820 (Shanahan 2010).

Protection and prevention

Wherever there is political instability, violence is rife, and this includes sexual and physical violence against women and girls. According to AusAID (2008b, p. 153), 'the four coups in recent history... have had a chilling effect on women's rights advocacy and programs. The coups are also a setback to gains made in reducing violence against women resulting in a stalling of relationships built between the women's movement, law and justice institutions'. Ronni Alexander (2006) points out that often political violence is used as an excuse for ignoring existing protections for women. Studies such as *The impact of the May 19 coup on women in Fiji* (FWCC 2001), *NGO report on the status of women in the Republic of the Fiji Islands* (FWRM, FWCC & Ecumenical Centre for Research Education and Advocacy 2002) and UNIFEM's (2007a) *Gender profile of the conflict in Fiji* document that, as well as being victims of targeted and orchestrated violence, women face further insecurity due to increased levels of domestic violence. 'Those married to soldiers or police said their husbands felt themselves above the law and therefore able to do as they pleased' (Alexander 2006, p. 20). Further, political instability also impacts on women's organisations, as leaders of the women's movement are often 'vocal human rights defenders [and] women's NGOs have also been specifically targeted during and following coups' (AusAID 2008b, p. 153).

AusAID's (2008b) report *Violence against women in Melanesia and East Timor* presents a comprehensive picture of the progress made in protecting women and girls from violence in Fiji. For instance, the report highlights the government's 'no drop policy', which sets a mandatory path of action for police officers to pursue when dealing with domestic and family violence, and which prevents individual officers from closing a case at their own discretion. The creation of Sexual Offences Units within the police force supports victims of sexual assault by taking their statements, providing transportation to hospitals and health centres for treatment and making appropriate referrals to agencies for services such as counselling and emergency housing. The Welfare/Employment Services Unit within the police force supports the welfare of police officers, including addressing the issue of domestic violence perpetrated by police (2008b, p. 73).

Preventing violence against women requires proactive efforts to change unequal power relations. This in turn necessitates working in partnership with men, 'in particular, involving men in movements to end violence against women, focusing on men's roles and responsibilities and emphasis on men as part of the solution' (UNESCAP 2010). The FWCC's three-year project titled Men's Program against Violence against Women, launched in 2002, goes beyond just training and awareness-raising. Rather than giving a generic workshop for men, the FWCC selected a group of men from strategic sectors, such as the police, education and religious institutions, and health and legal practices. 'The men were selected based on their potential influence in the community and workplace as advocates against violence against women' (UNESCAP 2003, p. 29). This group participated in a program that involved gender awareness-raising activities that explored male attitudes towards women, the cultural aspects of violence and how attitudes are perpetuated by individual and collective behaviour.

During the Program, men made commitments to become activists against violence by pledging to reflect in their behaviour and attitudes an acceptance of women as equal and to re-educate sons and daughters that men and women are equal. The Program encouraged advocating (in religious, youth and men's groups) that violence against women is a crime and must be eliminated. It also tried to create awareness among men in the community and workplaces of the impact that violence against women has on the family, economy and society. Thus, it actively supported all government and NGO programs that promote the elimination of violence against women and made itself accountable to the women's movement when conducting work in this area by involving it as a reference point (UNESCAP 2003). Participants in the Program also developed personal action plans that are monitored by the FWCC.

Women's Action for Change (WAC) focuses on working with perpetrators of violence (mainly male prisoners) through the use of community theatre to bring about behavioural and attitudinal change and to 'encourage non-violent ways of dealing with problems' (Moore 2003, p. 128). To achieve this aim, WAC works on building the self-esteem and confidence of prisoners through playback theatre, exercises and games 'designed to encourage participation on a non-competitive basis' (2003, p. 129). Their work is based on the principle that 'until the inner person feels good the outer person will not be able to change or survive' (2003, p. 137). Another of WAC's projects addresses sexual baiting, raising awareness of the issue as well as providing organisations with strategies on combating harmful practices. 'Sexual baiting' refers to 'the practice of discrediting and controlling people, organisations and political agendas through strategic use of allegations related to sexuality' (Rothschild 2005, p. 3).

A significant challenge facing Fiji (and other countries) is building a comprehensive rights-based framework to protect women and girls from violence that links with UNSCRs 1325, 1820, 1888 and 1889 and CEDAW:

> Women's advocacy groups in the Pacific have welcomed the move to stop sexual violence towards women in conflict situations. The formal leaders have decided that 1820 is a priority rather than 1325. We are going to remind them that while UNSCR 1820 is absolutely critical it should be viewed as an 'implementation strategy' to further the commitments made under UNSCR 1325 (femLINKpacific member).

This challenge can be addressed by creating a diagrammatic factsheet (translated into Fijian and Hindustani) that maps the links between UNSCRs 1325, 1820, 1888 and 1889, CEDAW and regional commitments. Some of the other challenges outlined in AusAID's

(2008b) *Violence against women in Melanesia and East Timor* report include difficulties in accessing the formal, largely urban-based justice system, continued reliance on gender-insensitive traditional justice systems that have an inconsistent implementation in terms of the 'no drop policy' referred to above and insensitive attitudes of the police. Yet, key actions can be taken. As the report recommends, what is required is support for multi-sectoral coordination and continued backing for reforms that strengthen women's access to justice. A better integration of anti-violence projects into the health system is advantageous. Support for primary and secondary education programs on ending violence against women can back projects that engage men and youth as allies in this. These are simply some of the strategic areas that donors, funding agencies, policy-makers, governments and civil society organisations might explore.

Peacekeeping

Protecting women and girls from violence includes finding ways to work with the military. Women from Fiji play active roles in UN peacekeeping missions, with deployments in peace and security operations in Cambodia, Croatia, Kosovo and the Solomon Islands (UNSC 2003). According to the International Women's Development Agency (IWDA) (2009), a significant number of the Royal Fiji Military Forces' employees serve in conflict zones as UN peacekeepers (in Egypt, Iraq, Lebanon, Sudan and Timor-Leste). Many are ill equipped emotionally to deal with the complex nature of conflicts and the high levels of stress and trauma, and this is 'compounded by the organisation's limited gendered awareness and ability to cater for the increasing numbers of women entering into peacekeeping roles' (IWDA 2009). Lack of appropriate training also means that existing notions of gendered social roles have a considerable impact on how these soldiers behave in conflict zones. The problem does not end there but continues when soldiers return home after their missions abroad. Most male peacekeepers return to a family life that may have undergone significant changes in their absence, with women taking new responsibilities for areas traditionally considered male domains. For female peacekeepers, in addition to having access to a high income (which may challenge gender roles), they may be subject to suspicions of unfaithfulness. In both cases, the gap between stereotypical gender roles and the actual situation compounds existing trauma and stress, and often results in a violent response, by way of physical abuse of wives and families (IWDA 2009). A member of the FWRM told us: '*It should not only be about parliament... The military needs to encourage more women to join. It is an institution and somehow, women's organisations, feminist organisations have to find a way to influence it*'. Efforts to engage with the military take two central forms, namely, capacity development around gender issues, such as the gender training conducted by the FWCC for some Fiji police and military units, particularly those involved in peacekeeping activities, and challenging dominant masculinity within the armed forces.

The Pacific Centre for Peacebuilding (PCP) points out that a significant (and often underappreciated) trial that men who serve in the defence forces face is the dominant construction of masculinity that centres on 'violence, aggression, a sense of invulnerability' (Skjelsbæk 2007, p. 13). This construction is problematic not just within the military, but also when soldiers return to civilian life (Higate 2003). It is vital to work with serving men and women on issues surrounding dominant masculinity, trauma and the stress of serving in violent situations during times of peace. Adopting a gendered rights-based framework, the PCP's trauma-healing workshop series for soldiers and officers, their partners and families, encourages participants to understand their stress within a gendered framework and learn to deal with it using nonviolent means. At the same time, the workshops supported by UNIFEM, the IWDA and AusAID promote an understanding of women's rights and the impact of conflict on women and girls. More recently, the PCP has been working with the military's personnel division to reform and refine human resource policies with the aim of changing the organisation's masculine culture and poor management of stress and trauma. According to a member of the PCP, the key to running successful workshops is

> when you go and talk to them about gender issues, you have to break it down into roles and responsibilities... because when we started doing these workshops, they [the soldiers and policemen] used to tell us things like 'I've been away a long time and I come home – where do I fit in again? She [the wife] will not let me do this, that and the other. We don't talk the same language... she is not sharing about what is going on in the house'. So while we are talking about gender issues, we are really focussing on gender relations.

A significant problem for many soldiers is dealing with the acts of violence they have committed. A member of the PCP told us that many people '*are scared to go back home. Because, they knew what they had done, and they were already getting comments thrown at them and thrown to their children and their wives. So they were also afraid of how to deal with these comments and not use violence. We would not have known that, if we did not work with this group of people*'.

The necessity to provide soldiers and police with access to trauma counselling and stress management as means to prevent violence cannot be overemphasised. Support to organisations like the PCP that work with military and ex-military personnel on trauma and stress management is warranted. Fiji also has a number of army and ex–armed forces personnel working for private military and security contractors as guards, escorts and other security staff, especially in

Iraq and Kuwait. In an economy that has felt the impact of coups, such employment opportunities are a significant source of income through remittances (Mohanty 2005). Hence, donors, funding agencies and policy-makers could consider extending financial support so that organisations like the PCP can extend their services to this group as well.

As Fiji is a troop-contributing nation to UN peacekeeping missions, issues raised in the final report of the *Policy dialogue to review strategies for enhancing gender balance among uniformed personnel in peacekeeping missions* are of significance to the country. The report is the outcome of a policy dialogue organised by the UNDPKO in order to address 'the paradox that there is very little systematic action to increase female deployment to peacekeeping operations, despite the widespread understanding that women in meaningful numbers make a major contribution to the successful implementation of complex, multidimensional peacekeeping mandates' (UNDPKO 2006b, p. 1). The UNDPKO recommends creating a roster of female peacekeepers who possess requisite experience to be called upon especially for short-term assignments in areas such as DDR and elections. Reviewing recruitment policies to promote a gender-sensitive culture is an area in which donors can make a significant contribution through cross-learning initiatives. Improving home-based support services such as housing, childcare centres, schools and transportation for women in military and police services can help to assure women that welfare provisions are in place for their families when they are deployed. Adapting pre-deployment training to ensure that gender mainstreaming considerations are incorporated in training for all personnel and translating training materials provided by the UNDPKO into Fijian and Hindustani can help to develop the capacity of peacekeepers to be more responsive to gender considerations while on a mission.

Participation of women in decision-making

In addition to participating in peacekeeping missions, women in Fiji play a significant role in shaping their country's politics. As a member of the Women and Theological Education Committee of South Pacific Association of Theological Schools (Weavers) told us, *'I think women highlight things that men do not realise – do not understand. There are always loopholes when there are no women... when women are there, they actively contribute a lot to what the men don't see'*. From the late 1960s, when the Young Women's Christian Association played a leading role in the anti-nuclear movement, to more recent political crises, women in Fiji have been 'visible as supporters of peace, although invisible from formal peace processes' (Bhagwan-Rolls 2006a). Peace vigils such as the Blue Ribbon Peace Vigil in 2000 serve as a platform for a collective women's call for peace and to highlight their security concerns. The FWRM acknowledges that women play a significant role in peace talks, not just in Fiji but across the Pacific. A member of this Movement told us how she accepts that there are conscientious efforts to ensure that women's voices are heard in terms of developing peace strategies; however, *'once it [conflict] has been resolved, and you sort of move onto some democratic process, I always find, that they put women to the side'*.

In order to address this issue, the Women's Plan of Action 1999–2008 draws attention to the requirement for gender-balanced decision-making. In the lead-up to the 2006 elections, all major political parties made commitments to set aside a significant percentage of seats for women. However, the results of the elections have been described as 'bitter sweet: bitter, because there had been a reduction in women candidate numbers, but sweet because a total of eight women won seats in the House of Representatives' (Nicholl 2007, p. 161). Overall, if we take into account the Senate as well, women hold 13.6 per cent of all Parliamentary seats. Speaking at the

Fifty-fourth Session of the Commission on the Status of Women, the Minister for Social Welfare, Women and Poverty Alleviation alluded to 'plans to address the issue of women's representation in Parliament under Fiji's new Constitution to be developed in preparation for the general Election in 2014' (Government of the Republic of Fiji 2010). If implemented, these are significant plans.

Other initiatives include the Bottom-Up Governance Leadership Program (a Pacific region program including Fiji), conducted by the Foundation for Development Cooperation and funded by the UN Democracy Fund with other partners like the University of the South Pacific and TorqAid, a humanitarian and community development consultancy that operates in Australia and overseas. This two-year Program, which commenced in September 2008, has two phases. The first provides an e-learning and knowledge platform, to help women familiarise themselves with governance issues, and a series of training programs in leadership skills. The second funds small-scale women's initiatives that aim to improve governance in their own local communities. UNIFEM's Women in Politics (WIP) program focuses on providing training in politics for women, identifying potential female leaders in key government decision-making bodies and strengthening their capacities and political skills. It also develops a database on the participation of Pacific women at all levels of decision-making. UNIFEM is working with the Fiji College of Advanced Education and the Centre for Training and Development (the Fijian government's training centre for civil servants) to test the WIP modules in their training program. In addition, as part of the WIP program, UNIFEM funded an assessment of the electoral system and, as UN Women, now works closely with stakeholders to back reform in the Electoral Act and in regulations that impede women's full participation in the decision-making process at all levels of governance (UNIFEM 2005).

The idea that women's voices should be heard in formal, not just in informal, spaces emerged repeatedly in our research. A member of femLINKpacific told us that *'we know that women mobilise, but how do we take it to that next level – how do we get into the formal spaces?'* We suggest that to enable women to access formal spaces, donors and funding agencies could consider three ideas.

- They could provide technical and financial support for the development of a women's dialogue forum, to create a women's agenda for the proposed elections in 2014. This idea was originally mooted by femLINKpacific (Bhagwan-Rolls 2009). However, what we propose is a slightly different model, which seeks to bring the different women's organisations under one roof when it comes to campaigning for a role in the formal spaces. The women's dialogue forum could have sub-forums that focus on specific issues.[2]
- The forum could be supported to develop a framework for action that explicitly links the pillars of human rights, democracy and the rule of law. As a member of the FWRM put it, *'[t]he only way that women's participation has a chance is by having all those three pillars working together'*.
- Regular Asia-Pacific regional forums would bring together women who have worked through the process of mediated dialogue and engagement in formal peace processes to share the learning.

Part of the problem in accessing formal spaces is trying to foster the capacity to understand how those spaces work and having the skills to work in those spaces. A member of femLINKpacific stressed that *'we can continue to negotiate for women's spaces, but, unless we are investing in their preparation, what are they going to say when they get to the table?'* The 'peace talks' model might be seen as a good practice in developing a capacity to work in and negotiate formal spaces. It is noteworthy that femLINKpacific developed its Peace Talks model precisely for such a purpose, that is, to enhance the capacity of a core group of women to participate in the formal peace process. The model comes from the effort to engage with the FRSC. It is a training and advocacy program in which the focus is not just on raising awareness on UNSCR 1325, but also on building effective lobbying skills to engage with relevant government departments, politicians and community leaders. The forum created by this model not only brings women together to discuss peace and security issues, but also invests time in building their capacity to liaise with significant government stakeholders. The major value gained from being part of a process based on this approach was articulated by a member of Weavers:

> *There was a workshop that femLINKpacific organised on UNSCR 1325. One of the things we did in the workshop was meet with different government officials as representatives of the different organisations to present to them what they should know about, especially how we feel about UNSCR 1325. That was a real good experience because I have never gone face-to-face and present my case to government and talk to them and we asked them questions. It was a real stepping stone for me.*

While it is important for women to gain access to formal spaces, participation in these spaces often is buttressed by discussions that take place outside formal frameworks. Women ought to be part of these too. For instance, Dialogue Fiji acts as a space for non-political leaders, including women, with different (often opposing) political views to discuss critical issues facing the country. The aim of Dialogue Fiji is to develop a bottom-up approach: 'What we are trying to do now, is just create space for people to talk. One of the things we are hoping is that we would be able to create some – a critical mass *so that the regime is going to have no choice but to be able to have a national dialogue . . . that is inclusive*' (FWRM member). We argue that policy-makers, donors and other funding agencies should promote inclusive dialogue as a central process of engagement with civil society and government stakeholders. This dialogue might involve consideration of a possible national truth and reconciliation commission for Fiji. Dialogue Fiji certainly expresses its aim to develop a national reconciliation commission. According to a member of the FWRM, it is hoped that Dialogue Fiji can serve as a platform, '*a spin-off of the dialogue*', to push forwards a transitional justice program.

Additionally, there is an urgency to encourage another type of dialogue in Fiji: one that seeks to bridge the divide within the women's movement. According to the women we interviewed, ideological differences, tensions resulting from political affiliations, and perceived lack of support for issue-based action that some women's organisations are engaged in are just some of the factors causing a discernible divide in the women's movement. These tensions have serious implications for presenting, if not a unified women's voice, at least one that speaks to common purposes (Marks 2005). A member of the Pacific Foundation for the Advancement of Women (PFAW) told us: '*Because of a political situation, you have different views as the women align themselves to different positions and there is conflict within the women's organisations, to the point, they don't even want to hear somebody . . . even if that person has all the expertise*'. To bridge the divide within the women's movement, there is a pressing need to support a transparent and honest dialogue between civil society organisations, especially women's organisations. Such a dialogue is consistent with the feminist goal of accepting differences and similarities, and celebrating diversity. It is important that such a dialogue is facilitated by someone who is respected and trusted by a wide range of women's organisations, which should be consulted to ascertain whom they regard as a good facilitator.

A further dilemma lies in the perception that young women lack the space to build and demonstrate their capacity for leadership and hence remain an untapped potential. This message is reiterated by organisations like the FWRM and femLINKpacific. 'How can society say that young people are not concerned about politics or national issues when they don't ask young people? Maybe they should ask... and then they'll get the answer' (in Bhagwan-Rolls 2001, p. 47). Projects like Be the Change You Want to Be, the Emerging Leaders' Forum (FWRM) and Generation Next (femLINKpacific) try to address the concerns of young women and to assist them in finding their voice on national issues.

> *We need an entirely new bunch of leaders. You need some succession planning in women's civil society organisations. A lot of people are just holding onto the keys of the kingdom. They are not really training the next generation of leaders; they are not pushing them out there, in the open. You have got gatekeepers there. They have got to let go of the keys and they have got to take a few young people under their wings, and say, let's train you, let's give you the reins and then let them go* (Anonymous).[3]

The point was also made to us that many organisations have the capacity to nurture young female leaders. Hence, the focus can shift from building the capacity of these organisations to '*mentoring others, bringing them on par, emerging leadership – changing all of that, and I think they [older organisations that have received funds from international donors for several years] are well-placed to do that. They will serve Fiji well by doing that*' (Anonymous). Donors, funding agencies and civil society organisations should support initiatives that build young women's (and men's) leadership capacities and skills as policy-makers. This might involve integrating a young women's program as a component of any project focusing on increasing women's participation in decision-making. For instance, it might be advisable to set up (or build into an existing program) a mentoring project for young women – a future leaders program with training, mentoring and networking components. Providing resources and financial support to young women to attend national, regional and international dialogues, such as supporting the FWRM to attend the processes concerned with the Universal Periodic Report Review,[4] go a long way in developing capacity to engage with a wide range of stakeholders on significant women's issues. Organisations receiving funding from donors, funding agencies and governments should demonstrate succession planning that includes a young women's leadership component.

It is widely acknowledged that women's political participation should be promoted. The manifestos of political parties emphasise the requirement to increase the number of female Members of Parliament; however, they have little to say about how they plan to accomplish this goal. Fiji's alternative electoral system acts as a barrier to women's participation, as voters are not able to rank candidates in order of preference. As Rae Nicholl (2007, p. 170) points out, 'in any system with single-member electorates, there is a strong tendency to choose "safe" candidates, who will not offend any citizens within the voting community'. Such systems typically do not assist those groups in society who traditionally are under-represented in Parliament.

A significant barrier to standing for office is the high cost of election campaigns, combined with the relatively poor financial status of women (Siwatibau 2007). To address this issue, initiatives such as the FWRM's Women in Politics Appeal stand out as good practices. The Appeal has two aims. On the one hand, it enables the organisation to raise funds for female candidates, irrespective of their political affiliation, to campaign, and on the other hand, it serves to mobilise female voters. The FWRM also produced a leaflet titled

Women ask, outlining strengths and strategies proposed by political parties to address the concerns of women.

Another challenge that women face is pressure from male family members and community leaders to vote for specific candidates (Nicholl 2007). It is therefore imperative that emphasis is placed on civic education, especially during elections. A good illustration of such an initiative is the collective effort of femLINKpacific, the FWRM, the FWCC and WAC during the 2006 elections. They placed full-page advertisements in the daily newspapers titled 'No-one sees who you vote for. No-one will ever know'. The advertisements encouraged female voters to examine the party manifestos, pay attention to the campaigns being run and critically question what politicians had done for their community. The advertisements ended by reminding women that '[t]his is your choice, your vote – yours alone' (Nicholl 2007).

Attention also should be paid to how best to engage men in promoting women's participation. *'There is so much emphasis on women's leadership – well, what about men's leadership? You need to train men to think about women, involving women and including women in decision-making'* (Anonymous). Political participation, according to a member of the PFAW, includes another angle as well:

> *People tend to think that all decision-making is done at the political level. No. So much work is really initiated by the civil service and if we have good civil servants they know how to influence the Minister. We need women Ministers; we need in Parliament women who can raise the issues for debate. At the same time I think we tend to forget the real decision-makers out there in those civil service offices. We need to work equally hard to get more women in as heads of departments, as head of Ministries, not just as Ministers, but as permanent secretaries.*

As discussed in Chapter 5, to enable the implementation of an affirmative action model to promote women's political participation, policy-makers will want to consider a quota system or a system of reserved seats for women in both houses of Parliament. In addition, continued support (through resources and finances) for building the capacity of women is called for, as well as for helping women to fulfil the role they are called upon to play once elected to office. Civil society organisations, especially women's organisations, must continue to rouse political parties to set up a special fund to support female candidates to cover the costs of campaigning, and work with them to develop concrete plans to build a pool of female candidates. Policy-makers, donors and funding agencies must invest in civic education campaigns generally as well as in specific programs targeted at women. Electoral Commission reforms will go a long way in enabling the independence of women's votes if they ensure that women are polling clerks (both Indigenous Fijian and Indo-Fijian) and present in polling stations, especially in rural locations, to assist women in filling out their ballot papers, and that female enumerators (especially Indo-Fijian) are engaged and provide necessary support to the registration of female voters.

Comments such as those made by Nanise Nagusuca (Assistant Minister for Culture and Heritage in 2006) demonstrate the difficulty faced in attempting to change the attitude that women are subordinate to men:

> The traditional Fijian set-up does not make mention of the woman being superior or even on equal standing with men. A lot of Fijian women know that they should be subservient to their husbands and be good mothers to their children. They should see that the home is well looked after and that the life of the family members is comfortable. Women's rights are a western concept and shouldn't be adopted (in Nicholl 2007, p. 171).

In order to change such attitudes, it is essential to deconstruct ideas regarding culture, cultural practices and gender roles. This is neither an easy process nor one that can be accomplished in a short period of time. However, it is imperative that gender awareness programs are designed with the primary aims of encouraging deep reflection on existing ideas about cultural gender norms and equipping equality advocates to argue against using cultural relativism as a reason to discriminate against women (Porter & Every 2009).

The Foundation of the Peoples of the South Pacific International (FPSPI), a network of independent community-based organisations working in the Pacific, recommends designing workshops that examine participants' currently held values on rights and equality, linking them to common values about humanity and the dignity of human life. This recommendation tallies with UN declarations and is a way of *'shattering that myth of [rights and equality] being an external import of western view'* (FPSPI member). Workshops on gender awareness must help participants to understand who is representing their culture, who is speaking on their behalf, the extent of heterogeneous interpretations of culture, the political context within which culture is being discussed, how culture has changed over time and what has brought about these changes. Finally, donors, funding agencies, policy-makers and civil society organisations must recognise that one-off workshops have limited results. Changing attitudes requires persistent effort and constant reiteration. Finding entry points, such as within the school curriculum, is also important.

Relief and recovery

Many of our participants expressed views of peace and security that confirm arguments made in the earlier chapters that human security is a holistic, all-encompassing concept. For example, some emphasised political stability and personal security. *'When you are looking at the policy level it is often considered to be the political security. We are* very much aware that it is a much broader issue around human security – it's personal security as well' (FPSPI member). Others referred to a deeply personal experience. *'To me, peace is all about that inner absence of negative emotions that come up, that can manifest itself in various ways that would hurt other people'* (PFAW member). Another commented, *'Peace has to come within you. If you get peace with yourself, you will be at peace with your family, then your community, then the nation'* (Weavers member). Others stressed a respect for equal rights:

> *You can't have security if women are not given equal rights ... we can't have peace and security if equality is not emphasised. If we are not treated equally women will be not at peace – they will be insecure – insecure in the church, insecure in the family, insecure in every sphere of life. There will be insecurity everywhere. Because I'm not respected – how can I feel secure? How can I feel at peace when I'm not accepted?* (Weavers member).

Another linked peace with access to justice: *'Justice, women being able to assert their rights in terms of the right housing, having right to decent food, education, health'* (FWRM member). Other views emphasised cross-cultural understanding and respect: *'We know that so much of the conflict in the world is created by this lack of understanding or ignorance or willingness to perceive another person's point of view. When it comes to gender, women, peace and security it is creating opportunities for that [creating a space to build understanding] to happen'* (FPSPI member).

Drawing on the above conceptualisations, it is clear that engendering peace and security is seen by Fijian women simultaneously as a bottom-up and a top-down process, at the heart of which lies transforming existing structures to address root causes of conflicts. As a member of the PFAW told us, *'[t]hat to me, is the test of the kind of work you need to do if you want to resolve conflicts. You have to begin with the people at the community level and the decision-makers at the village level and the tribal level, at the family level, the self level'.* The key focus in Fiji has been bridging the bottom-up and top-down processes so that they work in tandem. The contribution made by the WPS Fiji CC and the National Council of Women Fiji to the National Security and Defence Review in 2003 is an excellent illustration of engaging with SSR. In their submission, women's organisations raised critical issues regarding the manner in which the review had been conducted, who had been consulted, issues that were identified as security threats and the manner in which UNSCR 1325 was incorporated into the review and reform process. In particular, they highlighted that the review lacked a DDR process and was more focused on downsizing the military. The lack of acknowledgment that the military comprises not just the soldiers, but also their families, was criticised, as was the framing of women exclusively as victims of violence rather than as key resource persons to facilitate reform (Bhagwan-Rolls 2009). Apart from articulating the role that women's organisations could play in setting the security agenda of policy advice, monitoring, capacity development, identifying early warning indicators, raising public awareness and acting as links with the community, their submission addressed structural issues that constrain women's voices from being heard. It called for the inclusion of the Minister of Women as a member of the National Security Council, the Permanent Secretary of the Ministry of Women as a permanent member of the National Security Advisory Committee and women on provincial and district security committees and in the National Security Assessment Unit.

Approaching the issue of relief and recovery from a local perspective, there is a strong belief held by Fijian women in conflict prevention through empowering communities and encouraging peace education. *'What I think peacebuilding is... it starts with strengthening communities. So it is about community empowerment that enables them to deal with conflicts at all levels. It requires working with all parties that are involved in a conflict and acknowledging that it is not only the victim and offender, but there is also community impact of all conflicts*' (FPSPI member). The PFAW's peace education program is a good example of a multilayered approach. We were told: '*We are working on a peace education program for the community, for the women, for the non-formal sector. At the same time, we can use the program for the teachers as well. We have a curriculum – a five modular program – and we are hoping to train the trainers*' (PFAW member). Their peace education program is based on the principle that while legislation and laws are important, they '*don't change the people from within and if we don't change people from within nothing will change. So, our approach is to begin with the self. We have to have the people who love peace*'.

Focusing on peace education in schools, the Cool Schools pilot in Fiji, which commenced in 2007,[5] is an excellent example of a peer mediation program that teaches school students at all levels skills that resolve conflict effectively and peacefully. The hallmark of this project is that it takes a 'whole school' approach, involving not just students, but staff and support staff. The success of the project rests on teaching students mediation skills and then giving them opportunities to apply those skills. The teachers train their students in a seven-part course. Students are then invited to apply to be mediators and, once selected, are rostered to work in the playground and sometimes in the classroom as well. The mediators are identified by a special uniform, and children caught up in conflicts, including bullying, have the option of approaching a mediator or a teacher for help. If both parties are willing, a mediation session takes place with students agreeing to tell the truth, suggest a resolution, not interrupt and so forth. Ninety per cent of the time, agreement is reached and a contract signed. Once the program is implemented in the school, the parents and wider community are invited into the school to take part in the Bring Cool Schools Home program. This involves the student mediators modelling the mediation skills to their parents or caregivers, who are also taught mediation and conflict resolution skills to resolve conflict at home and in the community (Global Peacebuilders 2008, p. 16).

Part of empowering communities is recognising and validating existing conflict resolution, mediation and reconciliation mechanisms. As a member of the FPSPI said to us, '*[w]e feel that if we can address conflict at the community level, then you will prevent violence and conflict being spread out to the national level*'. To adopt this approach, the FPSPI is trying to develop a resource package that captures

> [u]seful tools and approaches that have been used by communities in the past in addressing violence. We really want to tap into that and not place too much emphasis on a western style of conflict mediation, but really extract what works for us, or what has worked for us in the past. We are also looking at the reconciliation processes in each and we are capturing that to ensure that whoever intends to work in the Pacific on peacebuilding is aware that these approaches exist and does not duplicate the process.

Remaining challenges

As some of the initiatives we have discussed illustrate, civil society organisations and women's organisations in Fiji have some innovative ideas for transitions from conflict to sustainable peace. However, women's organisations in Fiji work under considerably constrained circumstances that offer limited opportunities for them to fulfil the multiple roles they play as service providers, watchdogs, policy experts and voices of community concerns. Hence, linking the work of women's organisations with formal decision-making spaces is essential. This requires a shift in the way we think about what constitutes women's participation in decision-making. In addition to a focus on increasing the number of women who participate, it is important to nurture links between women's organisations (as an entity) and formal decision-making spaces. At a practical level, this translates into improving information dissemination on when critical meetings are being held, identifying key entry points to lobby leaders and developing capacity to undertake gender analysis of the issues on the agenda. Continued support for dialogues like Peace Talks and Dialogue Fiji, with dedicated funds to facilitate the participation of women's organisations in consultations (for example, providing funding for security, accommodation, food, transport and child care), is critical if women's voices are to be heard in formal decision-making processes. As we highlighted in Chapter 6, supporting women's organisations that participate in local inclusive dialogues for peace to attend international and regional forums on peace and security engender feelings of solidarity and guard against feelings of isolation and powerlessness.

The media have a significant role to play, not just as information providers but as shapers of public opinion. While there is a discernible presence of women in Fiji's media, women rarely are called upon by mainstream media to comment as experts in a particular field. According to Sharon Bhagwan-Rolls (2000, p. 69), women are often consulted in their role as 'ordinary people or persons in the street whose occupation may be considered unimportant to the opinion they are asked to express'. This makes community media important vehicles to bridge the information gap. It also provides opportunities for locally driven relevant content to form the basis for discussion and to

> conduct outreach to women and women's groups to disseminate the accords, particularly in local languages and through

multi-media presentations so that illiteracy is not a barrier and by doing so provide a 'safe network' so that women representatives in all mechanisms can not only monitor implementation of the peace agreement, including early warning for a resurgence of conflict, but also communicate these to relevant authorities (Bhagwan-Rolls n.d., p. 5).

To do what Sharon Bhagwan-Rolls recommends, the issues related to project-based funding, which by its very nature takes a short-term approach, have to be addressed. Project-based funding means that *'you can only achieve so much in one year in terms of trying to change the behaviours of men, developing the proper capacity within community systems or within the justice system – you can't do that in a year'* (FPSPI member). Members of the FPSPI point to another significant concern that smaller NGOs raise. Organisations that have received a significant amount of funding over a sustained period become gatekeepers averse to partnering and thus stifle opportunities to work with smaller organisations. Some organisations have become

> *big gatekeepers rather than partners. Yes, they are important leaders in our community, but there has to be initiatives allowed by others, and that is where we are struggling to keep negotiations and the discussions open to inform them what we are actually doing and then seeking their advice and requesting their support . . . I would like to see us having more of a coalition rather than saying, 'everything has got to go through this mechanism'* (FPSPI member).

Thus, there is an urgent requirement to facilitate information-sharing between organisations and strengthen regional links, *'just to find out what each other are doing at the ground level, institutional level, policy level as well. So you kind of get a fair idea of what is happening, what the gaps are in terms of the peace and security work'* (FPSPI member).

One way to ensure a strengthening of regional links is to advocate for the PIFS to have a Senior Gender Adviser with oversight of women, peace and security issues located in the Political Governance and Security Programme. Alternatively, the PIFS could appoint a conflict prevention adviser whose job description includes promoting a gendered framework for conflict prevention and resolution (Shanahan 2010). To stimulate action on the ground, support for regional mechanisms, such as regular region-wide information-sharing conferences for civil society organisations on women, peace and security, is advised. If all project and program funding were allocated resources for information-sharing and dissemination, then greater links would be forged between organisations. Finally, there is a tendency to depend on international consultants rather than using local expertise in designing programs. *'The development of any kind of program has to come from the people themselves. We have too many consultants. We have donors bringing in people from South Africa and other places – this is crazy. We are really qualified people; our skills should be better used'* (PFAW member).

Addressing these challenges in ways that implement UNSCR 1325 will require donors and funding agencies to adopt a programmatic view leading towards the establishment of a women, peace and security fund that could operate on a consultative basis with women's organisations collectively identifying priority areas and potential collaborations between them in the delivery of projects. This would also help in ensuring that more local experts are used, serving a dual purpose: better contextualisation and acknowledgment of the expertise of qualified people in Fiji and the Pacific region.

In addition to adopting a programmatic view, a balance is needed between responsive, strategic and project-based funding. Responsive funding works well 'when resources are scarce or where donor funds can be used as a lever to mobilise complementary funds or resources at the community level... support for one-off, or niche activities well-suited for testing, developing or piloting new or innovative approaches'. Strategic funding takes a longer term view; 'there may be considerable value, for instance, in looking at how civil society is evolving in a country and identifying ways of reinforcing the sector as a whole' (Canadian International Development Agency 2001, p. 13) and providing core funding to develop and maintain capacity. Organisations call for core funding in order to be innovative in a longer term way.

There are many women in Fiji who demonstrate broad understandings of peace and security and who continue to do the work of UNSCR 1325, some unwittingly, others intentionally. In this chapter, we have shown why there is a need for international donors to adopt a programmatic rather than a project-based approach to supporting the country's transition from instability to sustained peace. In giving examples of ways to bridge gaps between bottom-up and top-down strategies to participate in conflict transformation processes, we have offered reasons why inclusive dialogue in Fiji is a crucial part of peacebuilding.

CHAPTER 9

Sri Lanka

We make a distinction between post-war and post-conflict. We can say that the armed conflict between the Sri Lankan Army and the LTTE is over. So in that sense we are in a post-war scenario. But that doesn't mean we are in a post-conflict context. Conflict still exists and will continue to exist until we can make sure that human rights are not violated.
National Peace Council of Sri Lanka member, 2010

In this chapter we draw on our field-based interviews to examine the progress made in implementing UNSCR 1325 with respect to our interpretation of its four pillars: protecting women and girls and preventing conflict, enabling gender-sensitive peacekeeping, promoting women's participation in decision-making and ensuring gender-responsive relief and recovery. We make three central arguments.

- Women are active in furthering peaceful security, doing the work of UNSCR 1325, consciously or otherwise. Having been largely left out of peace talks, many seek a much more explicit role in a new post-conflict stage.
- In order to address the complex issues faced, donors should contemplate funding both long-term programs and short-term projects in supporting the country's transition from instability to sustained peace.

- The long-term affect of trauma requires creative approaches that work simultaneously to mitigate and heal deep psychological pain and build trust between different ethnic groups.

Conflict and insecurity

The ethnic conflict in Sri Lanka between the Tamils, Sinhalese and other groups is just one of three simultaneous and interconnected conflicts occurring in the country. The other two are the armed conflict between the Sri Lankan army and the Liberation Tigers of Tamil Eelan (LTTE) and the struggle for political power between the Sri Lanka Freedom Party, the United National Party and the Tamil Tigers (Manikkalingam 2008). At the heart of these conflicts is a sense of discrimination in relation to language, employment, education and political participation in governance. This prompted a violent call for a separatist Tamil state on the one hand and political violence during elections on the other. To resolve the ethnic tensions that erupted into a full-scale military conflict in 1983, attempts were made to bring about peace through negotiations between the Sri Lankan government and the LTTE (in 1985, 1987, 1989–90, 1994–95 and 2002–03). Each attempt failed. In 2008, the Sri Lankan government announced its intention to pursue a military solution to the conflict.

Conflict lasting over two decades has had a significant impact on human development in Sri Lanka. According to the 2009 Human Development Report (UNDP 2009), Sri Lanka ranks 102 out of 182 countries (down from 84 out of 174 in 1998). It ranks 83 out of 155 countries on the GDI and 98 out of 109 countries on the gender empowerment measure, with only 6 per cent of seats in Parliament held by women. There are an estimated 40,000 war widows in Sri Lanka, and, according to UNIFEM's (2008b) country profile, women made up one-third of the fighting force of the LTTE, which experts estimate to be 15,000. UNIFEM's profile on Sri Lanka also notes that women experience rape, detainment, harassment and other violations of personal security at checkpoints. Women and children are overrepresented as refugees and IDPs. According to the International Crisis Group (2010, p. 5) report *Sri Lanka: a bitter peace*, 'there have been numerous credible reports of prostitution networks in the IDP camps which function with the knowledge and involvement of Sri Lankan security forces'. This report also suggests that female LTTE ex-combatants were raped while held in detention centres. Equally disturbing is the fact that 'levels of fear are so high and with no independent monitors allowed access to the camps; it has not been possible to confirm or disprove these accusations'.

Implementation of UNSCR 1325

Sri Lanka does not have an NAP on UNSCR 1325. The women's organisations we interviewed suggested that it is possible that issues of protection, prevention, participation, and relief and recovery raised in UNSCR 1325 will be incorporated in the section 'Women and conflict' in the government's five-year plan for women. At the time of conducting this research, the National Plan of Action for Women (2010–14) was still being drafted. Some women we spoke with argued that a separate action plan on UNSCR 1325 runs the risk of being under-resourced, and that a preferable option is to incorporate it in a broader plan for women with the intention of developing a more holistic response. Other women are not convinced. According to them, despite the existence of UNSCR 1325, women were largely excluded from the formal peace talks held between the government of Sri Lanka and the LTTE in September 2002. It was only after intense lobbying by local and international women's organisations that a Sub-Committee for Gender Issues (SGI) was established. Hence, these women believe that a separate NAP on UNSCR 1325 will result in greater accountability.

In line with the requirements of UNSCR 1325, the UN Development Assistance Framework for Sri Lanka (2008–12), which has been endorsed by the government of Sri Lanka, adopts a human security approach. As such, it explicitly lists among its focus areas 'promoting women's active participation in and contribution to peacebuilding at national, regional and community levels; strengthening institutional mechanisms for women's empowerment, and increasing the substantive contribution of women in decision-making processes at all levels; and reducing gender-based violence through multi-sectoral interventions, and the effective implementation of laws and policies' (UN 2007, pp. 30–1).

From the perspective of civil society's involvement in promoting UNSCR 1325, Sarala Emmanuel (2008) draws attention to the fact that women's activism for peace in Sri Lanka has a long history that pre-dates UNSCR 1325. Her report makes a significant point in noting that

> women's peace activism has been a part of their broader work towards addressing issues of socio-economic marginalisation, cultural oppression, political rights and justice. Peace work was not a separate or isolated activity, and women's engagement with these other dimensions were seen as inherently important, and as being both inter-connected with and independent from issues of war and armed conflict (2008, p. 16).

This activism continues, with women's organisations involved in a range of activities from service delivery in running women's shelters, counselling to deal with trauma and support of microcredit programs to advocacy work and awareness-raising.

Protection and prevention

Emmanuel (2008) raises concerns for women's safety due to the increasing incidents of violence against women. According to members of the Gender-Based Violence Forum,[1] women in the north and the east (conflict zones) and in post-tsunami shelters and institutions form high-risk populations, '[t]he most prevalent types of violence against women being rape, domestic violence, sexual harassment, sexual violence, forced prostitution and trafficking' (IRIN News 2008).

This vulnerability comes despite the fact that gender equality, non-discrimination based on sex and affirmative action for the advancement of women all find mention in Sri Lanka's constitution. The country ratified CEDAW in 1981 and, as part of its commitment to tackling gender-based violence, signed the Vienna Declaration on the Elimination of Violence against Women in 1993. These actions were given further impetus with the drafting of the first National Action Plan for Women in 1996, in which special attention was given to legislative reforms, establishing crisis centres for female victims of violence, raising public awareness on the issue of violence and educating law enforcement agencies and the judiciary.

There have been positive steps taken to protect women and girls from violence and to facilitate their access to justice. The Supreme Court of Sri Lanka recognises that state violence against women while in police custody constitutes an infringement of the right to protection against torture and inhuman and degrading treatment (CEDAW 1999). Steps taken to protect women and girls include amendments to the penal code, removing the clause stating that acts of sexual violence qualify as such only if it can be demonstrated that they were committed against a woman's will. It also increases the age of consent for statutory rape from twelve to sixteen years,[2] stipulating that custodial and gang rapes constitute graver crimes and incur more severe punishment. It removes provisions that allowed for suspended sentences, even in the case of grave violations, and makes it mandatory to impose at least minimum terms of incarceration. In addition, the Ministry of Child Development and Women's Empowerment has initiated programs to strengthen the women and children's desks in police stations by creating mobile counselling units and pilot projects. Centres have been established in hospitals for victims of SGBV. Women's centres run by NGOs complement legal reforms.

Women's organisations provide support and services to victims of SGBV. For example, Women in Need (WIN), an NGO working towards woman and child abuse prevention and education, and Suriya Women's Development Centre provide shelter, psychosocial support and legal help. Women for Peace works with political prisoners, supporting them and their families through services such as accessing legal assistance and facilitating family visits. Other organisations like the Women and Media Collective (WMC) and the Sri Lankan Women for Peace and Democracy (a broad coalition of women's organisations) actively participate in efforts to reform legal processes to ensure better protection for women.

However, the 2001 NGO shadow report on CEDAW (CENWOR 2001) points out significant gaps in measures taken to protect women and girls. The report notes the necessity of tackling persistent structural and institutional barriers to accessing justice. These include inadequate resourcing of the women and children's desks set up in police stations and the often unacceptable attitudes of judges, law enforcement officers, medical professionals and lawyers towards female victims of violence. The report also highlights how the adversarial nature of the legal system proves frequently insensitive to gender concerns and sometimes hostile to women. In addition, it underscores a lack of awareness among women regarding their rights and, perhaps more alarmingly, an equally significant lack of awareness among law enforcement officers, judges and lawyers of the full potential of the law (CEDAW 1999). A member of WIN who spoke to us said:

> *The biggest challenge facing us is the attitude of the police and other law enforcement people (like the judiciary). The police, lawyers and judges must be sensitised about the need for protection and see*

domestic and sexual violence as a violation that must be treated with seriousness. So they need training – rights-based training so that they accept the seriousness of the issue.

Some of these issues can be addressed by developing the capacity of women's and legal aid organisations to better strive for legal reforms. While it is important to continue supporting and resourcing programs that focus on raising awareness of women's rights, attention also needs to be paid to instituting a justice sector reform project in collaboration with relevant government departments and legal aid, civil society and women's organisations. This project should adopt a holistic approach to protection by addressing critical procedural, attitudinal and capacity issues.

Developing appropriate gender-sensitive responses to enable the protection of women and girls from violence requires comprehensive data on the extent and nature of the problem. These are sorely lacking in Sri Lanka, making it difficult for civil society and women's organisations to convince major stakeholders of the seriousness of the problem. It is not just a practical issue of collecting data, but also of making them accessible to relevant stakeholders – women's organisations, police, the Attorney-General's Department, lawyers, judges, paralegals, medical professionals and human rights organisations. A first step is the initiation of a sustainable data collection project that brings together relevant stakeholders with the aim of building a national database on violence against women.

A significant reason for the wisdom of collecting this data is the lingering psychological impact of over two decades of conflict. We were told by a member of WIN that '*[o]ne of the other reasons why we don't see much investment in mental health is because the impact of violence on women's psychology is unseen – women tend to have a lot of tolerance and don't openly talk about any emotional imbalance that they might be experiencing and so this aspect of health is not prioritised*'.

In calling for the development of a mental health and well-being program for women and girls, with a special focus on the conflict-affected zones of the north and the east, women's organisations are eager to see greater investments in enhancing their capacity to fill the vacuum that exists in providing good, sensitive, psychological and mental health services. A possible solution lies in the establishment of multidisciplinary women's crisis centres, especially in the north and east, and in facilitating knowledge-sharing initiatives that draw on good practices from other regions also affected by conflict.

Peacekeeping

The Sri Lankan security forces are not the only groups accused of committing acts of SGBV. During its three-year presence in the country (1987–89), the Indian Peace Keeping Force was accused of acts of rape and molestation, mostly during house-to-house searches for the LTTE (Sebastian 1994). More recently, in 2007, some Sri Lankan troops were expelled from the UN Stabilisation Mission in Haiti on suspicion of sexual exploitation of Haitian women and girls (BBC News 2007).

While this track record of ensuring gender perspectives in peacekeeping is less than impressive, efforts are being made now to ensure that the Sri Lankan armed forces are well versed in international law on women and armed conflict. The Institute for Human Rights (IHR) is supporting the Institute of Peace Support Operations Training by conducting sessions on gender law as part of the basic instructor training program for officers and senior non-commissioned officers. In addition, the IHR contributes to a potential observers staff officers course by conducting sessions on human, women's and children's rights (IHR 2009). As a member of the Association for War Affected Women (AWAW) suggested, organisations like hers '*need to start advocating for an all-women peacekeeping contingent. India's women contingent to Liberia was a small one but it still had an impact in terms of reducing women's vulnerability'*. In this regard, women's organisations would like to explore the possibility of the Sri Lanka Army Women's Corps playing a more central role in local and international peacekeeping. Currently, the women's corps is responsible for carrying out civilian tasks, including the welfare of IDPs.

There has been no official UN mission to Sri Lanka. In 2002, following the ceasefire agreement, the international Sri Lanka Monitoring Mission was organised by the Norwegian government upon the request of the government of Sri Lanka and the LTTE. The Mission ended in 2008 with the abrogation of the ceasefire agreement. More recently, in June 2010, the UN Secretary-General's Panel of Experts on Accountability in Sri Lanka was appointed. The Panel's mandate is to advise the Secretary-General on the issue of accountability with regard to alleged violations of international human rights and humanitarian law in Sri Lanka. The Panel has found credible allegations of rape committed by the Sri Lankan army and the LTTE (UN n.d.). Sri Lanka faces a significant hurdle in ending impunity.

The breakdown of law and order during times of conflict and insecurity, and the lack of institutions to protect women, create a sense of impunity that must be addressed. In May 2010, President Mahinda Rajapaksa announced the appointment of the Lessons Learnt and Reconciliation Commission, whose mandate includes investigating violations of internationally accepted norms of conduct during the conflict. It is empowered to make recommendations on the nature of compensation to be granted to the victims or their dependants, as well as on the institutional, administrative and welfare measures that will need to be instituted to effect reconstruction, rehabilitation and reconciliation. The Commission's report is not yet released, and we wait to see to what extent issues related to human rights violations, especially violations of women's rights, are reported and what recommendations are made.

Participation of women in decision-making

Women's groups had been campaigning since the early 1980s for a negotiated political solution. Following the ceasefire agreement in February 2002, an international consultation on women, peacebuilding and constitutional development was organised by the International Centre for Ethnic Studies (ICES). This resulted in the drafting of the Women's Peace Memorandum, which made a strong case for including 'women's concerns in the peace process and articulated the basic elements of a gendered framework for conflict resolution and peacebuilding. It called for women's full and equal participation in peace negotiations and in decision-making in all phases of the reconstruction, rehabilitation, and transformation process' (UNDAW 2003, p. 7). However, while women play pivotal roles in pushing for peace and security, they were largely left out of formal peace talks held between the government of Sri Lanka and the LTTE in September 2002. (Only one women representative from the LTTE attended the discussions.) This is a damning scenario, given that UNSCR 1325 was passed in 2000.

Undeterred, an international women's mission was organised to assess women's concerns and prepare specific recommendations to the plenary of the peace talks. This report served as a basis on which women's organisations lobbied extensively for the inclusion of women in the formal peace talks. As a result of these negotiations, an SGI was established, comprising ten women. The LTTE appointed five high-level female cadres, and the government appointed the rest from bipartisan women's NGOs. However, when the peace talks stalled, the SGI was unable to continue its work. Nonetheless, Michelle Page, Tobie Whitman and Cecilia Anderson (2009, pp. 17–18) point out that the above initiative qualifies as a good practice, because

> [t]he SGI was the only subcommittee given the freedom to formulate its own terms of reference ... The SGI was an

unprecedented attempt to involve women in formal peace negotiations. It built on the Kosovo, Northern Ireland, and Burundi peace processes and reflected a growing awareness of the need to include women at all stages of negotiations, peacebuilding, and reconstruction.

The establishment of the SGI demonstrates the importance of external pressure and evidence-informed lobbying. It mandates the representation of women in peace talks and provides a means of connecting female delegates to the peace negotiations. The SGI had its fair share of problems, primarily stemming from its lack of autonomy, as its members were bound by limitations of their appointments.

Recognising that political participation is linked to engaging in decision-making roles in the peace process, women's organisations are relentless in their demand to increase women's participation in decision-making.[3] Considerable efforts are made to build the capacity of women for political leadership. According to Chulani Kodikara (2009, p. 2), 'over 5,000 women appear to have been trained by different organisations in the period 2000–2008'. She points out that such programs serve a dual purpose of developing capacity and confidence as well as 'inspiring and motivating women to pursue a career in politics which otherwise they might not have wanted to do'. Raising awareness on the issue of women's low level of representation in politics with different stakeholders has been another endeavour. All forms of the media are used. From women's journals to mainstream media, women are active in articulating a collective call for political and electoral reform to overcome barriers to women's active participation. Newspaper campaigns such as those run by the Sri Lanka Women's Non-Governmental Organisations Forum, the WMC and the gender unit of the National Peace Council (NPC) target the general population. Television and radio are used to having women's voices heard on the issues. The initiative supported by the Women

Defining Peace (WDP) project[4] in 2008–09, for instance, designed and aired a television program played every Monday. It used different formats, such as documentaries, tele-dramas, panel discussions and debates with experts and ordinary citizens. It encouraged the participation of Parliamentarians, provincial councillors and public servants (Kodikara 2009).

Many organisations call for affirmative action strategies (such as reserved seats and quotas) to be implemented at the national and local levels of government. In 2003, the ICES, the WMC, Mothers and Daughters of Lanka and Muslim Women's Research and Action Forum submitted a memorandum to the Parliamentary Select Committee on Electoral Reform (this was reconstituted in 2006). The memorandum presented a sophisticated case for far-reaching electoral reforms at the local, provincial and national government levels, including reserving seats for women (50 per cent in local elections and 30 per cent in provincial and Presidential elections); the use of closed lists, with every second name on the list being a woman in the case of local elections, and on the proposed national lists of all parties in the case of Presidential elections; the abolishment of the preferential electoral system; and the retention of only the proportional representation system.[5] However, while the Parliamentary Select Committee on Electoral Reform's interim report in July 2007 recognised the need to increase women's representation in politics, it put forth only conservative recommendations of how political parties should ensure nominations of more female candidates. It modestly proposed the introduction of legal provisions to make it mandatory for every third candidate nominated by a party secretary from the national list to be a woman (Kodikara 2008). More recently, in March 2010, prior to the Parliamentary elections in April, Sri Lanka's largest opposition party, the United National Front,[6] released its women's manifesto, titled Deya Dinawana Eya, the first of its kind released by a political party in Sri Lanka (Samath

2010). Among other things, the manifesto promises to ensure 25 per cent female representation at the provincial and national levels and in Parliamentary decision-making committees.

What stands out in Sri Lanka is the extent to which women's organisations have engaged with political parties by lobbying through 'media campaigns, press conferences, one-to-one to meetings and direct correspondence with political party leaders' (Kodikara 2009, p. 51). Most of these engagements are multifaceted, combining a range of activities. For instance, a project initiated by the ICES in 2000 combined research on the quota for women with various stages of dialogue on the issue, including discussions among grassroots women, and national-level interactions between grassroots representatives and national-level activists. At the national-level dialogue, a session was devoted to discussing recommendations with the Minister of Women's Affairs and other political parties' representatives. The recommendations were also formally presented to the Minister of Women's Affairs.

A partnership between the Northern Illinois University, Agromart, the Centre for Women's Research (Sri Lanka) (CENWOR) and the Sarvodaya Women's Movement, called Grow (2002–04), combined capacity-building with a national-level symposium. The resulting declaration was presented to the Prime Minister and the Minister for Women's Empowerment and Social Welfare and was sent to secretaries of all the major political parties. The National Committee for Women organised a well-orchestrated campaign prior to the 2006 local government elections, which involved raising community awareness, training women, media engagement, one-to-one meetings with the secretaries of political parties and creating a list of trained female candidates that was made available to political parties. The AWAW's Team 1325 project not only looks to build capacity but also engages in writing to Members of Parliament. It mobilises the Central Province Women's Voice, a network of women from political parties in the central province designed to undertake a signature campaign in support of a quota system; it also meets elected Members of Parliament, including the Women's Parliamentary Caucus, to discuss an affirmative action policy.

The Sinhala Tamil Rural Women's Network (STRWN) led the way by creating a women's group to contest a provincial council election in 1999 as independents not affiliated with a political party. This strategy was adopted by other women's organisations in 2006 at the provincial level and received support from two national-level organisations. The WMC provided both financial and media support, and the NPC provided training and financial assistance. Although the women's group conducted a door-to-door campaign appealing for one vote from every household to be given to a woman in their group, it was unsuccessful in winning a single seat. Even so, the WMC continues to be active in utilising a provision under the Local Governance Ordinance to participate as observers at local government meetings as a means to ensure accountability on women's issues.

Despite ongoing efforts to promote both proactive participation of women in politics and an increased representation of women in decision-making, Sri Lanka still has a long way to go. Repeatedly, women cite the lack of financial resources as a major impediment to political participation. One of many factors that set women like Sirimavo Bandaranaike and Chandrika Kumaratunga apart is their access to, and control over, financial resources required to contest elections. Not all women come from politically well-established families. Partnering with and supporting women's organisations to set up a non-partisan election fund for prospective female candidates could play a significant role in encouraging more women to stand in elections.[7]

The absence of an affirmative action policy makes it difficult for women's organisations to hold political parties accountable for election promises and manifestos. There is significant resistance to implementing a quota within political parties. As a member from the WMC told us,

> *I think the main challenge we are facing today is that there are very few women in decision-making positions in the government and this is because there is little willingness among most political parties to nominate women to stand for elections. We need to advocate for quotas and also get women on the electoral list. Training alone is not enough.*

Structural inequalities, resulting from the manner in which political parties are run and managed, do little to promote women's participation. Although women's wings exist in most parties, these have little political clout. They mainly mobilise the female constituency during elections. Most parties are boys' clubs, enjoying extensive networks linking national and local levels. According to a member of CENWOR, much more needs to be done to '*work with political parties – and with the women's wing in these parties*'. This includes establishing transparent and accountable practices for the selection of candidates and engaging men in political parties and in the broader community to promote a greater role for women both within their parties as well as in other decision-making levels of government. CENWOR also works on building effective networks between the women's caucus, women's wings in political parties, grassroots women's organisations and urban women's organisations.

Training and capacity development programs often target women from the south and the Sinhalese community. There remains a gap between the knowledge and skills imparted by these programs and those demanded by political parties from potential candidates or by organisations doing advocacy work. Finally, most programs tend to be generic in nature, designed to cater to a wide range of women, even those not interested in entering active politics. A member of WDP was categorical about a need for change:

> [w]e need to stop supporting anything and everything in the name of leadership. Some programs are just using leadership training to get funds. There is a need to review what we mean by leadership training, what should a curriculum look like. The focus must be on building capacity to 'act, influence and negotiate'.

Elections have often been marred by political violence. This is a disincentive for women who are targeted deliberately. According to a member of the AWAW, 'we have a very aggressive election system that uses violence to intimidate candidates and shape voting patterns. Families, who have seen the violence in Sri Lankan politics, hesitate (and understandably) to allow women to run for office'. Women's groups need support in lobbying the government to ensure the implementation of effective measures to prevent and control election-related violence. The election commissioner's rulings, if implemented effectively by the police and other law enforcement authorities, would assist security.

Female voters are an untapped resource in Sri Lanka. Large numbers of women turn out to vote, and anecdotal evidence suggests that their decisions regarding candidates are autonomous. However, this does not necessarily translate into votes for women candidates. The reason remains unclear. In the 2010 elections, IDPs faced difficulties in casting their votes. There were outdated voter lists, lack of proper identification, confusion about where to vote and security concerns. Also disenfranchised are migrant workers, many of whom are women. The necessity of engaging with young women to build a group of emerging leaders is an untouched area. We were told by a member of WDP that 'at the moment we don't have a second tier of women leaders emerging. Young women's participation in *women's organisations has been slow. We really need to widen the circle of women advocating for women's rights!'*

Darini Rajasingham-Senanayake (2004, p. 161), in her analysis on women's agency in post-conflict Sri Lanka, provides insight into why this might be the case. She points out that in Sri Lanka 'most women's groups are mobilised by and large along ethnic lines', with notably few exceptions. This situation offers limited opportunities for young women's agency, especially when they are questioning stereotypical gender norms. Rajasingham-Senanayake (2004, p. 147) uses the example of young widowed Tamil women who take on non-traditional roles by working to sustain their families and suggests that they are 'redefining the perception of widows (and to a lesser extent unmarried women), as inauspicious beings by refusing to be socially and culturally marginalised and ostracised because they have lost husbands'. Women's groups mobilised along ethnic lines might not offer these young women the space or the power to express their struggles for a new identity. Supporting women's organisations that are working across ethnic lines to engage with young women opens new spaces for young women to express and articulate their leadership.

Relief and recovery

There is a stark contrast between how women understand peace compared to the official position of the Sri Lankan government. According to the government, 'after several decades of fighting, in which many thousands of people lost their lives, Sri Lanka is at peace. We have celebrated the end of the terror that threatened us for so long, and the country is now looking to the future, confident that it is going to be bright' (Secretariat for Coordinating the Peace Process 2009). On the other hand, a member from the AWAW articulated what peace means to her:

> *Peace means more than just the absence of war. You can't have peace without security which is more than just physical security, it's also about things like food and the future – when these securities are 'relatively' fulfilled then we will have peace. I say relatively because I am not an idealist but a realist. One of the reasons why we have conflict is that there is no respect for human dignity and when this is combined with persistent inequalities it becomes a deadly mix.*

Thus, while the official discourse focuses on ensuring 'state security from internal as well as external threats' (Bastian 2009, p. 88), most civil society and women's organisations in Sri Lanka adopt a rights-based human security approach. They underscore the obligation to respect human rights and ensure greater equity in health, education, economic opportunity and physical safety. A member of the NPC told us: '*Peace is about enjoying human rights and being able to participate in the political process so that your voice is heard and security is the knowledge that your human rights cannot be violated by any group whether state or non-state*'. A member of CENWOR phrased it in another way, saying,

> *We need to think at a broader level – in terms of economic, social and physical security. I think the challenge we face at the moment is that all the focus has been on the armed conflict with the LTTE but the more qualitative aspects such as better education and health have been put on the back burner. But poor health and education can also lead to insecurity. It's really a complex web of factors that contribute to insecurity.*

Civil society and women's organisations emphasise the need for communal harmony. For a member from the STRWN, '*[p]eace means living together in harmony, where there is a solution for the economic problem, there is no violence against women. We can't have peace if there is no trust'.*

With the aim of working towards reconciliation, in 2010, the Sri Lankan government announced the establishment of the Lessons Learnt and Reconciliation Commission. At the time of writing this book, the terms of reference are still to be finalised. Women's organisations support the proportional inclusion of women in the Commission and drafting gender-sensitive terms of reference, and call for the exclusion of amnesty to those who have committed acts of violence against women. The published mandate is expressed in gender-neutral terms (that is, no specific reference is made to violations of women's rights). In terms of representation, only one woman has been nominated to the eight-member Commission.

Civil society initiatives adopt a broad approach to relief and recovery. Peace education is a critical focus in Sri Lanka. Organisations like the NPC and the Berghof Foundation for Conflict Studies focus on adult peace programs that target government officials, teachers, religious and community leaders, journalists and civil society organisations (Srinivasan 2009). Initiatives like the Butterfly Peace Garden in Batticaloa, established in 1997 and continuing its work even today, demonstrate innovative approaches to working with children traumatised by war. In a safe environment, through a range of activities drawn from the visual, dramatic and musical arts, young girls and boys participate in after-school and weekend creative play programs designed to open up children to new experiences, like meeting children from different ethnic backgrounds, and also to demonstrate, by modelling nonviolent behaviour, alternative ways to resolve conflict (Chase 2000). Extending benefits of such a project to the broader community, the Butterfly Peace Garden explores how the experiences of children can foster reconciliation. The projects that the children work on are put on display for parents, teachers and religious leaders either as 'travelling theatre, sometimes as a town parade, sometimes as an opera or art exhibition' (Barbara 2004, p. 233).

Another form of peace education takes the form of interracial dialogues to debunk ethnic and racial stereotypes and myths. As a member of CENWOR told us, '[w]e need to change people's mindset through inter-racial dialogues. For too long we have been divided along ethnic lines... sometimes we women in the south don't really understand what it is like for women in the north and the east who have grown up with the war'. The STRWN adopts a community-based approach to peacebuilding through peace dialogues. This encourages the community to discuss the problems they face, explore why tensions exist in their communities and how language, trust and fear exacerbate tensions. The point is to look for potential solutions to bring about peace in a way that addresses the fears raised by the community. Recalling one such workshop, which formed part of the WDP project, a member from the AWAW said:

> We brought together 60 women from six districts and gave them training in conflict resolution and then connected them with women in the war-threatened areas where we held a workshop which was really about sharing knowledge and experiences of insecurity and what it means. As far as impact goes – one woman (a seamstress) whose husband is a soldier told us that before this workshop she refused to stitch clothes for a Tamil woman even though she knew that in the school where her daughter studied there were Tamil teachers. After the workshop, she felt that there was a lot she could do to change attitudes towards Tamils like engaging with other mothers in her child's school, speaking to her clients and people in her street. So this is an example of how with the least amount of effort lots can be changed.

The Centre for Peacebuilding and Reconciliation has a Young Visionary Project that seeks to build the capacity of youth (both girls and boys) to set up peer groups to encourage interracial dialogue, to bring together more young people and to develop their understanding of each other and the issues facing the country. The Young Visionaries run workshops and use drama, sports and art to communicate ideas of peace and nonviolent solutions to conflict.

Organisations like the AWAW have developed train-the-trainer projects to support women's leadership in relief and recovery efforts. The Team 1325 is one such project, in which workshops on UNSCR 1325 are held in villages and form the basis for selecting a group of women to attend a nine-month train-the-trainer program that focuses on women and leadership. The aim of the program is for the group to go back to their villages and promote women's political participation. Building on this first initiative, the AWAW has started another, called Club 1325, targeting female politicians.

> *Here we have women politicians from all levels of government – a cross-party senior women's coalition. We took this group to South Africa and then to the Harvard Law School to learn about negotiation and mediation. The purpose of this group is to try and change the political culture in Sri Lanka. There is a lot of infighting and conflict both within and between parties. Such a culture is detrimental to society, so we thought it's a good idea to get a group of women together to see how they can change it by understanding the responsibility that comes with being in a position of power* (Anonymous).

Relief and recovery efforts also focus on the resettlement and reintegration of IDPs. According to the 2007–08 *Report of the Representative of the Secretary-General on the human rights of internally displaced persons*, the 2004 tsunami and the re-escalation of armed conflict in 2006 resulted in widespread displacement (Human Rights Council 2008). Resettlement and reintegration of IDPs, especially women and girls, are significant, and it has been difficult to access information on what progress has been made. Reports by organisations such as Amnesty International (2009) and Human Rights Watch (2009) suggest that camps are overcrowded and fail to meet international standards, due to poor sanitation, insufficient water, inadequate food and medical care, and high restrictions on mobility. Since the government of Sri Lanka does not permit independent monitoring of the camps, it is difficult to form a picture of what is working and what gap remains (International Crisis Group 2010). As a member of WDP mentioned, this program is concerned about the plight of women '*who have grown up in IDP camps and now are being resettled. We really need to talk with these women and work towards a common platform to promote reconciliation and harmony*'. In addition, a member of CENWOR pointed out that there is a tendency to talk in generalised terms such as 'women's issues' rather than adopt a more nuanced approach that recognises that, while there might be common issues faced by all women, those in IDP camps or in resettled areas have specific concerns.

> *A significant issue facing us is the number of internally displaced people – many of whom are women and girls. Often we say 'what are the main issues for women' – but really we should not treat women as one group. No doubt there are some common concerns but some issues faced by say widows or women soldiers or internally displaced women might be different as well. We have to go beyond a one-size-fits-all work and we really need to look closely at internally displaced people – most often we only think of the Tamils but the Muslims in Sri Lanka and the Sinhalese are also part of this group.*

This reflection highlights the importance of looking beyond the collection of sex-disaggregated data. Organisations working in the area of relief and recovery have to be cognisant that gender analysis involves understanding intersectionality – 'how different sets of identities impact on access to rights and opportunities' (Association of Women in Development 2004, p. 1) – and experiences of oppression and privilege. A fundamental question in undertaking gender analysis should be which men and women, boys and girls are we talking about?

Remaining challenges

The prevailing sense of physical insecurity and the pervading culture of violence in politics have led to a proliferation in small arms. A significant challenge in dealing with this issue is the lack of adequate empirical evidence needed to make decisions about controlling it. Women's organisations are particularly concerned, because this increases the vulnerability of women in the community. In order to develop a comprehensive program to address the issue, women's organisations are willing to be supported to work with the Sri Lankan police force, not just to investigate the extent of the problem, but also to develop community-based initiatives aimed at controlling it.

Also, there is no formal DDR process in Sri Lanka. There is an urgent need to tackle DDR issues because of the ever-present threat of increasing militarisation. The *Global monitoring checklist on women, peace and security* (Onslow 2009) documents the work done by the International Organisation for Migration on reintegrating ex-combatants. Some organisations, like the AWAW, are active in ensuring that female home guards[8] are included in this reintegration program (2009, p. 133). A gender-responsive reconstruction program includes education, training and employment for female ex-combatants to support women's organisations devoted to developing community sensitisation programs that enable the reintegration of these women into civilian life. Additionally, a forum that brings together women's organisations to discuss how they can respond to militarisation supports the spaces for women's discourse to question prevailing militarist tendencies.

Without efforts being made towards reconciliation, DDR programs will have only a limited impact. Many women's organisations feel that reconciliation should be more of a priority, in particular, continued dialogue between Tamil, Muslim and Sinhala communities, in order to build trust and mutual respect. Supporting peace education by integrating it into the school curriculum is a sustainable approach to bring about generational change. Recognising the importance of language, the STRWN believes that there should be greater support for Tamil and Sinhala language classes as part of reconciliation efforts. As a member of this organisation put it, '*language and trust are main issues in Sri Lanka – they are important to address peace. If we don't speak the same language it is difficult for us to understand each other so there is no trust. Language classes are therefore important*'. In addition to supporting women's organisations to hold community dialogues, cultural exchange programs and awareness campaigns on trust and reconciliation, a member of CENWOR suggested the desirability of reaching out to the younger generation through online technologies. These could serve as a platform to bring different groups of young women together to engage in dialogues on peace and reconciliation.

Keeping with this theme of bringing women together, better networking between women's organisations is essential. Women's organisations are working simultaneously, at different levels, across a range of similar issues. Networking could prove highly beneficial in terms of pooling expertise and providing a consolidated platform for women's issues. A member of WIN articulated this as '*NGOs working in an ad hoc manner around the country so much so that it is unclear who is doing what. If we know this we can better collaborate*'. There is a reluctance to fund such efforts, as the immediacy of their impact cannot be easily measured.

This issue of what is and is not funded is a major concern. As in the case of Fiji, relying on project-based funding is a significant obstacle in working for sustainable peace. The lack of core funding means that

> [i]t's hard to deliver services. Plus there are outreach and awareness programs that have to be run. We have built certain credibility with the communities we work with. We have gained their confidence and so we have a responsibility to them. If there is only project-based funding then when the funding runs out what do we do? We can't just close down our services and shelters (Anonymous).

Another critique of donor funding relates to the lack of flexibility. The demand that organisations change their mandates or tweak their projects to fit donor priorities does not give due credit to the work NGOs do, sometimes well before donor funding is made available.

> Donors sometimes want us to modify our mandates to suit their funding priorities – at times this is not difficult to do. So for instance I have been asked if we can talk about peace and security instead of protection and prevention with respect to mental health. But it's a matter of principles. We are the experts in the field providing much needed services in a particular field so why should we modify our mandate to suit what is currently attractive to donors? (Anonymous)

Yet, sometimes donors fail to recognise the dangers involved in raising contentious women's rights issues in Sri Lanka. A member of another women's organisation who also wished to remain anonymous said:

> *I think donors need to understand that when we talk about peace and security for women we are dealing with a very sensitive and delicate issue because of Sri Lanka's record with respect to human rights. Not many women's organisations want to deal with this issue head on because of the risks involved in doing so. We have to be careful in how we approach this issue as you don't want to put anyone in danger.*

A possible approach to addressing these issues is a bottom-up strategy in which the agenda is set by the community and pre-project funding is included to support community-based agenda-setting.

> *Donors have their own priorities and often have already decided (at least broadly) what needs to be done and we are asked to fit into their framework. This is not how it should be. We need a bottom-up approach where the communities develop their own project and we facilitate that development. Donors need to support a project from phase zero – that is, support pre-project preparation where we go to a community and talk with them about the issues they face and how they think these can be addressed. This will be truly empowering* (Anonymous).

Other funding-related issues include difficulties experienced by regional and community-based organisations compared to nationally based organisations. Although not expressively framed as such, there are concerns over changing aid modalities, such as a preference for direct budget support to governments and pooled funding schemes for supporting civil society. Pooled funding often comes with high entry requirements, including a minimum financial size, making it inaccessible to the many women's organisations that have small annual budgets. The lack of support for and capacity to develop grants that meet donor requirements mean that many women's organisations lose out on whatever funding is available.

In Chapter 8, we discussed the need to adopt a programmatic approach in Fiji with balance between responsive, strategic and project-based funding. We also spoke about establishing a women, peace and security fund and initiating a consultative process with women's organisations to identify priority areas and potential collaborations between organisations. These suggestions apply to Sri Lanka as well. Other options include mainstreaming gender in donor budgets by explicitly developing targeted budget lines for gender equality and women's empowerment projects. Working with local and international businesses to establish corporate social responsibility funds that target women's organisations is another possibility that remains to be explored. In order to harmonise aid delivery and increase the pool of resources available to women's organisations, donors should explore the possibility of basket funding. In Kenya, for instance, several donors jointly support either a program or a sector such as the Gender and Governance Programme basket fund, which provides support to strengthen women's representation on boards, networking and leadership (Alami & Goetz 2006). In a bottom-up approach, the agenda is set by the community, as recommended by many women's organisations.

Finally, the donors and multilateral aid agencies must find a collective voice in advocating and pressuring the Sri Lankan government to include women's rights in policies and programs. There are restrictions on the work that women's organisations are allowed to do in conflict-affected regions. For instance, women's organisations can be funded to initiate microcredit projects that support livelihoods, but not those that tackle domestic violence or SGBV. The international community is aware of these restrictions. Women's organisations want a collective voice that pressures the government to open up entry points to tackle women's rights issues in Sri Lanka.

In this chapter, we have explored the implementation of UNSCR 1325 and its related resolutions and have emphasised three central points.

- We have shown how many women are operating in building peaceful security. Some do the work of UNSCR 1325 in a deliberate, knowledgeable fashion. Others do the work inadvertently; it is simply what they have been doing throughout the long years of war. Having been largely excluded from the negotiation table, many are trying to find inroads into more definite positions in a fresh post-conflict stage.
- To support the transition from instability to sustained peace we have suggested innovative flexible funding mechanisms that adopt a programmatic approach and support better alignment with community needs and aspirations.
- We have shown that, despite the enduring distress of suffering that remains, many women's groups continue to work creatively, often in insecure contexts, to help others work through deep psychological pain and in building trust with different ethnic groups, to further reconciliation.

Appendix

United Nations Security Council Resolution 1325 (2000)

Adopted by the Security Council at its 4213th meeting, on 31 October 2000

The Security Council,

Recalling its resolutions 1261 (1999) of 25 August 1999, 1265 (1999) of 17 September 1999, 1296 (2000) of 19 April 2000 and 1314 (2000) of 11 August 2000, as well as relevant statements of its President, and *recalling also* the statement of its President to the press on the occasion of the United Nations Day for Women's Rights and International Peace (International Women's Day) of 8 March 2000 (SC /6816),

Recalling also the commitments of the Beijing Declaration and Platform for Action (A/52/231) as well as those contained in the outcome document of the twenty-third Special Session of the United Nations General Assembly entitled "Women 2000: Gender Equality, Development and Peace for the Twenty-First Century" (A/S-23/10/Rev.1), in particular those concerning women and armed conflict,

Bearing in mind the purposes and principles of the Charter of the United Nations and the primary responsibility of the Security

Council under the Charter for the maintenance of international peace and security,

Expressing concern that civilians, particularly women and children, account for the vast majority of those adversely affected by armed conflict, including as refugees and internally displaced persons, and increasingly are targeted by combatants and armed elements, and *recognizing* the consequent impact this has on durable peace and reconciliation,

Reaffirming the important role of women in the prevention and resolution of conflicts and in peace-building, and *stressing* the importance of their equal participation and full involvement in all efforts for the maintenance and promotion of peace and security, and the need to increase their role in decision-making with regard to conflict prevention and resolution,

Reaffirming also the need to implement fully international humanitarian and human rights law that protects the rights of women and girls during and after conflicts,

Emphasizing the need for all parties to ensure that mine clearance and mine awareness programmes take into account the special needs of women and girls,

Recognizing the urgent need to mainstream a gender perspective into peacekeeping operations, and in this regard *noting* the Windhoek Declaration and the Namibia Plan of Action on Mainstreaming a Gender Perspective in Multidimensional Peace Support Operations (S/2000/693),

Recognizing also the importance of the recommendation contained in the statement of its President to the press of 8 March 2000 for specialized training for all peacekeeping personnel on the protection, special needs and human rights of women and children in conflict situations,

Recognizing that an understanding of the impact of armed conflict on women and girls, effective institutional arrangements to guarantee their protection and full participation in the peace process can significantly contribute to the maintenance and promotion of international peace and security,

Noting the need to consolidate data on the impact of armed conflict on women and girls,

1. *Urges* Member States to ensure increased representation of women at all decision-making levels in national, regional and international institutions and mechanisms for the prevention, management, and resolution of conflict;
2. *Encourages* the Secretary-General to implement his strategic plan of action (A/49/587) calling for an increase in the participation of women at decision-making levels in conflict resolution and peace processes;
3. *Urges* the Secretary-General to appoint more women as special representatives and envoys to pursue good offices on his behalf, and in this regard calls on Member States to provide candidates to the Secretary-General, for inclusion in a regularly updated centralized roster;
4. *Further urges* the Secretary-General to seek to expand the role and contribution of women in United Nations field-based operations, and especially among military observers, civilian police, human rights and humanitarian personnel;
5. *Expresses* its willingness to incorporate a gender perspective into peacekeeping operations, and *urges* the Secretary-General to ensure that, where appropriate, field operations include a gender component;
6. *Requests* the Secretary-General to provide to Member States training guidelines and materials on the protection, rights and the particular needs of women, as well as on the importance of involving women in all peacekeeping and peacebuilding measures, invites Member States to incorporate these elements as well as HIV/AIDS awareness training into their national

training programmes for military and civilian police personnel in preparation for deployment, and *further requests* the Secretary-General to ensure that civilian personnel of peacekeeping operations receive similar training;

7. *Urges* Member States to increase their voluntary financial, technical and logistical support for gender-sensitive training efforts, including those undertaken by relevant funds and programmes, inter alia, the United Nations Fund for Women and United Nations Children's Fund, and by the Office of the United Nations High Commissioner for Refugees and other relevant bodies;

8. *Calls on* all actors involved, when negotiating and implementing peace agreements, to adopt a gender perspective, including, inter alia:

    (a) The special needs of women and girls during repatriation and resettlement and for rehabilitation, reintegration and post-conflict reconstruction;

    (b) Measures that support local women's peace initiatives and indigenous processes for conflict resolution, and that involve women in all of the implementation mechanisms of the peace agreements;

    (c) Measures that ensure the protection of and respect for human rights of women and girls, particularly as they relate to the constitution, the electoral system, the police and the judiciary;

9. *Calls upon* all parties to armed conflict to respectfully international law applicable to the rights and protection of women and girls, especially as civilians, in particular the obligations applicable to them under the Geneva Conventions of 1949 and the Additional Protocols thereto of 1977, the Refugee Convention of 1951 and the Protocol thereto of 1967, the Convention on the Elimination of All Forms of Discrimination against

Women of 1979 and the Optional Protocol thereto of 1999 and the United Nations Convention on the Rights of the Child of 1989 and the two Optional Protocols thereto of 25 May 2000, and to bear in mind the relevant provisions of the Rome Statute of the International Criminal Court;

10. *Calls on* all parties to armed conflict to take special measures to protect women and girls from gender-based violence, particularly rape and other forms of sexual abuse, and all other forms of violence in situations of armed conflict;

11. *Emphasizes* the responsibility of all States to put an end to impunity and to prosecute those responsible for genocide, crimes against humanity, and war crimes including those relating to sexual and other violence against women and girls, and in this regard stresses the need to exclude these crimes, where feasible, from amnesty provisions;

12. *Calls upon* all parties to armed conflict to respect the civilian and humanitarian character of refugee camps and settlements, and to take into account the particular needs of women and girls, including in their design, and recalls its resolutions 1208 (1998) of 19 November 1998 and 1296 (2000) of 19 April 2000;

13. *Encourages* all those involved in the planning for disarmament, demobilization and reintegration to consider the different needs of female and male ex-combatants and to take into account the needs of their dependants;

14. *Reaffirms* its readiness, whenever measures are adopted under Article 41 of the Charter of the United Nations, to give consideration to their potential impact on the civilian population, bearing in mind the special needs of women and girls, in order to consider appropriate humanitarian exemptions;

15. *Expresses* its willingness to ensure that Security Council missions take into account gender considerations and the rights of

women, including through consultation with local and international women's groups;

16. *Invites* the Secretary-General to carry out a study on the impact of armed conflict on women and girls, the role of women in peace-building and the gender dimensions of peace processes and conflict resolution, and *further invites* him to submit a report to the Security Council on the results of this study and to make this available to all Member States of the United Nations;

17. *Requests* the Secretary-General, where appropriate, to include in his reporting to the Security Council progress on gender mainstreaming throughout peacekeeping missions and all other aspects relating to women and girls;

18. *Decides* to remain actively seized of the matter.

[UNSCR 1325 taken from UN website: http://www.un.org/events/res_1325e.pdf]

Acknowledgements

This book stems from a project funded in 2009–10 by the Commonwealth of Australia, Australian Agency for International Development (AusAID), Gender Policy and Coordination Section. We are very grateful to AusAID for this funding and for the enthusiasm and moral and practical support we received from Barbara O'Dwyer, then Gender Adviser, and Sarah Boyd, then policy officer, in the Gender Policy and Coordination Unit. In particular, we are grateful to all the women and men in Timor-Leste, Fiji and Sri Lanka who gave to us their time, views and reflections in such a generous fashion. We learned so much from them. Their insights have helped to shape many of the ideas in the book. Dr Danielle Every was part of the initial research project but was unable to work on the book. We sincerely appreciate her foundational work with us on the early stages of the research. Our thanks go to the staff of the Gender Consortium, Flinders University, particularly Genevieve Chaffey, who typed the transcripts of the interviews with efficiency and clarity, and Cara Ellickson for her encouragement and support. We thank Dr Ravi Raghupathi for his review of our early draft. We are very appreciative to Dr Norman Porter for his careful reading and suggestions for the (almost) final draft. Penny Mansley has done a sterling job in helping to make the book read clearly. We thank also all those we have worked with at UQP, particularly Kirsty Burow for her careful checking of the proofs. Co-authoring a book is not an easy task; yet, we have done so with serious intent and with humour, in friendship and mutual respect.

Endnotes

Introduction

1. A significant difference between this important edited collection and our book is the focus in the former on conflicts in which peace support operations have or have not been deployed, and their case studies include Kosovo, Liberia, Nepal, Nigeria, Rwanda, Sierra Leone, Sudan and Timor-Leste as well as regional case studies on the African Union, Economic Community of West African States, Southern African Development Community and the European Union. While there is some overlap in their content and our objectives, our focus is on providing theoretical analysis of the pillars used to measure the Secretary-General's indicators (UNSC 2010a) with case studies on Timor-Leste, Fiji and Sri Lanka.
2. This project was funded for one year in 2009–10 by AusAID's Gender Policy & Coordination Section. The book has been written collaboratively. Danielle Every conducted background research for the chapters on peacekeeping and participation but was unable to work on the book.
3. This research was approved by both the University of South Australia Human Research Ethics Committee and the Flinders University Social and Behavioural Research Ethics Committee. Porter and Mundkur conducted the fieldwork interviews in Timor-Leste and Fiji, and, while Mundkur hoped to conduct interviews in Sri Lanka, political unrest meant that people felt unsafe to come to Colombo, so she interviewed Sri Lankans on phone and via Skype from India.
4. We have not included discussion on UNSCR 1960, which was adopted in December 2010, because we had completed the bulk of the writing. This resolution reaffirms the other resolutions and especially calls for regular reporting on sexual violence in armed conflict in the hope of an end to impunity of perpetrators.

5. We conducted in-depth interviews with 13 people in Timor-Leste, with fifteen in Fiji and with six Sri Lankans. We took the advice of our funders as the starting point for who to interview. While the number of people interviewed does not reflect a large base, we make no claims to this being a definitive empirical study; rather, the materials gained from the interviews are used to inform our readings and analysis. Consent was given to us by the majority of interviewees to publish their names, but we have elected to identify them in their role and organisation rather than with their names, to protect them in the work they do.

Chapter 1

1. The dataset for the selection of armed conflicts referred to by Bastick, Grimm and Kunz (2007) was developed by the Uppsala Conflict Data Program and the Centre for the Study of Civil War at the Peace Research Institute Oslo. Places like the Central African Republic, East Timor, Haiti, Indonesia, Papua New Guinea, the Solomon Islands and Zimbabwe had conflicts that do not meet the exact criteria above, but there is significant evidence of conflict-related sexual violence in each of these countries.
2. The September 11, 2001, attacks on the United States killed 3,025 people and prompted the war on terror, but this conflict differs from the armed conflicts discussed here.
3. The index has 23 indicators that measure ongoing domestic and international conflict, measures of safety, militarisation and security, and a secondary dataset of 33 drivers that include women in Parliament, gender inequality and gender ratio of population, women to men.
4. Despite this ranking, there have been conflicts in Aceh, Ambon, Jayapura, Timor-Leste and West Papua.
5. References to UNIFEM concern work done prior to the 2011 UN Women, when UNIFEM became part of this new entity.
6. We acknowledge a rich diversity within a multitude of feminisms that cover differing theoretical, political and practical stances, but do not differentiate between feminisms unless it is immediately pertinent. We assume no homogeneity among women but clarify when we are referring to specific differences among women.
7. For example, in Pakistan, in the national language, Urdu, *khud-mukhtar* (being autonomous) and *ba-ikhtiar* (having authority/power) are not common terms. In Indonesia, the word has been translated as *pemberdayaan* (a state of being energised) or *penguatan* (a state of being strengthened). In

avoiding the word 'power' (*kuasa*) to avoid threatening those in power, 'the very concept of "empowerment" has been disempowered from the outset' (Wee & Shaheed 2008, p. 39).

Chapter 2

1. The Beijing conference gathered the largest number of NGOs at any UN conference at that time and is regarded as a crucial precursor to UNSCR 1325.
2. While this is often referred to as the resolution on 'sexual violence in conflict', it, along with UNSCRs 1888 and 1889, is on 'women and peace and security'.
3. The Project monitored mandate renewals, sanctions and general country situations for 20 states, a total of 432 resolutions from November 2000 to August 2010 (Butler, Mader & Kean 2010, p. 7).
4. Italics are in the original and refer to the 'six Cs' of UNSCR 1820.
5. It is inevitable that by the time this book is published more NAPs will have been released. There is some discrepancy in dates NAPs are adopted, released and launched, so the dates used are derived from the PeaceWomen website, specifically <www.peacewomen.org/pages/about-1325/national-action-plans-naps>.
6. In order of release, this includes Denmark in 2005; in 2006 the United Kingdom, Norway and Sweden; in 2007 the Netherlands, Côte d'Ivoire, Switzerland, Austria and Spain; in 2008 Iceland, Finland and Uganda; in 2009 Liberia, Belgium, Chile and Portugal; in 2010 Bosnia and Herzegovina, the Philippines, Sierra Leone, Rwanda, DRC, Canada, Estonia and France; and in 2011 Nepal.
7. UNIFEM has been the lead agency on UNSCR 1325 yet was the UN's smallest entity. It is now part of UN Women.
8. This is in contrast to Chapter VII, whose resolutions are binding on Member States and usually invoked when there is a threat to international peace and security.
9. This is a network of individuals and thirteen organisations based in the United Kingdom who work to promote UNSCR 1325.
10. The initiative was organised by UNDPKO, the UN Department of Political Affairs, UNIFEM and the UNDP. Participating localities were Afghanistan, Bosnia and Herzegovina, Burundi, Côte d'Ivoire, Croatia, DRC, Guinea-Bissau, Haiti, Iraq, Kenya, Kosovo, Lebanon, Liberia, Nepal, the Occupied Palestinian Territories, Pakistan, Senegal/West Africa, Serbia, Sierra Leone,

Somalia, Sri Lanka, Sudan, Tajikistan/Asia and Timor-Leste. Sri Lanka and Western Sahara held different versions of the open days.
11. In 2010, the Minister for Foreign Affairs in Australia, the Hon. Kevin Rudd, announced that Australia will provide AU$14.4 million to UN Women over two years from 2011 to support international efforts to promote equality and empower women.
12. Many references throughout this book refer to work done by these agencies prior to the establishment of this Entity.
13. This was in Aceh, Colombia, Liberia, the Middle East, Sri Lanka and Uganda. Additional contributors to this report included Cerue Garlo, Shyamala Gomaz, Suraiya Kamaruzzaman, Turid Smith Polfus, Elena Roy and Lina Zedriga.

Chapter 3

1. The 1998 Commission on the Status of Women focused on gender-sensitive justice, the specific needs of women affected by armed conflict, increasing women's participation in all stages of peace processes, and reconstruction and disarmament.
2. The ICISS was established by the government of Canada in September 2000 to respond to the UN Secretary-General Kofi Annan's challenge to arrive at a consensus around the basic questions of principle and process involved in humanitarian interventions.
3. Dragoljub Kunarac, a Commander of a special reconnaissance unit in the Bosnian Serb army, was accused of participating in a campaign to rid the Foča area of its non-Serb inhabitants. The Muslim civilian population was targeted, and many women were subjected to sexual violence. On 22 February 2001, Kunarac was sentenced to 28 years' imprisonment for torture, rape and enslavement as crimes against humanity, and for torture and rape as violations of the laws or customs of war. (See *Kunarac, Dragoljub* n.d.)
4. The Special Measures for Protection from Sexual Exploitation and Abuse adopt a zero tolerance policy on SGBV applicable to all peacekeeping personnel and call for compulsory training on sexual exploitation and abuse for all operation personnel.
5. This is a phrase used by Indonesian NGOs working with women and disability issues. It points to the fact that only a few elite women are given opportunities to participate in decision-making and are expected to speak on behalf of all women, especially women with disabilities.

Chapter 4

1. Many of the examples used in this chapter come from research conducted by Danielle Every, who participated early in the project.
2. We acknowledge aggressive dominant masculinity that characterises most militaries. However, in this book we do not enter into debates about women joining the armed forces. We focus our attention on what can be done to make peacekeeping forces responsive to the gendered impacts of conflicts so that they can take action in an appropriate manner.
3. This report was written by Letitia Anderson, and the publication was made possible through funding provided by AusAID.
4. UNSCR 1820 makes explicit the links between justice, SSR and gender.
5. Often, the term 'sexual exploitation and abuse' is used in relation to peace-keeping, particularly in instances of misconduct, but sexual exploitation and abuse is a form of SGBV, so the latter is used for consistency.
6. This was renamed as the UN Organization Stabilization Mission in the DRC, 28 May 2010.
7. An FPU is a team of 140 police officers deployed as a group, which undertakes crowd control, protects UN staff and material, and escorts UN personnel when they must visit insecure regions of a mission area.
8. This summary derives from Porter's notes taken during the address made by Sahi entitled 'Strategic policing: women as peacekeepers' (at Women PeaceMakers 2010; see also Simoni 2010).
9. This summary derives from Porter's notes taken during the address made by Tiwari entitled 'Women and peacekeeping: lessons learned and next steps' (at Women PeaceMakers 2010; see also Simoni 2010).
10. In the long-term, competence in these areas rests on their inclusion in school curricula.
11. NGOs play an important role in mainstreaming gender into peacekeeping operations. For example, Women in International Security is a global network that seeks to advance women's leadership in the international peace and security field. It was established in 1987 by female experts in foreign affairs and defence and is a part of the Centre for Peace and Security Studies at Georgetown University, Washington DC.
12. AusAID has formed a civilian corps to respond to emergencies.

Chapter 5

1. Darby and Mac Ginty (2008, p. 3) analyse the criteria required for a successful peace accord: negotiate in good faith, include key actors, address the central issues in dispute, do not use force, and commit to a sustained process.

2. These authors base their analysis on data from the Uppsala Conflict Data Program of 2008 on peace agreements.
3. This research was limited to a representative sample of 24 peace processes, for which some data were available.
4. Chinkin (2003b, p. 9) notes 'the tension between gender mainstreaming and women-specific provisions' in the content and implementation of peace agreements.
5. Porter has made some of these arguments previously in conference presentations. Small sections here are modified from Porter 2010a and another small section from Porter 2010b.
6. The Indonesian government did not include any women in its negotiating team.
7. Writing the constitution was at the core of the peace process, and women argued for being put on voters' lists by the democratic parties or for the option to create separate women's lists.
8. These principles closely align with the three central rationales presented in this chapter for why women should be included in peace processes.
9. Out of the total 601 seats, 240 members were to be elected through the 'first past the post' system from single-member constituencies. (The winning candidate in this system is the one who gains more votes than any other candidate, even if this is not an absolute majority of valid votes. Candidates rather than political parties are voted for.) A further 335 members were to be elected through the proportional representation system (in which each political party presents a list of candidates for a multi-member electoral district; parties are voted for and receive seats in proportion to their overall share of the vote); and the remaining 26 members were to be nominated by the Interim Council of Ministers.
10. 'The women's councils are grass-roots structures elected at the cell level (the smallest administrative unit) by women only, and then through indirect election at each successive administrative levels (sector, district, province). They operate in parallel to general local councils and represent women's concerns. The ten-member councils are involved in skills training at the local level and in awareness-raising about women's rights. The head of the women's council holds a reserved seat on the general local council, ensuring official representation of women's concerns and providing links between the two systems' (Powley 2005, p. 156).
11. These statistics were valid on 31 July 2010. In Tonga, while no women were elected in 2008, one woman was appointed to the Cabinet and thus she was one of thirty-two Members sitting in Parliament.

Chapter 6

1. At the time of writing their chapter, Goetz was UNIFEM's thematic adviser on governance, peace and security, while Sandler was the Deputy Director of UNIFEM.
2. Juliet Hunt prepared these for the Geneva Centre for the Democratic Control of Armed Forces, UN-INSTRAW, Organisation for Security and Cooperation in Europe & Office for Democratic Institutions and Human Rights workshop, Geneva, 2007.
3. Case studies were written by Kathryn Lockett, Annie Matunda Mbambi, Marie-Claire Farray, Lesley Abdela, Kate McCullough, Irene Miskimmon and Tim Symonds.
4. In particular, this includes the UN NGO Working Group on Women and Peace and Security and also the Civil Society Advisory Group co-chaired by Mary Robinson and Bineta Diop. There was a technical working group on global indicators for UNSCR 1325.
5. The Consortium has eight key partners: Centre for Environment, Gender and Development, Hong Kong; Department of Community Health Sciences, Aga Khan University, Pakistan; International Gender Studies Centre, Oxford; Semarak Cerlang Nusa, Indonesia; Shirkat Gah Women's Resource Centre, Pakistan; Solidaritas Perempuan, Indonesia; Southeast Asia Research Centre, City University, Hong Kong; and Women Living Under Muslim Laws, Senegal, Pakistan and London.

Chapter 7

1. 'East Timor' refers to pre-independence times and 'Timor-Leste' to post-independence. Not all literature makes this distinction.
2. This was not recognised by the UN, which, from 1960, listed East Timor as a non-self-governing territory.
3. Mandates that have included women, peace and security include Afghanistan (2002), Burundi (2004 and 2006), Chad (2010), Côte d'Ivoire (2003 and 2004), Darfur (2007), the DRC (2010), Guinea-Bissau (2009), Haiti (2004), Liberia (2003), Sierra Leone (2006 and 2009) and Sudan (2005 and 2007) (UNSC 2010b, p. 16).
4. It is ongoing as we write.
5. This was derived from 2003 statistics from the UNDP Human Development Report (Wandita, Campbell-Nelson & Leong Pereira 2006).
6. The placement of Gender Advisers in Sierra Leone, Kosovo and East Timor was an important advance in peacekeeping missions, paving the way for the expectation of gender mainstreaming in subsequent missions.

7. Many of these achievements were listed in personal correspondence by a member of UNMIT, 21 August 2009.
8. This Charter has ten articles relating to equality and rights to security of the person, politics, health, education, social rights, labour, tradition and women's rights, freedom from exploitation and children's rights.
9. The *NGOs alternative report (*NGOs Working Group 2009, p. 6) is a result of 87 NGO representatives' work in different areas and 'presents the real life of women in Timor-Leste during the period of ratification of the CEDAW (2003–2008)'. Examples of discrimination include placing women as fourth on candidates lists; failing to recognise widows who helped during the struggle for independence; no exception for abortion for victims of rape and incest; pregnant students forced to drop out of school; victims remaining silent in judicial processes when intimidated by perpetrators; and gender focal points having insufficient power to be effective.
10. These include Convention on the Elimination of All Forms of Racial Discrimination (1965), International Covenant on Civil and Political Rights (1966), International Covenant on Economic, Social and Cultural Rights (1966), Convention against Torture and Other Cruel, Inhuman or Degrading Treatment or Punishment (1984) and Convention on the Rights of the Child (1989).
11. A policy officer from AusAID present at the conference remarked, '*It was interesting to note the limited awareness of 1325 (and even more so with 1820)*' (personal correspondence, 17 August 2009).
12. FOKUPERS plays a strong counselling role to female political prisoners, wives of political prisoners, war widows and survivors of violence.
13. These views are personal observations and do not reflect the views of the UN (personal communication, 29 April 2010).
14. According to UNIFEM (2008a, p. 83), statistics for 2006 show that only in Australia and South Africa did women make up 29 per cent of the police force; they formed under 20 per cent in all the other Member State police forces.
15. This includes AusAID funding of AU$10 million over five years, 2009–13.
16. This was previously the Office for the Promotion of Equality (OPE). Its predecessor was the Gender Affairs Unit of UNTAET. OPE became SEPI after the 2007 elections.
17. Grenfell et al. (2009, p. 25) explain how there are not straightforward English translations for the terms *suco* and *aldeia*. The former can incorporate 'groups of families, clans, and a number of small villages', while the latter typically 'is territorially confined to a single area' and so 'is geographically smaller'.

18. The UNSC report (UNSC 2010b, p. 18) states 11 female *suco* chiefs.
19. Redefeto is an umbrella organisation for eighteen women's groups. It was established in 2000 during the first National Women's Congress. It seeks to empower women and push for gender equality.
20. Literacy rates recorded by the Human Development Report 1995–2005 indicate 52 per cent literacy for women and 65 per cent for men (AusAID 2008b, p. 82). Other reports indicate that 'almost two-thirds of adult women are illiterate' (NGO Working Group 2009, p. 11).
21. This recommendation is adapted from the recommendations made at the Second International Women for Peace Conference, Dili, 5–6 March 2009.
22. PRADET has been asked to establish services in the five peripheral hospitals. '*Our medical/forensic protocol has been approved by Dr Ana Pesoa, Prosecutor General . . . so we are now training our staff to train the rest of the country . . . [S]till lots more to be done however*' (personal correspondence, 28 April 2010).
23. In this report, the authors document the organisational gender profiles of 27 organisations in Timor.
24. This final paragraph has been adapted from Porter (2011).

Chapter 8
1. The GDI measures achievement in the same basic capabilities as the Human Development Index but takes note of inequality in achievement between women and men. Both are developed by the UNDP.
2. The Women's Parliamentary Caucus in Timor-Leste serves as a model.
3. This participant asked to be identified in this way.
4. The Universal Periodic Report Review reviews human rights records of all 192 UN Member States every four years.
5. Supported by NZAid, four schools participated in the pilot: DAV College, Dudley Intermediate, John Wesley Primary and Nasinu Secondary.

Chapter 9
1. The Forum was set up in August 2005 to facilitate greater coordination, understanding and sharing of information and resources, and to strengthen multi-sectoral responses to sexual violence (Women and Media Collective n.d.).
2. According to the new amendment, when a woman under the age of 16 is raped, proof of consent is not necessary; proof of the act of intercourse is sufficient (CENWOR 2001).

3. There are three levels of government in Sri Lanka: national, provincial and local government bodies.
4. WDP is a project based in Sri Lanka that focuses on preventing and responding to SGBV and increasing women's voices and influence in peacebuilding processes. It is supported financially by the Canadian International Development Agency and implemented by a consortium consisting of Cowater International, Match International and the World University Service of Canada.
5. In Sri Lanka, Presidential elections are based on a preferential voting system in which voters rank candidates in order of preference. In addition, 225 Members of Parliament are elected by an open list proportional representation system.
6. The party is also credited with establishing the Women's Bureau and the Ministry of Women's Affairs, and with developing a women's charter that it sought to legalise through a women's rights bill, but it lost the elections in 2010.
7. These could be along the lines of EMILY's List or the Wish List.
8. In 1986, the Home Guard Service was created by the Minister of National Security under the command of local Sri Lankan police units, and two years later women joined the service. In 2006, the Home Guard was renamed the Civil Security Force.

Bibliography

Academic books, chapters and journal articles

Aguirre, D & Pietropaoli, I 2008, 'Gender equality, development and transitional justice: the case of Nepal', *International Journal of Transitional Justice*, 2, pp. 356–77.

Alexander, R 2006, 'Political violence in the South Pacific: women after the coups in Fiji', *Journal of International Cooperation Studies*, 141, pp. 1–31.

Alton, J 2002, 'We've come a long way: engendering peacebuilding and the new diplomacy', *Canadian Woman Studies*, 22:2, pp. 72–7.

Anderlini, SN 2005, 'Women and peace through justice', *Development*, 48:3, pp. 103–10.

—— 2007, *Women building peace: what they do, why it matters*, Lynne Rienner, Boulder, CO.

Anderson, L 2010, 'Politics by other means: when does sexual violence threaten international peace and security?', *International Peacekeeping*, 17:2, pp. 244–60.

Ayata, AG & Tütüncü, F 2008, 'Critical acts without a critical mass: the substantive representation of women in the Turkish Parliament', *Parliamentary Affairs*, 61:3, pp. 461–75.

Babcock, L & Lashever, S 2007, *Women don't ask: the high cost of avoiding negotiation and positive strategies for change*, Bantam Books, New York.

Bagshaw, D & Porter, E (eds) 2009, *Mediation in the Asia-Pacific region: transforming conflicts and building peace*, Routledge, London.

Barbara, JS 2004, 'Medicine and peace: the Butterfly Peace Garden', *Croatian Medical Journal*, 45:2, pp. 232–3.

Barnes, K & Olonisakin, 'F 2011, 'Introduction', in 'F Olonisakin, K Barnes & E Ikpe (eds), *Women, peace and security: translating policy into practice*, Routledge, London, pp. 3–14.

Barrow, A 2009, '"[It's] like a rubber band": assessing UNSCR 1325 as agenda mainstreaming process', *International Journal of Law in Context*, 5:1, pp. 51–68.

Bedont, B & Hall-Martinez, K 1999, 'Ending impunity for gender crimes under the International Criminal Court', *Brown Journal of World Affairs*, 6, pp. 65–85.

Bell, C & O'Rourke, C 2007, 'Does feminism need a theory of transitional justice? An introductory essay', *International Journal of Transitional Justice*, 1, pp. 23–44.

—— & —— 2010, 'Peace agreements or pieces of paper? The impact of UNSC Resolution 1325 on peace processes and their agreements', *International and Comparative Law Quarterly*, 59, pp. 941–80.

Bellamy, AJ 2009, *Responsibility to protect*, Polity Press, Cambridge, UK.
Bellamy, AJ & Williams, PD with Griffin, S 2010, *Understanding peacekeeping*, Polity Press, Cambridge, UK.
Bere, MA 2005, 'Women and justice in Timor-Leste', *Development Bulletin*, 68, pp. 55–7.
Bhagwan-Rolls, S 2000, 'Gender and the role of the media in conflict and peacemaking: the Fiji experience', *Development Bulletin*, 53, pp. 65–9.
—— 2001, 'fem'TALK: young women's perspectives from the Fiji islands', *Development Bulletin*, 56, pp. 46–8.
Booth, C & Bennet, C 2002, 'Gender mainstreaming in the European Union: towards a new conception and practice of equal opportunities?', *European Journal of Women's Studies*, 9:4, pp. 430–46.
Brown, M 2009, 'Security, development and the nation-building agenda – East Timor', *Conflict, Security and Development*, 92, pp. 141–64.
Bunch, C 2004, 'A feminist human rights lens', *Peace Review*, 16:1, pp. 29–34.
Cahn, N, Haynes, D & Ní Aoláin, F 2010, 'Returning home: women in post-conflict societies', *University of Baltimore Law Review*, 393, pp. 339–69.
Caprioli, M 2004, 'Democracy and human rights versus women's security: a contradiction?', *Security Dialogue*, 354, pp. 411–28.
Caprioli, M, Nielsen, R & Hudson, VM 2010, 'Women and post-conflict settings', in J Hewitt, J Wilkenfeld & TR Gurr (eds), *Peace and conflict 2010*, Centre for International Development and Conflict Management, University of Maryland, Boulder, CO, pp. 91–102.
Carroll, S (ed.) 2001, *The impact of women in public office*, Indiana University Press, Bloomington, IN.
Celis, K 2008, 'Studying women's substantive representation in legislatures: when representative acts, contexts and women's interests become important', *Representation*, 44:2, pp. 111–23.
Charlesworth, H 1994, 'Transforming the united men's club: feminist futures for the United Nations', *Transnational Law and Contemporary Problems*, 4, pp. 421–54.
Charlesworth, H & Wood, M 2002, 'Women and human rights in the rebuilding of East Timor', *Nordic Journal of International Law*, 71, pp. 325–48.
Chinkin, C 2003a, 'Gender, human rights and peace agreements', *Ohio State Journal of Dispute Resolution*, 18:3, pp. 867–86.
Cockburn, C 2004, 'The continuum of violence: a gender perspective on war and peace', in J Hyndman & W Giles (eds), *Sites of violence, gender and conflict zones*, University of California Press, Los Angeles, CA, pp. 24–44.
Cohn, C, Kinsella, H & Gibbings, S 2004, 'Women, peace and security', *International Feminist Journal of Politics*, 61, pp. 130–40.
Copelon, R 2000, 'Gender crimes as war crimes: integrating crimes against women into international criminal law', *McGill Law Journal*, 46, pp. 217–40.
Corcoran-Nantes, Y 2009, 'The politics of culture and the culture of politics – a case study of gender and politics in Lospalos, Timor-Leste', *Conflict, Security and Development*, 92, pp. 165–87.
Crenshaw, K 2003, 'Mapping the margins: intersectionality, identity politics, and violence against women of colour', in L Alcoff & E Mendieta (eds), *Identities: race, class, gender, and nationality*, Blackwell Publishing, New York, pp. 175–200.

Darby, J & Mac Ginty, R (eds) 2008, *Contemporary peacemaking: conflict, peace processes and post-war reconstruction*, Palgrave Macmillan, Basingstoke.

Devlin, C & Elgie, R 2008, 'The effect of increased women's representation in Parliament: the case of Rwanda', *Parliamentary Affairs*, 61:2, pp. 237–54.

Diaz, MM 2005, *Representing women? Female legislators in west European Parliaments*, ECPR Press, Oxford.

Dijkstra, AG 2002, 'Revising the UNDP's GDI and GEM: towards an alternative', *Social Indicators Research*, 57:3, pp. 301–38.

Donais, T 2009, 'Empowerment or imposition? Dilemmas of local ownership in post-conflict peacebuilding processes', *Peace and Change*, 341, pp. 3–26.

Durham, H & O'Byrne, K 2010, 'The dialogue of difference: gender perspectives on international humanitarian law', *International Review of the Red Cross*, 92:877, pp. 31–52.

Emmanuel, S 2008, *Strategic mapping of women's peace activism in Sri Lanka*, Women and Media Collective, Colombo.

Enloe, C 1993, *The morning after: sexual politics at the end of the Cold War*, University of California Press, Berkeley, CA.

Evans, G 2008, *The responsibility to protect: ending mass atrocity crimes once and for all*, Brookings Institution Press, Washington DC.

Eyben, R & Napier-Moore, R 2009, 'Choosing words with care? Shifting meanings of women's empowerment in international development', *Third World Quarterly*, 302, pp. 285–300.

Fairlie, MA 2003, 'Affirming Brahimi: East Timor makes the case for a model criminal code', *American University International Law Review*, 18:5, pp. 1059–102.

Franceschet, S & Piscopo, J 2008, 'Gender quotas and women's substantive representation: lessons from Argentina', *Politics and Gender*, 4:3, pp. 393–425.

Freeman, M 2006, *Truth commissions and procedural fairness*, Cambridge University Press, Cambridge, UK.

Galtung, J 1964, 'An editorial', *Journal of Peace Research*, 11, pp. 1–4.

Gardam, J 1997, 'Women and the law of armed conflict: why the silence?', *International and Comparative Law Quarterly*, 46:1, pp. 55–80.

Gardam, J & Charlesworth, H 2000, 'Protection of women in armed conflict', *Human Rights Quarterly*, 22:1, pp. 148–66.

Gizelis, T 2009, 'Gender empowerment and United Nations peacebuilding', *Journal of Peace Research*, 46:4, pp. 505–23.

Goetz, A-M 1998, 'Women in politics & gender equity in policy: South Africa & Uganda', *Review of African Political Economy*, 25:76, pp. 241–62.

Goetz, A-M & Sandler, J 2007, 'Swapping gender: from cross-cutting obscurity to the sectoral security?', in A Cornwall, E Harrison & A Whitehead (eds), *Feminisms in development: contradictions, contestations and challenges*, Zed Books, London, pp. 161–73.

Goldsmith, A & Harris, V 2009, 'Out of step: multilateral police missions, culture and nation-building in Timor-Leste', *Conflict, Security and Development*, 92, pp. 189–211.

Gould, C 1996, 'Diversity and democracy: representing differences', in S Benhabib (ed.), *Democracy and difference: contesting the boundaries of the political*, Princeton University Press, Princeton, NJ, pp. 171–86.

Greenberg, ME & Okani, R-C 2001, *Strengthening women's participation in decision-making at the local level in Mali*, WidTech, Washington DC.

Greenberg, ME & Zuckerman, E 2009, 'The gender dimensions of post-conflict reconstruction: the challenges in development aid', in T Addison & T Brück (eds), *Making peace work: the challenges of social and economic reconstruction*, Palgrave MacMillan & UNU-WIDER, Helsinki, pp. 2–33.

Grenfell, D & Trembath, A 2007, *Challenges and possibilities: international organisations and women in Timor-Leste*, Globalism Research Centre, RMIT University, Melbourne.

Grenfell, D, Walsh, M, Trembath, A, Moniz Noronha, C & Holthouse, K 2009, *Understanding community: security and sustainability in four aldeia in Timor-Leste*, Globalism Research Centre, RMIT University, Melbourne.

Grenfell, L 2009, 'Promoting the rule of law in Timor-Leste', *Conflict, Security and Development*, 9:2, pp. 213–38.

Grey, S 2002, 'Does size matter? Critical mass and New Zealand's women MPs', *Parliamentary Affairs*, 55:1, pp. 19–29.

Harris Rimmer, S 2010, *Gender and transitional justice: the women of East Timor*, Routledge, London & New York.

Hewitt, JJ, Wilkenfeld, J & Gurr, TR 2010, *Peace and conflict 2010: executive summary*, Centre for International Development and Conflict Management, University of Maryland, Boulder, CO.

Higate, P 2003, '"Soft clerks" and "hard civvies": pluralizing military masculinities', in P Higate (ed.), *Military masculinities, identity and the state*, Praeger, Westport, CT, pp. 27–43.

Higate, P & Henry, M 2004, 'Engendering insecurity in peace support operations', *Security Dialogue*, 354, pp. 481–98.

Hogg, N 2010, 'Women's participation in the Rwandan genocide: mothers or monsters?', *International Review of the Red Cross*, 92:877, pp. 69–102.

Hudson, H 2005a, '"Doing" security as though humans matter: a feminist perspective on gender and the politics of human security', *Security Dialogue*, 362, pp. 155–74.

—— 2005b, 'Peacekeeping trends and their gender implications for regional peacekeeping forces in Africa: progress and challenges', in D Mazurana, A Raven-Roberts & J Parpart (eds), *Gender, conflict, and peacekeeping*, Rowman & Littlefield, Lanham, MD, pp. 111–33.

Hunt, S & Posa, C 2001, 'Women waging peace: inclusive security', *Foreign Policy*, 124, pp. 38–47.

Institute for Economics and Peace 2009, *Global peace index: 2009 methodology, results and findings*, Institute for Economics and Peace, Sydney.

—— 2010, *Global peace index: 2010 methodology, results and findings*, Institute for Economics & Peace, Sydney.

Jahan, R 1995, *The elusive agenda: mainstreaming women in development*, Zed Books, London.

Kaldor, M 2007, *Human security: reflections on globalization and intervention*, Polity Press, Cambridge, UK.

Kegley, C & Blanton, SL 2010, *World politics: trend and transformation*, 12th edn, Wadsworth, Boston, MA.

Kilmurray, A & McWilliams, M 2011, 'Struggling for peace: how women in Northern Ireland challenged the status quo', *Solutions Journal*, 2:2, pp. 2–14.
Kittilson, M 2005, 'In support of gender quotas: setting new standards, bringing visible gains', *Politics and Gender*, 1:4, pp. 638–45.
Landgren, K 1995, 'Safety zones and international protection: a dark grey area', *International Journal of Refugee Law*, 7:3, pp. 436–58.
Laracy, H 2008, 'An historic view of Fiji', in B Lala & M Pretes (eds), *Coup: reflections on the political crisis*, Australian National University E Press, Canberra, pp. 18–24.
Lederach, JP 1997, *Building peace: sustainable reconciliation in divided societies*, United States Institute Peace Press, Washington DC.
Lewis, DA 2009, 'Unrecognized victims: sexual violence against men in conflict settings under international law', *Wisconsin International Law Journal*, 27:1, pp. 1–49.
Lodhia, S 2003, 'Coups in Fiji: a personal perspective and analysis of an ethnic Indian', *Fijian Studies*, 11, pp. 163–76.
Longwe, S 1991, 'Gender awareness: the missing element in the third world development project', in T Wallace & M Candida (eds), *Changing perceptions: writings on gender and development*, Oxfam, Oxford, pp. 149–57.
McDonald, R 2008, *Safety, security, and accessible justice: participatory approaches to law and justice reform in Papua New Guinea*, Pacific Islands Development Series No. 3, East-West Center, Hawaii.
Mack, A (ed.) 2005, *Human security report 2005: war and peace in the 21st century*, Oxford University Press, New York.
Mackay, A 2005, 'Mainstreaming gender in United Nations peacekeeping training: examples from East Timor, Ethiopia, and Eritrea', in D Mazurana, A Raven-Roberts & J Parpart (eds), *Gender, conflict, and peacekeeping*, Rowman & Littlefield, Lanham, MD, pp. 265–79.
MacKenzie, M 2009, 'Empowerment boom or bust? Assessing women's post-conflict empowerment', *Cambridge Review of International Affairs*, 222, pp. 199–215.
Mani, R 2002, *Beyond retribution: seeking justice in the shadows of war*, Polity Press, Oxford.
Manikkalingam, R 2008, 'What I have learned from being a part of Sri Lanka's civil war', *Polity*, 4:6, pp. 35–9.
Mansbridge, J 2005, 'Quota problems: combating the dangers of essentialism', *Politics and Gender*, 1:4, pp. 622–38.
Marks, J 2005, 'Understand the differences: act on the commonalities', in P van Tongeren, M Brenk, M Hellema & J Verhoeven (eds), *People building peace II: successful stories of civil society*, Lynne Rienner, Boulder, CO, pp. 185–6.
Mazurana, D, McKay, S, Carlson, K & Kasper, J 2002, 'Girls in fighting forces and groups: their recruitment, participation, demobilization, and reintegration', *Journal of Peace Psychology*, 8:2, pp. 97–123.
Mazurana, D, Raven-Roberts, A, Parpart, J & Lautze, S 2005, 'Introduction: gender, conflict and peacekeeping', in D Mazurana, A Raven-Roberts & J Parpart (eds), *Gender, conflict, and peacekeeping*, Rowman & Littlefield, Lanham, MD, pp. 1–26.
Miranda, A 2006, *Women and political violence: female combatants in ethno-national conflict*, Routledge, London & New York.

Mobekk, E 2010, 'Gender, women and security sector reform', *International Peacekeeping*, 17:2, pp. 278–91.
Moore, P 2003, 'Rehabilitation for change in Fiji: a women's initiative', in D Sinclair (ed.), *A kind of mending: restorative justice in the Pacific Islands*, Pandanus Books, Canberra, pp. 123–37.
Moran, MH 2010, 'Gender, militarism, and peace-building: projects of the post-conflict moment', *Annual Review of Anthropology*, 39, pp. 261–74.
Nakaya, S 2004, 'Women and gender equality in Somalia and Mozambique', in T Keating & WA Knight (eds), *Building sustainable peace*, UN University Press, Tokyo, pp. 142–66.
—— 2011, 'Women and gender issues in peacebuilding: lessons learned from Timor-Leste', in 'F Olonisakin, K Barnes & E Ikpe (eds), *Women, peace and security: translating policy into practice*, Routledge, London, pp. 155–69.
Nanivadekar, M 2006, 'Are quotas a good idea? The Indian experience with reserved seats for women', *Politics and Gender*, 2:1, pp. 119–28.
Neuwirth, J 2002, 'Women and peace and security: the implementation of UN Security Council Resolution 1325', *Duke Journal of Gender Law and Policy*, 9, pp. 253–60.
Ní Aoláin, F & Rooney, E 2007, 'Underenforcement and intersectionality: gendered aspects of transition for women', *International Journal of Transitional Justice*, 1, pp. 338–54.
Ní Aoláin, F & Turner, C 2007, 'Gender, truth and transition', *UCLA Women's Law Journal*, 16, pp. 229–79.
Nicholl, R 2007, 'Broken promises: women and the 2006 Fiji election', in J Fraenkel & S Firth (eds), *From election to coup in Fiji: the 2006 campaign and its aftermath*, Australian National University E Press, Canberra, pp. 160–74.
Njoki Wamai, E 2011, 'UNSCR on 2 to 5 implementation in Liberia: dilemmas and challenges', in 'F Olonisakin, K Barnes & E Ikpe (eds), *Women, peace and security: translating policy and practice*, Routledge, London, pp. 52–65.
Nussbaum, MC 2000, *Women and human development: the capabilities approach*, Cambridge University Press, Cambridge, UK.
Olonisakin, 'F, Barnes, K & Ikpe, E (eds) 2011, *Women, peace and security: translating policy into practice*, Routledge, London.
Olonisakin, 'F & Ikpe, E 2011, 'Conclusion', in 'F Olonisakin, K Barnes & E Ikpe (eds), *Women, peace and security: translating policy into practice*, Routledge, London, pp. 225–35.
Olsson, L & Tryggestad, T 2001, *Women and international peacekeeping*, Frank Cass, London.
Oosterhoff, P, Zwanikken, P & Ketting, E 2004, 'Sexual torture of men in Croatia and other conflict situations: an open secret', *Reproductive Health Matters*, 12:23, pp. 68–77.
Paina, DT 2000, 'Peacemaking in Solomon Islands: the experience of the Guadalcanal women for peace movement', *Development Bulletin*, 53, pp. 47–8.
Pollard, A 2000, 'Resolving conflict in Solomon Islands: the women for peace approach', *Development Bulletin*, 53, pp. 44–6.
Porter, E 2003, 'Women, political decision-making, and peace-building', *Global Change, Peace and Security*, 153, pp. 245–62.
—— 2006, 'Can politics practice compassion?', *Hypatia: A Journal of Feminist Philosophy*, 21: 4, pp. 97–123.

—— 2007, *Peacebuilding: women in international perspective*, Routledge, London & New York.

—— 2011, 'Gender-inclusivity in transitional justice strategies: women in Timor-Leste', in S Buckley-Zistel & R Stanley (eds), *Gender and transitional justice*, Palgrave Macmillan, Basingstoke, pp. 221–40.

Porter, E & Every, D 2009, 'Peacebuilding: women peaceworkers', in D Bagshaw & E Porter (eds), *Mediation in the Asia-Pacific region: transforming conflicts and building peace*, Routledge, London, pp. 31–49.

Puechguirbal, N 2010, 'Discourses on gender, patriarchy and Resolution 1325: a textual analysis of UN documents', *International Peacekeeping*, 17:2, pp. 172–87.

Rajasingham-Senanayake, D 2004, 'Between reality and representation: women's agency in war and post-conflict Sri Lanka', *Cultural Dynamics*, 16:2/3, pp. 141–68.

Raven-Roberts, A 2005, 'Gender mainstreaming in United Nations peacekeeping operations: talking the talk, tripping over the walk', in D Mazurana, A Raven-Roberts & J Parpart (eds), *Gender, conflict, and peacekeeping*, Rowman & Littlefield, Lanham, MD, pp. 43–64.

Rees, T 1998, *Mainstreaming equality in the European Union: education, training and labour market policies*, Routledge, London.

Reingold, B 2000, *Representing women: sex, gender, and legislative behaviour in Arizona and California*, University of North Carolina Press, Chapel Hill, NC.

Richmond, O 2007, 'Emancipatory forms of human security and liberal peacebuilding', *International Journal*, 62:3, pp. 459–77.

—— (ed.) 2010, *Palgrave advances in peacebuilding: critical developments and approaches*, Palgrave Macmillan, Basingstoke.

Roberts, A 2010, 'Lives and statistics: are 90% of war victims civilians?', *Survival*, 523, pp. 115–36.

Rubio-Marín, R 2006, 'The gender of reparations: setting the agenda', in R Rubio-Marín (ed.), *What happened to the women? Gender and reparations for human rights violations*, Social Science Research Council, New York, pp. 20–47.

Sarkin, J 2009, 'The role of the United Nations, the African Union and Africa's sub-regional organisations in dealing with Africa's human rights problems: connecting humanitarian intervention and the responsibility to protect', *Journal of African Law*, 53, pp. 1–33.

Sawers, M 1998, 'Are women more likely to vote for women's issue bills than their male colleagues?', *Legislative Studies Quarterly*, 23, pp. 435–48.

—— 2002a, *The difference women make: the policy impact of women in congress*, University of Chicago Press, Chicago, IL.

—— 2002b, 'Transforming the agenda? Analyzing gender differences in women's issue bill sponsorship', in CS Rosenthal (ed.), *Women transforming congress*, University of Oklahoma Press, Norman, OK, pp. 260–83.

—— 2005, 'Connecting descriptive and substantive representation: an analysis of sex differences in co-sponsorship activity', *Legislative Studies Quarterly*, 30:3, pp. 407–32.

Schroeder, E 2004, 'A window of opportunity in the DRC: incorporating a gender perspective in the DDR process', *Peace, Conflict and Development*, 5, pp. 1–45.

Schwindt-Bayer, L & Mishler, M 2005, 'An integrated model of women's representation', *Journal of Politics*, 67:2, pp. 407–28.

Sebastian, R 1994, 'Ethnic conflict in Sri Lanka: its ecological and political consequences', in V Shiva (ed.), *Close to home: women reconnect ecology, health and development*, Earthscan, London, pp. 141–9.

Segal, L 2008, 'Gender, war and militarism: making and questioning the links', *Feminist Review*, 88, pp. 21–35.

Sellers, PV 2009, 'Gender strategy is not a luxury for international courts', *American University Journal of Gender, Social Policy and the Law*, 17:2, pp. 301–26.

Shepherd, LJ 2008, 'Power and authority in the production of United Nations Security Council Resolution 1325', *International Studies Quarterly*, 52, pp. 383–404.

Simić, O 2010, 'Does the presence of women really matter? Towards combating male sexual violence in peacekeeping operations', *International Peacekeeping*, 17:2, pp. 188–99.

Siwatibau, S 2007, 'Women and minority interests in Fiji's alternative electoral system', in J Fraenkel & S Firth (eds), *From election to coup in Fiji: the 2006 campaign and its aftermath*, Australian National University E Press, Canberra, pp. 379–85.

Standing, H 2007, 'Gender, myth and fable: the perils of mainstreaming in sector bureaucracies', in A Cornwall, E Harrison & A Whitehead (eds), *Feminisms in development: contradictions, contestations and challenges*, Zed Books, London, pp. 101–11.

Stemple, L 2009, 'Male rape and human rights', *Hastings Law Journal*, 60:3, pp. 605–46.

Subrahmanian, R 2007, 'Making sense of gender in shifting institutional contexts: some reflections on gender mainstreaming', in A Cornwall, E Harrison & A Whitehead (eds), *Feminisms in development: contradictions, contestations and challenges*, Zed Books, London, pp. 112–21.

Suhrke, A 2001, 'Peace-keepers as nation-builders: dilemmas of the UN in East Timor', *International Peacekeeping*, 8:4, pp. 1–20.

Thomas, S 1991, 'The impact of women on state legislative policies', *Journal of Politics*, 53:4, pp. 958–76.

Towns, A 2003, 'Understanding the effects of larger ratios of women in national legislatures: proportions and gender differentiation in Sweden and Norway', *Women and Politics*, 25:1, pp. 1–29.

Trembath, A & Grenfell, D 2007, *Mapping the pursuit of gender equality: non-government and international agency activity in Timor-Leste*, Globalism Institute, RMIT University, Melbourne.

Trembath, A, Grenfell, D & Moniz Noronha, C 2010, *Impacts of national NGO gender programming in local communities in Timor-Leste*, Globalism Institute, RMIT University, Melbourne.

Tryggestad, T 2009, 'Trick or treat? The UN and implementation of Security Council Resolution 1325 on women, peace, and security', *Global Governance*, 15, pp. 539–57.

—— 2010, 'The UN Peacebuilding Commission and gender: a case of norm reinforcement', *International Peacekeeping*, 17:2, pp. 159–71.

Valenius, J 2007, 'A few kind women: gender essentialism and Nordic peacekeeping operations', *International Peacekeeping*, 14:4, pp. 510–23.

Vayrynen, T 2004, 'Gender and UN peace operations: the confines of modernity', *International Peacekeeping*, 11:1, pp. 125–42.

Vega, A & Firestone, J 1995, 'The effects of gender on congressional behaviour and the substantive representation of women', *Legislative Studies Quarterly*, 20:2, pp. 213–22.

Walzer, M 1977, *Just and unjust wars*, Basic Books, New York.

Wandita, G, Campbell-Nelson, K & Leong Pereira, M 2006, 'Learning to engender reparations in Timor-Leste: reaching out to female victims', in R Rubio-Marín (ed.), *What happened to the women? Gender and reparations for human rights violations*, Social Science Research Council, New York, pp. 284–334.

Wängnerud, L 2000, 'Testing the politics of presence: women's representation in the Swedish Riksdag, *Scandinavian Political Studies*, 23:1, pp. 67–91.

Wee, V & Shaheed, F 2008, *Women empowering themselves: a framework that interrogates and transforms*, Southeast Asia Research Centre, Hong Kong.

Weldon, S 2002, 'Beyond bodies: institutional sources of representation for women in democratic policymaking', *Journal of Politics*, 64:4, pp. 1153–74.

Whip, R 1991, 'Representing women: Australian female Parliamentarians on the horns of a dilemma', *Women and Politics*, 11, pp. 1–22.

Whittington, S 2000, 'The UN transitional administration in East Timor: gender affairs', *Development Bulletin*, 53, pp. 74–6.

Whitworth, S 2004, *Men, militarism and UN peacekeeping*, Lynne Rienner, Boulder, CO.

Willett, S 2010, 'Introduction: Security Council Resolution 1325: assessing the impact on women, peace and security', *International Peacekeeping*, 17:2, pp. 142–58.

Wolbrecht, C 2000, *The politics of women's rights: parties, positions, and change*, Princeton University Press, Princeton, NJ.

Wolff, S 2006, *Ethnic conflict: a global perspective*, Oxford University Press, Oxford.

Reports and policy, NGO, government and working papers

Anderlini, SN, Conaway, CP & Kays, L 2004, 'Transitional justice and reconciliation', in International Alert & Women Waging Peace, *Inclusive security, sustainable peace: a toolkit for advocacy and action*, vol. 4 (*Justice, governance and civil society*), International Alert & Women Waging Peace, London & Washington DC, pp. 1–15.

Anderlini, SN & Stanski, V 2004, 'Conflict prevention, resolution and reconstruction', in International Alert & Women Waging Peace, *Inclusive security, sustainable peace: a toolkit for advocacy and action*, vol. 2 (*Conflict prevention, resolution and reconstruction*), International Alert and Women Waging Peace, London & Washington DC, pp. 1–15.

Anderlini, SN & Tirman, J 2010, *What the women say: participation and UNSCR 1325 a case study assessment*, MIT, Cambridge, MA.

Association of Women in Development 2004, *Intersectionality: a tool for gender and economic justice*, Women's Rights and Economic Change: Facts and Issues No. 9, AWID, Ontario.

AusAID 2002, *Peace, conflict and development policy*, Commonwealth of Australia, Canberra.

—— 2006, *Gender guidelines, peace-building*, Commonwealth of Australia, Canberra.

—— 2007a, *Gender equality in Australia's aid program – why and how*, Commonwealth of Australia, Canberra.

—— 2008a, *Gender equality: annual thematic performance report 2006–07*, Commonwealth of Australia, Canberra.
—— 2008b, *Violence against women in Melanesia and East Timor: building on the global and regional promising approaches*, Commonwealth of Australia, Canberra.
—— 2009, *Stop violence: responding to violence against women in Melanesia and East Timor: Australia's response to the ODE report*, Commonwealth of Australia, Canberra.
—— 2010a, *Women, peace and security: AusAID's implementation of UNSCR 1325*, Commonwealth of Australia, Canberra.
—— 2011, *Women leading change: AusAID's support for women's leadership and decision-making*, Commonwealth of Australia, Canberra.
Baechler, G 2010, *A mediator's perspective: women and the Nepali peace process*, Women at the Table: Asia Pacific 2010 Opinion Series No. 1, Centre for Humanitarian Dialogue, Geneva.
Barnes, K 2006, *Reform or more of the same? Gender mainstreaming and the changing nature of UN peace operations*, York Centre for International Security Studies Working Paper No. 41, York Centre for International and Security Studies, Ontario.
—— 2009, *Turning policy into impact on the ground: developing indicators and monitoring mechanisms on women, peace and security issues for the European Union*, Initiative for Peacebuilding Gender Cluster, Brussels.
Bastian, S 2009, 'Politics of social exclusion, state reform and security in Sri Lanka', *IDS Bulletin*, 40:2, pp. 88–95.
Bastick, M, Grimm, K & Kunz, R 2007, *Sexual violence in armed conflict: global overview and implications for the security sector*, Geneva Centre for the Democratic Control of Armed Forces, Geneva.
Basu, S 2004, *Building constituencies of peace: a women's initiative in Kashmir*, WISCOMP, New Delhi.
Bharadwaj, N, Dhungana, S, Hicks, N, Crozier, R & Watson, C 2007, *Nepal at a crossroads: the nexus between human security and renewed conflict in rural Nepal*, Friends for Peace & International Alert, Kathmandu.
Bouta, T, Frerks, G & Bannon, I 2005, *Gender, conflict, and development*, World Bank, Washington DC.
Bush, K 2000, 'Polio, war and peace', *Bulletin of the World Health Organization*, 78:3, pp. 281–2.
Butler, M, Mader, K & Kean, R 2010, *Women, peace and security handbook: compilation and analysis of United Nations Security Council Resolution language 2000–2010*, PeaceWomen Project of Women's International League for Peace and Freedom, New York.
Canadian International Development Agency 2001, *Gender equality and peacebuilding: an operational framework*, CIDA, Quebec.
CARE International 2010, *From resolution to reality: lessons learned from Afghanistan, Nepal and Uganda on women's participation in peacebuilding and post-conflict governance*, CARE International UK, London.
Clegg, I, Hunt, R & Whetton, J 2000, *Policy guidance on support to policing in developing countries*, Centre for Development Studies, University of Wales, Swansea.

Commission of the European Communities 1996, *Incorporating equal opportunities for women and men into all community policies and activities*, communication from the Commission, COM (96) 67, CEC, Brussels.

Council of Europe 1998, *Gender mainstreaming: conceptual framework, methodology and presentation of good practices*, final report of activities of the group of specialists on mainstreaming, Council of Europe, Strasbourg.

da Costa, R 2006, *The administration of justice in refugee camps: a study of practice*, UNHCR Legal and Protection Policy Research Series No. 10, UNHCR, Geneva.

Dahlerup, D 2005, 'Increasing women's political representation: new trends in gender quotas', in *Women in Parliament: beyond numbers: a revised edition*, International Institute for Democracy and Electoral Assistance, Stockholm, pp. 141–53.

DFID 2009, *Building the state and securing the peace: emerging policy paper*, Department for International Development UK, London.

El-Bushra, J 2003, *Women building peace: sharing know-how*, International Alert, London.

Escobar, LT 2009, *The critical route of action plans: women, peace and security perspectives of the Resolution 1325 in Latin America*, RESDAL Working Paper, Buenos Aires.

Esplen, E 2006, *Engaging men in gender equality: positive strategies and approaches. Overview and annotated bibliography*, Institute of Development Studies, University of Sussex, Brighton.

Etchart, L 2005, 'Progress in gender mainstreaming in peace support operations', in R Baksh, L Etchart, E Onubogu & T Johnson (eds), *Gender mainstreaming in conflict transformation: building sustainable peace*, Commonwealth Secretariat, London, pp. 56–81.

femLINKpacific 2008, *Women, peace and security: policy for peace in our Pacific region*, femLINKpacific Media Initiatives for Women, Suva.

—— 2009, *Women, peace and security: policy for peace in our Pacific region*, femLINKpacific Media Initiatives for Women, Suva.

FWCC 2001, *The impact of the May 19 coup on women in Fiji*, Fiji Women's Crisis Centre, Suva.

Garcia, E 2008, *Consolidating peace. Nepali constitution-making: a Filipino peace practitioner's perspective*, International Alert, London.

Giossi Caverzasio, S 2001, *Strengthening protection in war: a search for professional standards*, International Committee of the Red Cross, Geneva.

Government of Nepal 2007, *Election to Members of the Constituent Assembly Act, 2064 (2007)*, Article 7 [3] and Schedule 1.

ICISS 2001, *The responsibility to protect: report of the International Commission on Intervention and State Sovereignty*, International Development Research Centre, Ottawa.

Institute of Social Studies Trust 2007, *Progress of women in South Asia*, Institute of Social Studies Trust & UNIFEM, South Asia Office, New Delhi.

International Alert & Women Waging Peace 2004, *Inclusive security, sustainable peace: a toolkit for advocacy and action*, International Alert & Women Waging Peace, London & Washington DC.

International Crisis Group 2010, *Sri Lanka: a bitter peace*, Asia Briefing No. 99, International Crisis Group, Brussels.

Jabre, K & Palmieri, S 2005, 'Promoting partnership between men and women in Parliament: the experience of the Inter-Parliamentary Union', in *Women in Parliament: beyond numbers: a revised edition*, International Institute for Democracy and Electoral Assistance, Stockholm, pp. 214–30.

Johnston, N 2004, 'Peace support operations', in International Alert & Women Waging Peace, *Inclusive security, sustainable peace: a toolkit for advocacy and action*, vol. 2 (*Conflict prevention, resolution and reconstruction*), International Alert & Women Waging Peace, London & Washington DC, pp. 33–50.

Karam, A & Lovenduski, J 2005, 'Women in Parliament: making a difference', in *Women in Parliament: beyond numbers: a revised edition*, International Institute for Democracy and Electoral Assistance, Stockholm, pp. 187–212.

Kodikara, C 2009, *The struggle for equal political representation of women in Sri Lanka: a stocktaking report for the Ministry of Child Development and Women's Empowerment and the UNDP*, Women and Media Collective, Colombo.

Lyytikäinen, M 2007, *Gender training for peacekeepers: preliminary overview of United Nations peace support operations*, Gender, Peace and Security Working Paper 4, UN-INSTRAW, Dominican Republic.

McGrew, L, Frieson, K & Chan, S 2004, *Good governance from the ground up: women's roles in post-conflict Cambodia*, Institute for Inclusive Security, Washington DC.

Mackay, F & Bilton, K 2003, *Learning from experience: lessons in mainstreaming equal opportunities*, Scottish Executive Social Research, University of Edinburgh, Edinburgh.

Majoor, H & Brown, ML 2008, *Evaluating the Dutch national action plan on UNSCR Resolution 1325 after one year of implementation*, Working Group 1325, The Hague.

Mantilla, J 2006, *Gender, justice, and truth commissions*, World Bank, Washington DC.

March, C, Smyth, I & Mukhopadhyay, M 1999, *A guide to gender-analysis frameworks*, Oxfam, Oxford.

Marhaban, S 2010, *Aceh: the maintenance and dividends of peace*, Open Dialogue on Mediation for Peace, Centre for Humanitarian Dialogue, Geneva.

Morna, CL (ed.) 2004, *Ringing up the changes: gender in southern African politics*, Gender Links, Johannesburg.

Myrttinen, H 2009, *Poster boys no more: gender and security sector reform in Timor-Leste*, Policy Paper 31, Geneva Centre for the Democratic Control of Armed Forces, Geneva.

NDI 2010, *Democracy and the challenge of change: a guide to increasing women's political participation*, National Democratic Institute, Washington DC.

Nelson, C & Muggah, R 2004, *Solomon Islands: evaluating the weapons free village campaign small arms survey*, Working Paper, Graduate Institute of International and Development Studies, Geneva.

Nesiah, V 2006, *Truth commissions and gender: principles, policies and procedures*, International Centre for Transitional Justice, New York.

NGOs Working Group 2009, *NGOs alternative report: implementation of the Convention on the Elimination of All Forms of Discrimination against Women (CEDAW) in Timor-Leste*, NGOs Working Group, Dili.

Onslow, C (ed.) 2009, *Global monitoring checklist on women, peace and security: Afghanistan, Democratic Republic of Congo, Nepal, Northern Ireland, Sri Lanka*, GAPS UK, London.

Organisation for Security and Cooperation in Europe/Office for Democratic Institutions and Human Rights 2009, *Gender and early warning systems: an introduction*, OSCE/ODIHR, Warsaw.

Pankhurst, D 1999, *Mainstreaming gender in peacebuilding: a framework for action from the village council to the negotiating table*, International Alert & Women Waging Peace, London.

Pearson, AM 2004, 'The Mahila Shanti Sena: new women's peace movement in India', *Peace Magazine*, January–March, p. 15.

Pillay, A 2006, *Gender, peace and peacekeeping: lessons learned from South Africa*, Institute for Security Studies Paper No. 128, Institute for Security Studies, Pretoria.

Popovic, N 2008, 'Security sector reform assessment, monitoring & evaluation and gender', in M Bastick & K Valasek, *The gender and SSR toolkit*, DCAF & UN-INSTRAW, Geneva, pp. 1–24.

Potter, A 2011, *G is for gendered: taking the mystery out of gendering peace agreements*, Women at the Table: Asia Pacific 2011 Opinion Series No. 5, Centre for Humanitarian Dialogue, Geneva.

Powley, E 2005, 'Rwanda: women hold up half the Parliament', in *Women in Parliament: beyond numbers: a revised edition*, International Institute for Democracy and Electoral Assistance, Stockholm, pp. 154–63.

Powley, E & Anderlini, SN 2004, 'Democracy and governance', in International Alert & Women Waging Peace, *Inclusive security, sustainable peace: a toolkit for advocacy and action*, vol. 4 (*Justice, governance and civil society*), International Alert & Women Waging Peace, London & Washington DC, pp. 36–63.

PPC 2008, *Roundtable report: women in peace and humanitarian operations*, Pearson Peacekeeping Centre, Ottawa.

Schirch, L & Sewak, M 2005, *The role of women in peacebuilding*, Global Partnership for the Prevention of Armed Conflict, The Hague.

Schmeidl, S & Piza-Lopez, E 2002, *Gender and conflict early warning: a framework for action*, International Alert & Swiss Foundation for Peace, Bern.

Shvedova, N 2005, 'Obstacles to women's participation in Parliament', in *Women in Parliament: beyond numbers: a revised edition*, International Institute for Democracy and Electoral Assistance, Stockholm, pp. 34–50.

Slim, H & Bonwick, A 2005, *Protection: an ALNAP guide for humanitarian agencies*, Overseas Development Institute, London.

Standing Committee on Foreign Affairs, Defence and Trade 2008, *Australia's involvement in peacekeeping operations*, Commonwealth of Australia, Canberra.

Sudhakar, N & Wolden, S 2010, *Real change for Afghan women's rights: opportunities and challenges in the upcoming Parliamentary elections*, Peace Brief 44, US Institute for Peace, Washington DC.

Swithern, S & Hastie, R 2009, *Safety of civilians: a protection training pack*, Oxfam, London.

Valasek, K 2008, 'Security sector reform and gender', in M Bastick & K Valesek (eds), *Gender and security sector reform toolkit*, Geneva Centre for the Democratic Control of Armed Forces, Organisation for Security and Cooperation in Europe/Office for Democratic Institutions and Human Rights & UN-INSTRAW, Geneva, pp. 1–22.

Valji, N 2007, *Gender justice and reconciliation: dialogue on globalisation*, Occasional Paper No. 35, Friedrich-Ebert-Stiftung, Berlin.

VeneKlasen, L & Miller, V 2002, *New wave of power, people and politics: the action guide for advocacy and citizen participation*, World Neighbours, Oklahoma City, OK.

Verloo, M 2001, *Another velvet revolution? Gender mainstreaming and the politics of implementation*, IWM Working Paper No. 5/2001, Institute for Human Sciences, Vienna.

Vlachová, M & Biason, L (eds) 2005, *Women in an insecure world: violence against women – facts, figures and analysis*, Geneva Centre for the Democratic Control of Armed Forces, Geneva.

Wojkowska, E 2006, *Doing justice: how informal justice systems can contribute*, Oslo Governance Centre, Oslo.

World Bank 2011, *World development report: conflict, security and development*, World Bank, Washington DC.

Conferences and conference reports
(Online resources accessed November 2009 – September 2011)

Abugre, C 2008, *Reviewing the implementation of UNSCR 1325 and UNSCR 1820: what will it take?*, paper presented at the Women in the Land of Conflict Conference, Voksenaasen, Oslo, 23–25 November, <www.peacewomen.org/assets/file/Resources/NGO/1325-1820_ReviewingImpl_WLC_Nov2008.pdf>.

Berry, K & Reddy, S 2010, *Safety with dignity: integrating community-based protection into humanitarian programming*, Network Paper No. 68, Humanitarian Practice Network, Overseas Development Institute, London, March.

Bhagwan-Rolls, S 2006a, 'Women mediators in Pacific conflict zones: mediating cultures in the Pacific and Asia', Third Asia-Pacific Mediation Forum Conference, Suva, 26–30 June.

—— 2009, 'Gender and security sector reform – existing good practice in gender and security sector oversight', Security Sector Governance in the Pacific, UNDP/PIFS regional conference, Nuku'alofa, 27–30 April.

Celis, K, Childs, S, Kantola, J & Krook, ML 2007, 'Rethinking women's substantive representation', European Consortium for Political Research Workshops, Helsinki, 7–12 May.

Chase, R 2000, 'Healing and reconciliation for war-affected children and communities: learning from the Butterfly Garden of Sri Lanka's eastern province', International Conference on War Affected Children, Winnipeg, 10–17 September.

Childs, S & Krook, M 2005, 'The substantive representation of women: rethinking the "critical mass" debate', annual meeting of APSA, Washington DC, 1–4 September.

Cohn, C, Bhagwan-Rolls, S, Kande, M, Dobruna, V & Talabani, A 2004, *Workshop on strategies for grassroots implementation of Resolution 1325*, Boston Consortium on Gender, Security and Human Rights, Boston, MA.

da Costa, MPJ 2009, 'The voices and experiences of women Parliamentarians' caucus in promoting gender equality and women's empowerment in the national Parliament of Timor-Leste', Second International Women for Peace Conference, Dili, 5–6 March.

Edgren-Schori, M 2008, 'Training soldiers for peace', in G Greindl (ed.), *Training soldiers for peace*, proceedings of the Blue Helmet Forum Austria 2008, Salzburg, 10–12 July, Association of Austrian Peacekeepers, Vienna.

Garap, S 2005, 'Human rights program in village court services', Committee on the Elimination of Discrimination against Women Conference, Port Moresby, 24–25 November.

Gloub, S 2005, 'Challenging the rule of law orthodoxy: many roads to justice', Asia-Pacific Access to Justice Practitioner's Guide Launch and Training Workshop, Phnom Penh, 22–24 September.

Gregory, J 1999, 'Gender mainstreaming: closing the gap between theory and practice', Conference on Women and Political Action: Debating Ways Forward for Feminists, London, 18–19 June.

Kabui, F & Guthleben, A 2008, 'The establishment of a commission in Solomon Islands', Australasian Law Reform Agencies Conference, Port Vila, 10–12 September.

Krook, M, Franceschet, S & Piscopo, J 2009, 'The impact of gender quotas: a research agenda', First European Conference on Politics and Gender, Belfast, 21–23 January.

Longwe, S 2002, *Assessment of the gender orientation of NEPAD*, paper presented at the African Forum for Envisioning Africa, Nairobi, 26–29 April, South African Regional Poverty Network, <www.sarpn.org/documents/d0000065/P68_Longwe.pdf>.

Mangold, A 2003, 'The peaceable police woman? The practice of de-escalation in the eyes of female and male police officers', Fifth European Feminist Research Conference: Gender and Power in the New Europe, Lund, 20–24 August.

Menezes, FS 2009, 'Interaction between formal and traditional justice systems: local justice and formal justice – can the two systems work together in Timor-Leste?', Second International Women for Peace Conference, Dili, 5–6 March.

Nelson, C 2006, 'Women and disarmament: what can be learnt from conflicts in Solomon Islands, Bougainville and PNG?', International Firearms Safety Seminar, Christchurch, 21–24 February.

Paris Declaration on Aid Effectiveness 2005, High Level Forum, Paris, 28 February – 2 March.

Porter, E 2010a, 'Overcoming inequality: valuing women's participation in peacebuilding', Research Challenges on Women, Peace and Security, Peace Research Institute Oslo, Oslo, 11–12 November, available at <www.prio.no/Research-and-Publications/Gender/Gender-Research-Conference>.

—— 2010b, 'Why bother with a gender perspective in peacebuilding?', in B Offord & R Garbutt (eds), *A scholarly affair: proceedings of the Cultural Studies Association of Australasia 2010 National Conference*, Southern Cross University, Centre for Peace & Social Justice, Lismore, pp. 125–34.

SAP International 2008, *Second South Asian Regional Conference: Combating Violence against Women in Politics: Revisiting Policies, Politics and Participation*, proceeding report, South Asia Partnership International, Lalitpur.

Sawer, M 2004, 'When women support women: EMILY's List and the substantive representation of women in Australia', Australasian Political Studies Association Conference, Adelaide, 29 September – 1 October.

Simoni, A 2010, *Precarious progress: UN resolutions on women, peace and security: final report*, Joan B Kroc Institute for Peace & Justice, San Diego, CA.

Tiwari, S 2010 ,'Women and peacekeeping: lessons learned and next steps', Precarious Progress: UN Resolutions on Women, Peace and Security, Women PeaceMakers Program, San Diego, CA, 29 September – 1 October.

Whittington, S 2006, 'Women and decision-making in post-conflict transitions: case studies from Timor Leste and the Solomon Islands', Sixth Asia-Pacific Congress of Women in Politics, Makati City, 10–12 February.

Wisotzki, S 2003, 'Engendering security discourses in IR: theoretical insights and practical implications', Forty-fourth Annual Convention of the International Studies Association, Portland, OR, 22 February – 1 March.

Women for Peace 2009, *Second international conference 2009: Women for peace narrative report*, Alola Foundation, Timor-Leste.

Women PeaceMakers 2010, Precarious Progress: UN Resolutions on Women, Peace and Security, Women PeaceMakers Conference, San Diego, CA, 29 September – 1 October.

United Nations documents and agencies
(Online resources accessed January 2009 – May 2011)

Alami, N & Goetz, A-M 2006, *Promoting gender equality in new aid modalities and partnerships*, UNIFEM Discussion Paper, UNIFEM, New York.

Anderlini, SN 2000, *Women at the peace table: making a difference*, UNIFEM, New York.

Bertolazzi, F 2010, *Women with a blue helmet: the integration of women and gender issues in UN peacekeeping missions*, UN-INSTRAW Working Paper Series, UN-INSTRAW, Santo Domingo.

Boutros-Ghali, B 1995, *Supplement to an agenda for peace: position paper of the Secretary-General on the occasion of the fiftieth anniversary of the United Nations*, A/50/60 – S/1995/1, UN, New York.

Brahimi, L 2000, *Report of the panel on United Nations peace operations* (Brahimi report), A/55/305 – S/2000/809, UN, New York.

CEDAW 1979, *Convention on the Elimination of All Forms of Discrimination against Women*, CEDAW, New York, 18 December.

—— 1999, *Consideration of reports submitted by state parties under Article 18 of the Convention on the Elimination of All Forms of Discrimination against Women: Sri Lanka*, CEDAW/C/LKA/3-4, CEDAW, New York, 18 October.

—— 2009, *Concluding observations of the Committee on the Elimination of Discrimination against Women: Timor Leste*, CEDAW/C/TLS/CO/1, CEDAW, New York, 7 August.

Chinkin, C 2003b, *Peace agreements as a means for promoting gender equality and ensuring participation of women – a framework of model provisions*, Background Paper EGM/PEACE/2003/BP.1, UNDAW, Ottawa.

Human Rights Council 2008, *Report of the representative of the Secretary-General on the human rights of internally displaced persons*, A/HRC/8/6/Add.4, Human Rights Council, New York, 21 May.

Mayanja, R 2010, 'Armed conflict and women: 10 years of Security Council Resolution 1325', *UN Chronicle*, 47:1, pp. 16–18.

Ospina, S 2006, *Participation of women in politics and decision making in Timor-Leste: a recent history*, UNIFEM, Dili.

Powley, E 2007, *Rwanda: the impact of women legislators on policy outcomes affecting children and families*, The State of the World's Children Background Paper, UNICEF, New York.

Rehn, E & Johnson Sirleaf, E 2002, *Women, war and peace: the independent experts' assessment on the impact of armed conflict on women and women's role in peacebuilding*, UNIFEM, New York.

Roynestad, E 2003, *Are women included or excluded in post-conflict reconstruction: a case study from Timor-Leste*, Expert Paper EGM/PEACE/2003/EP.8, UNDAW, Ottawa.

Shanahan, T (UNDP Pacific Centre) 2010, personal correspondence, 31 March.

Sorensen, B 1998, *Women and post-conflict reconstruction: issues and sources*, War-torn Societies Project Occasional Paper No. 3, UN Research Institute for Social Development, Geneva.

UN 1996, *Report on fourth world conference on women*, UN, New York.

—— 2007, *United Nations Development Assistance Framework (UNDAF) Sri Lanka 2008–2012*, UN, New York.

UN Association in Canada 2007, *Peacekeeping to peacebuilding: lessons from the past, building for the future*, UNAC, Ottawa.

UNDAW 2003, *Expert Group meeting on peace agreements as a means for promoting gender equality and ensuring participation of women – a framework of model provisions*, EGM/PEACE/2003/EP.9, UNDAW, Ottawa, 10–13 November.

UNDP 1994, *New dimensions of human security*, Human Development Report 1994, Oxford University Press, Oxford & New York.

——1995, *Gender and human development*, Human Development Report, Oxford University Press, New York.

—— 2000, *Human rights and human development*, Human Development Report, Oxford University Press, New York.

—— 2006, *Women's issues now part of legal training in Nepal*, UNDP, 5 April, <http://content.undp.org/go/newsroom/2006/april/womens-legal-training-nepal-20060405.en;jsessionid=axbWzt...?categoryID=349437&lang=en>.

—— 2007, *Fighting climate change: human solidarity in a divided world*, Human Development Report 2007/2008, Palgrave Macmillan, Basingstoke.

—— 2008a, *Innovative approaches to promoting women's economic empowerment*, UNDP, New York.

—— 2008b, *Gender profile of the conflict in Sri Lanka*, UNIFEM, New York.

—— 2009, *Overcoming barriers: human mobility and development*, Human Development Report 2009, Palgrave Macmillan, Basingstoke.

UNDPKO 2004, *Gender resource package for peacekeeping operations*, UNDPKO, New York.

—— 2006a, *Background paper: enhancing the operational impact of peacekeeping operations – gender balance in military and police services deployed to UN peacekeeping missions*, UNDPKO, New York.

—— 2006b, *Policy dialogue to review strategies for enhancing gender balance among uniformed personnel in peacekeeping missions: final report*, UNDPKO, New York, 28–29 March.

—— 2007, *Implementation of Security Council Resolution 1325 (2000) on women, peace and security in peacekeeping contexts: a strategy workshop with women's constituencies*

from troop and police contributing countries: final report, UNDPKO, Pretoria, 7–9 February.
—— 2008, *Guidelines for integrating gender perspectives into the work of UN police in peacekeeping missions*, UNDPKO, New York.
—— 2009a, *Gender statistics*, UN Peacckeeping, <www.un.org/en/peacekeeping/resources/statistics/gender.shtml>.
—— 2009b, UN Peacekeeping, <www.un.org/Depts/dpko/dpko>.
—— 2010, *Ten-year impact study on the implementation of UN Security Council Resolution 1325 (2000) on women, peace and security in peacekeeping: final report*, UNDPKO, New York.
UNDPKO/Office of Military Affairs 2010, *Statistical report on female military and police personnel in UN peacekeeping operations prepared for the 10th anniversary of the SCR 1325*, UNDPKO/OMA, New York.
UNDPKO, UNDPA, UNIFEM & UNDP 2010, *Women count for peace: the 2010 open days on women, peace and security*, UNDPKO, UNDPA, UNIFEM & UNDP, New York.
UN Economic and Social Council 1998, *Commission on the Status of Women report on the forty-second session*, E/CN.6/1998/12 – E/1998/27, UN, New York, 2–13 March.
UN Economic Commission for Africa 2009, *African women's report 2009: measuring gender inequalities in Africa: experiences and lessons learned from the African gender and development index*, UNECA, Addis Ababa.
UNESCAP 2003, *Elimination of violence against women in partnership with men*, Gender and Development Discussion Paper Series No. 15, UNESCAP, Bangkok.
—— 2010, *Violence against women*, UNESCAP, <www.unescap.org/ESID/GAD/Issues/Violence>.
UNFPA 2008, *UNSCR 1325*, UNFPA Nepal, <www.unfpanepal.org/en/unscr1325>.
UNGA 1974, *Declaration on the protection of women and children in emergency and armed conflict*, A/RES/29/3318, UNGA, New York, 14 December.
—— 1982, *Declaration on the participation of women in promoting international peace and cooperation*, A/RES/37/63, UNGA, New York, 3 December.
—— 1993, *Declaration on the elimination of violence against women*, A/RES/48/104 20, UNGA, New York, December.
—— 1997, *Report of the Economic and Social Council for 1997*, A/52/318, UNGA, New York, September.
—— 1998, *The causes of conflict and the promotion of durable peace and sustainable development in Africa*, report of the Secretary-General, A/52/871 – S/1998/318, UNGA, New York, April.
—— 1999, *Optional Protocol to the CEDAW*, A/RES/54/4, UNGA, New York, 15 October.
—— 2010, *Women's participation in peace building*, report of the Secretary-General, A/65/354 – S/2010/466, UNGA, New York, 7 September.
UNHCR 1993, *The state of the world refugees 1993: the challenge of protection*, UNHCR, New York.
UNICEF 2007, *The state of the world's children: women and children: the double dividend of gender equality*, UNICEF, New York.
UNIFEM 2002, *Actions to end violence against women: a regional scan of the Pacific*, UNIFEM, Suva.
—— 2004, *Gender profile of the conflict in Timor-Leste*, UNIFEM, New York.

—— 2005, *Women in politics*, UNIFEM, <http://pacific.unifem.org/index.php?cat=15>.
—— 2007a, *Gender profile of the conflict in Fiji*, UNIFEM, Suva.
—— 2007b, *Women building peace and preventing sexual violence in conflict-affected contexts: a review of community-based approaches*, UNIFEM, New York.
—— 2008a, *Who answers to women? Gender and accountability*, Progress of the World's Women 2008/2009, UNIFEM, New York.
—— 2008b, *Report of the sixth South Asia regional ministerial conference commemorating Beijing*, UNIFEM, New Delhi.
—— 2009, *United Nations Security Resolution 1325*, fact sheet, UNIFEM Australian National Committee, <www.unifem.org.au/Content%20Pages/Gender%20Issues/peace-security>.
—— 2010, *Women's participation in peace negotiations: connections between presence and influence*, UNIFEM, New York.
UNIFEM & UNDPKO 2010, *Addressing conflict-related sexual violence: an analytical inventory of peacekeeping practice*, UNIFEM & UNDPKO, New York.
UN-INSTRAW 2007a, *Good and bad practices in gender training for security personnel: summary of a virtual discussion*, UN-INSTRAW, <www.un-instraw.org/data/images/documents/GPS/GPSTrainingDiscussion-Summary.pdf>.
—— 2007b, *Top ten recommendations for gender training*, UN-INSTRAW, New York.
—— 2008, 'India: female security officers to patrol border with Pakistan', *UN-INSTRAW E-Newsletter*, November, <www.un-instraw.org/es/newsletter/un-instraw-e-newsletter-november-2008.html>.
—— 2009 *Gender training community of practice*, UN-INSTRAW, <www.un-instraw.org/gtcop/en>.
—— 2010, *Algerian media professionals trained in gender approach*, Ensemble pour l'Égalité, <www.womenpoliticalparticipation.org/detail_agenda.php?code=22>.
UNMIL 2010, *UN envoy lauds Nigeria for enhancing women's role in peace-keeping missions*, Reliefweb, <www.reliefweb.int/rw/rwb.nsf/db900SID/KHII-82L9DV?OpenDocument>.
UNMIT 2007, 'Executive summary', in *Gender affairs unit quarterly report, July–September 2007*, UNMIT, <http://unmit.unmissions.org/LinkClick.aspx?fileticket=loJ2k%2bgAoQc%3d&tabid=434&mid=779>.
—— 2008, *UNMIT Gender quarterly report to DPKO HQ January–March 2008*, UNMIT, <http://unmit.unmissions.org/LinkClick.aspx?fileticket=B%2fJXTFGrFBM%3d&tabid=434&mid=779>.
UN News Service 2009, *UN peacekeeping missions urged to bolster number of women police officers*, UN News Centre, 7 August, <www.un.org/apps/news/story.asp?NewsID=31715&Cr=sexual+violence&Cr1=peacekeeping>.
UNRISD 2005, *Gender equality: striving for justice in an unequal world*, UN Research Institute for Social Development, Geneva.
UNSC 1999, *Resolution 1265 (1999) [on the protection of civilians in armed conflict]*, S/RES/1265 (1999), UNSC, New York, 17 September.
—— 2000a, *Resolution 1325 (2000) [on women and peace and security]*, S/RES/1325 (2000), UNSC, New York, 31 October.
—— 2000b, *Resolution 1296 (2000) [on the protection of civilians in armed conflict]*, S/RES/1296 (2000), UNSC, New York, 19 April.

—— 2003, *Women suffer disproportionately during and after war*, Press Release SC/7908, UNSC, New York, 29 October.
—— 2004, *Women and peace and security*, report of the Secretary-General, S/2004/814, UNSC, New York, 13 October.
—— 2006, *Resolution 1674 (2006) [on the protection of civilians in armed conflict]*, S/RES/1674 (2006), UNSC, New York, 28 April.
—— 2007, *Women and peace and security*, report of the Secretary-General, S/2007/567, UNSC, New York, 12 September.
——2008a, *Resolution 1820 (2008) [on women and peace and security]*, S/RES/1820 (2008), UNSC, New York, 19 June.
—— 2008b, *Women and peace and security*, report of the Secretary-General, S/2008/622, UNSC, New York, 25 September.
—— 2009a, *Women and peace and security*, report of the Secretary-General, S/2009/465 UNSC, New York, 16 September.
—— 2009b, *Resolution 1888 (2009) [on women and peace and security]*, S/RES/1888 (2009), UNSC, New York, 30 September.
—— 2009c, *Resolution 1889 (2009) [on women and peace and security]*, S/RES/1889 (2009), UNSC, New York, 5 October.
—— 2010a, *Women and peace and security*, report of the Secretary-General, S/2010/498, UNSC, New York, 28 September.
——2010b, *Cross-cutting report on women, peace and security*, UNSC Report No. 2, UNSC, New York, 1 October.
UN Secretariat 1992, *An agenda for peace: preventive diplomacy, peacemaking and peacekeeping*, report of the Secretary-General, A/47/277 – S/24111, UN Secretariat, New York, 17 June.
—— 1999, *Bulletin observance by United Nations forces of international humanitarian law*, ST/SGB/1999/13, UN Secretariat, New York, 6 August.
—— 2003, *Bulletin special measures for protection from sexual exploitation and sexual abuse*, ST/SGB/2003/13, UN Secretariat, New York, 9 October.
USAID n.d., *Women take their place in government*, USAID, <www.usaid.gov/stories/cambodia/ss_cambodia_government.html>.

Online references
(Accessed January 2009 – September 2011)
African Department of Defence 2009, *Bulletin: Department of Defence*, African Department of Defence, <www.dcc.mil.za/bulletins/Files/2009/40bulletin2009.pdf>.
America.gov 2007, *Maldives woman spearheads reform, pushes for women's rights*, America.gov, <www.america.gov/st/democracyht-english/2007/March/20070308151814ajesrom0.5691492.html>.
Amnesty International 2009, *Sri Lanka: displaced now trapped between the military and the impending monsoon*, Amnesty International, <www.amnesty.org/en/for-media/press-releases/sri-lanka-displaced-now-trapped-between-military-and-impending-monsoon-2>.
Anderson, I 2005, *Fragile states: what is international experience telling us?*, AusAID, Australian Government, <www.ausaid.gov.au/publications/pdf/fragile_states.pdf>.

Asian Development Bank 2006, *Republic of the Fiji Islands: country gender assessment*, Asian Development Bank, <www.adb.org/Documents/Reports/Country-Gender-Assessments/fij.asp>.

ASK 2009, 'National Parliamentary election in Bangladesh: a perspective from women representation', *Breaking the Silence*, 3, <www.sapint.org/newsletter/newsletter3/through-gendered-lens.html>.

AusAID 2007b, *Women in blue*, AusAID, Australian Government, <www.ausaid.gov.au/closeup/women_in_blue.cfm>.

—— 2010b, *Fiji*, AusAID, Australian Government, <www.ausaid.gov.au/country/country.cfm?CountryId=15>.

BBC News 2007, *Sri Lanka to probe UN sex claims*, BBC News, http://news.bbc.co.uk/2/hi/south_asia/7076284.stm.

Bell, C & O'Rourke, C n.d., *The transitional justice peace agreements database*, International Conflict Research Institute, <www.peaceagreements.ulster.ac.uk>.

Bhagwan-Rolls, S n.d., *Use of community radio to encourage women's involvement in peace building and conflict resolution*, AMARC, <www.amarc.org/documents/articles/Use_of_CR.pdf>.

—— 2006b, *Security Council Resolution 1325: national implementation of women, peace and security – ways forward*, NGO Working Group on Women, Peace and Security, <www.womenpeacesecurity.org/media/doc-waysforward.doc>.

Bhutan Women and Children Organisation n.d., *Status of women in Bhutan*, Bhutan Women and Children Organisation, <www.wspacework.net/n_w/pol_net.htm>.

CAVR n.d., *Women and Chega: making recommendations reality*, CAVR, <www.cavr-timorleste.org/updateFiles/english/Dissemination/Women%20and%20Chega.pdf>.

—— 2005, *Chega! The report of the Commission for Reception, Truth, and Reconciliation Timor-Leste*, East Timor and Indonesia Action Network, <www.etan.org/news/2006/cavr.htm>.

CENWOR 2001, *Sri Lanka shadow report on the UN CEDAW*, International Women's Rights Action Watch Asia Pacific, <www.iwraw-ap.org/using_cedaw/srilanka.doc>.

Coalition to Stop the Use of Child Soldiers 2008, *Child soldiers global report 2008*, Coalition to Stop the Use of Child Soldiers, <www.childsoldiersglobalreport.org>.

Crook, M 2009, *The quality of women is very important*, Inter Press Service News Agency, <http://ipsnews.net/print.asp?idnews=48535>.

Fawcett Society 1997, *Fawcett briefing: the four C's*, Fawcett Society, <www.fawcettsociety.org.uk/documents/The_four_Cs(1).pdf>.

Fearon, K 2002, *Northern Ireland Women's Coalition: institutionalizing a political voice and ensuring representation*, Conciliation Resources, <www.c-r.org/our-work/accord/public-participation/ni-womens-coalition.php>.

Forum-Asia: Asian Forum for Human Rights and Development 2008, *Shaping progress and standing up for human rights*, Forum-Asia, <www.forum-asia.org/index.php?option=com_content&task=view&id=1546&Itemid=132>.

FWRM, FWCC & Ecumenical Centre for Research Education and Advocacy 2002, *NGO report on the status of women in the Republic of the Fiji Islands*, International Women's Rights Action Watch Asia Pacific, <www.iwraw-ap.org/using_cedaw/fiji.doc>.

Global Peacebuilders 2008, *Peace: approaches to peacebuilding*, Global Peacebuilders, <www.globalpeacebuilders.org/english/peacebuilding.html>.

Government of Liberia 2010, *The Liberia national action plan for the implementation of United Nations Resolution 1325*, UNDP, <www.undp.org/cpr/documents/gender/lnap_gender.pdf>.

Government of the Republic of Fiji 2010, *Statement by the Minister for Social Welfare, Women & Poverty Alleviation: 54th session of the Commission on the Status of Women*, Permanent Mission of Fiji to the United Nations, <www.fijiprun.org/index.php?option=com_content&view=article&id=108,54th-csw&catid=24,commission-on-the-status-of-women&Itemid=19>.

Gun Free South Africa 2009, *Gender-based violence project WC and KZN*, Gun Free South Africa, <www.gca.org.za/OurProjects/GenderBasedViolenceProjectWC/tabid/1803/language/en-US/Default.aspx>.

Human Rights Watch 2009, *Sri Lanka: tensions mount as camp conditions deteriorate*, Human Rights Watch, <www.hrw.org/en/news/2009/10/09/sri-lanka-tensions-mount-camp-conditions-deteriorate>.

Hunt, S 2007, *Let women rule*, Foreign Affairs, <www.foreignaffairs.com/articles/62617/swanee-hunt/let-women-rule>.

IANWGE n.d., *Taskforce on women, peace and security*, Inter-Agency Network on Women and Gender Equality, <www.un.org/womenwatch/ianwge/taskforces/wps/history.html>.

IDEA 2009, *Nepal*, International Institute for Democracy and Electoral Assistance, <www.idea.int/asia_pacific/nepal>.

IHR 2009, *Human rights education and training*, IHR, <http://ihrsrilanka.org/category/human-right>.

International Association of Women Judges n.d., *What we do*, International Association of Women Judges, <www.iawj.org/what/other.asp>.

International Women's Tribune Centre n.d., *Women talk peace*, International Women's Tribune Centre, <www.iwtc.org/2983/index.html>.

Inter-Parliamentary Union 2010, *Women in national Parliaments*, Inter-Parliamentary Union, <www.ipu.org/wmn-e/world.htm>.

IRIN News 2008, *Sri Lanka: violence against women on the rise*, IRIN News, <www.irinnews.org/Report.aspx?ReportId=81693>.

Isis: Women's International Cross Cultural Exchange n.d., *Programmes*, Isis: WICCE, <www.isis.or.ug/programmes>.

IWDA 2009, *Trauma healing and stress management*, IWDA, <www.iwda.org.au/au/programs/promote-safety-security/trauma-domestic-violence>.

Karama 2009, *Towards an enhanced participation of women in decision-making positions in the Arab world*, Karama, <www.el-karama.org/sites/default/files/Policy%20Paper-%20English_0.pdf>.

Kaushik, S 2008, 'Women in democratic governance: a south Asian experience', *Breaking the Silence*, 2, <www.sapint.org/newsletter/newsletter2/outlook.html>.

Kinoti, K 2009, *Setbacks to democracy in Fiji: women's experiences*, Association for Women's Rights in Development, <www.awid.org/Library/Setbacks-to-democracy-in-Fiji-Women-s-experiences>.

Kodikara, C 2008, *Women and politics in Sri Lanka: the challenges to meaningful participation*, Groundviews, <http://groundviews.org/2008/09/02/women-and-politics-in-sri-lanka-the-challenges-to-meaningful-participation>.

Kofe, SS & Taomia, F n.d., *Advancing women's political participation in Tuvalu*, Pacific Islands Forum Secretariat, <www.forumsec.org.fj/resources/uploads/attachments/documents/Report_5_-_Advancing_Women_s_Representation_in_Tuvalu_209_-_255.pdf>.

Kunarac, Dragoljub n.d., The Hague Justice Portal, <www.haguejusticeportal.net/eCache/DEF/6/082.html>.

Latin American Security & Defense Network 2009, *Challenges and opportunities in peace operations: the incorporation of women*, Peacewomen, <www.peacewomen.org/resources/Peacekeeping/Resdal_brochure_eng.pdf>.

Lechte, R 2009, *Ruth Lechte, veteran activist, on crisis in Fiji*, Women Leading Change, <http://womenleadingchange.wordpress.com/2009/04/27/ruth-lechte-veteran-activist-on-crisis-in-fiji>.

Malik, A 2007, 'Woman Minister killed by fanatic', *Dawn*, <www.dawn.com/2007/02/21/top2.htm>.

Mallick, K 2006, 'India's Women Peace Corps: embodying Gandhi's idea for a peace army', *PeaceWork*, 368, <www.peaceworkmagazine.org/india-s-women-s-peace-corps-embodying-gandhi-s-idea-peace-army>.

Ministry for Women and Culture, Republic of Fiji 1998, *The Women's Plan of Action 1999-2008*, UNESCAP, <www.unescap.org/esid/psis/population/database/poplaws/law_fiji/fiji_017.htm>.

Mohanty, M 2005, 'Globalisation, new labour migration and development in Fiji: the changing nature of labour migration in Fiji', in S Firth (ed.), *Globalisation and governance in the Pacific Islands*, Australian National University E Press, Canberra, <http://epress.anu.edu.au/ssgm/global_gov/mobile_devices/ch06s06.html#d0e2342>.

Mojumdar, A 2010, *Afghanistan: women's rights movement slowly taking shape in Kabul*, Eurasianet.org, <www.eurasianet.org/departments/civilsociety/articles/eav030810a.shtml>.

NGO Working Group on Women, Peace and Security 2008, *Women's equal participation and full involvement in all efforts for the maintenance and promotion of peace and security*, statement at the UN Open Debate, NGO Working Group on Women, Peace and Security, <www.womenpeacesecurity.org/media/pdf-2008_October_29_Security_Council_Open_Debate_Statement.pdf>.

Page, M, Whitman, T & Anderson, C 2009, *Strategies for policymakers: bringing women into peace negotiations*, Hunt Alternatives Fund, <www.huntalternatives.org/pages/8105_strategies_for_policymakers_bringing_women_into_peace_negotiations.cfm>.

PeaceWomen n.d., *Security Council Resolution 1325 – local language translations*, PeaceWomen, <http://peacewomen.org/translation_initiative/security-council-resolution-1325>.

—— 2010, *National commitments on SCR 1325*, PeaceWomen, <http://peacewomen.org/commitments>.

Pearson, E 2008, *Demonstrating legislative leadership: the introduction of Rwanda's gender-based violence bill*, Initiative for Inclusive Security, Hunt Alternatives Fund, <www.huntalternatives.org/download/1078_demonstrating_legislative_leadership.pdf>.

PIFS 2005, *The Pacific plan for strengthening regional cooperation and integration*, Pacific Islands Forum Secretariat <www.forumsec.org.fj/resources/uploads/attachments/documents/Pacific_Plan_Nov_2007_version.pdf>.

Porter, E 2005, 'Women and security: "you cannot dance if you cannot stand"', *Open-Democracy*, 19 October, 50.50 Inclusive Democracy, <www.opendemocracy.net/democracy-resolution_1325/dancc_2937.jsp>.

PPC 2009a, *Who we are*, Pearson Peacekeeping Centre, <www.peaceoperations.org/web/la/en/pa/25D32889DA43494098B2BAA8F3D3F4FA/template.asp>.

—— 2009b, *Female UNPOL officers participate in Secretary General report*, Pearson Peacekeeping Centre, <www.peaceoperations.org/_CMS/Files/MA_UNPOLper cent20Officers_ENper cent20per cent28PDFper cent29.pdf>.

—— 2009c, *Seminar report: women in peace operations*, Pearson Peacekeeping Centre, <www.peaceoperations.org/wp-content/uploads/2010/02/Seminar-Report_Women-in-POs_Zambia-Oct.09.pdf>.

Puechguirbal, N 2008, 'Gender and peacekeeping: a few challenges', *Peace and Conflict Monitor*, <www.monitor.upeace.org/printer.cfm?id_article=505>.

Rothschild, C (ed.) 2005, *Written out: how sexuality is used to attack women's organising*, Center for Women's Global Leadership, <www.cwgl.rutgers.edu/globalcenter/publications/written2005.pdf>.

Samath, F 2010, *First political manifesto for women in Sri Lanka*, Inter Press Service News Agency, <http://ipsnews.net/news.asp?idnews=50787>.

Schoetzau, B 2007, *Women peacekeepers can work with female victims, set example for male colleagues*, 51VOA, <www.51voa.com/voa_standard_english/VOA_Standard_10680.html>.

Secretariat for Coordinating the Peace Process 2009, *Monthly Bulletin*, July, Peace and Reconciliation: Unity and Prosperity, <www.peaceinsrilanka.org/userfiles/file/Final%20Bulletin.pdf>.

Skjelsbæk, I 2007, *Gender aspects of international military interventions: national and international perspectives*, Peace Research Institute Oslo, <www.prio.no/files/file49891_gender_aspects_of_international_military_interventions.pdf>.

South-South Opportunity Case Stories n.d., *Ireland-Liberia-Timor Leste – trilateral learning on women, peace and security*, Impact Alliance, <www.impactalliance.org/ev02.php?ID=49071_201&ID2=DO_TOPIC>.

Srinivasan, A 2009, *A survey of civil society peace education programmes in South Asia*, Educational Policy Research Series, Prajnya Initiatives for Peace, Justice and Security, <www.prajnya.in/eprsI2.pdf>.

Sterling, SR, O'Brien, J & Bennett, JK 2007, *AIR: advancement through interactive radio*, Computer Science, University of Colorado, <www.cs.colorado.edu/department/publications/reports/docs/CU-CS-1006-06.pdf>.

Styles-Power, C, Hamilton, C & Hall, E 2008, *The VPU in Timor-Leste: an independent assessment of its role and function*, Technical Paper Series, UNICEF Timor-Leste,

<http://webapps01.un.org/vawdatabase/uploads/Timor%20Leste%20-%20VPU%20Report%20UNICEF.pdf>.
UN n.d., *Secretary-General's Panel of Experts on Sri Lanka*, UN, <www.un.org/en/rights/srilanka.shtml>.
US Department of State n.d., *Bureau of East Asian and Pacific Affairs*, US Department of State, <www.state.gov/p/eap>.
US Institute of Peace 2011, *Truth Commission Digital Collection*, US Institute of Peace, <www.usip.org/publications/truth-commission-digital-collection>.
WACky Peace 2009, 3, December, International Women's Development Agency Inc., <www.iwda.org.au/au/2009/12/01/women%E2%80%99s-action-for-change-releases-september-2009-peacebuilding-newsletter-%E2%80%93-wacky-peace>.
Women and Media Collective n.d., *Gender Based Violence Forum (GBV Forum)*, Women and Media Collective, <www.womenandmedia.net/network/GBV_FORUM.htm>.
Women for Prosperity n.d., *Country background*, Women for Prosperity, <http://wfpcambodia.org/country_bg.htm>.
Women in International Security n.d., *Programs*, Women in International Security, <wiis.georgetown.edu/programs>.
Women's International League for Peace and Freedom 2007, *UN rights expert welcomes appointment of first female judges in the Maldives*, 1325 Australia, <www.1325australia.org.au/html/femaleJudge.html>.
WUNRN 2011, *Nepal adopts national action plan on UN SC Res 1325 & 1820*, Women's UN Report Network, 10 February, <www.wunrn.com/news/2011/02_11/02_07/020711_nepal.htm>.

Index

Aakar, 74
access to justice, 6, 18, 38, 54, 142 *see also* transitional justice
    Afghanistan, in, 68
    criticism of initiatives, 75–6
    feminist approach, 23–5, 75–6
    Fiji, in, 215
    gender-responsive judicial systems, 61, 65–6
    JSMP, 180–1
    Nepal, in, 67
    PNG, in, 67–8
    policing reforms, 68
    protection from violence, nexus with, 63–70
    Solomon Islands, in, 66
    Sri Lanka, in, 228–30
    support services, affordable, 68–9
    Timor-Leste, in, 65–6, 175, 176, 177, 180–1, 192, 202
    traditional justice systems, 67–8, 178, 179
    truth and reconciliation commissions, 64–6
    UNSCR 1889, 142
activism *see also* affirmative action
    Sri Lanka, in, 227
    UNSCRs as basis, 35–6
affirmative action
    advantages, 128–9
    gender-inclusive peace and, 131
    political involvement of women, 120, 127–31, 136, 214, 228, 235, 237–8

Afghan Women's Summit, 124
Afghanistan
    empowerment of women, initiatives for, 165
    peace process, women's participation in, 124
    policing reforms, 68
Annan, Kofi
    empowerment of women, 25
    gender perspective on peacekeeping, 82–3, 156
    Kofi Annan International Peacekeeping Training Centre, 101
    protection of citizens during conflict, 55
armed conflict, 253–4, 255 *see also* conflict; war
    change in nature, 11, 12
    civilians, effect on, 12, 37–8, 55–6, 57
    concern under BPFA, 34
    Declaration on the Protection of Women and Children in Emergency and Armed Conflict, 55
    gendered nature, 15–16, 19
    global locations, 11, 12–13
    poverty, nexus with, 13–14
    reasons, 11–12
    sexual violence, 18, 58
    UN reports, 55–6
    war, 12

armed conflict (*Cont.*)
  women and children as participants,
    16, 21–2, 79, 103, 202–3
AusAID
  Fmali Seif hotline, 69
  Male Advocates Program, 74
  peacebuilding, 72
  RAMSI Law and Justice Program, 66
  UNSCR 1325 project, 2
  Violence against women in Melanesia and East Timor report, 199, 201–2
  women's rights workshops, 204

Beijing Declaration, 252
Beijing Platform for Action 1995 (BPFA), 34, 55, 114–15, 171

CARE International, 165
Commission for Reception, Truth and Reconciliation (CAVR), 65–6, 175, 178, 189
Commission on the Status of Women, 55
conflict *see also* armed conflict; war
  capacity development approach, 73
  Fiji, in, 196
  human toll of, 10
  injustice, relevance of, 63
  prevention and protection of citizens, 54–6, 58, 62, 70–4, 95
  Sri Lanka, in, 225–6
  Timor-Leste, in, 168–71
  UNSCR 1325, approach to, 35
Convention on the Elimination of All Forms of Discrimination against Women 1979 (CEDAW), 34, 71, 255–6
  Optional Protocol 1999, 34
  Sri Lankan ratification, 228
  Timor-Leste, in, 176–7
  women's participation in decision-making, 114–15, 123, 129, 139
crimes against humanity, 34 *see also* Sexual and gender based violence (SGBV); war crimes
  R2P approach, 57

culture
  empowerment of women, nexus with, 7–8, 10, 21, 25–6, 191

decision-making, women's participation in, 6–7, 8, 20, 62, 70–1, 77, 164, 253, 254
  activism and affirmative action, 120, 127–31, 136, 214, 227–8, 235, 237–8
  CEDAW strategies, 114–15
  challenges, 123–4, 132, 137–40, 212–13
  critical mass of women, 117
  data, 115–16
  Fiji, in, 206–15, 220
  good governance, for, 111
  participation, nature of, 114
  peace process, in *see* peace negotiations
  principles and priorities, 112–15
  reasons for involvement, 111–12, 117–21, 132–7
  Sri Lanka, in, 233–40
  Timor-Leste, in, 172, 173, 184–91
  UNSCR 1325, under, 35, 77, 114–15, 139
Declaration on Participation of Women in Promoting International Peace and Cooperation, 114
Declaration on the Elimination of Violence against Women 1993, 55
Declaration on the Protection of Women and Children in Emergency and Armed Conflict, 55
'developing regions', 13
Dili Declaration on Women, Peace and Security, 173, 177, 192
disarmament, demobilisation and reintegration (DDR), 37, 58, 79, 84, 119, 139, 145, 160
  Fiji, in, 205, 217
  gender-responsive programs, 79, 91, 107
  Sri Lanka, in, 246–7

domestic violence
  Fiji, in, 196, 199–201
  militarised cultures, in, 17
  Timor-Leste, in, 171, 175–6, 177, 178–9, 182, 183, 184, 192

empowerment of women, 7
  culturally-sensitive, 7–8, 11, 21, 25–6
  examples of initiatives, 164–6
  feminist approach, 25–6, 162
  framework levels, 163–4
  goal, 162
  human rights context, 191
  Islamic states, in, 163
  meaning, 25, 163, 165
  relief and recovery, relevance to, 161–6
  UN Secretary-General Kofi Annan's statement, 25
  UN Women see UN Entity for Gender Equality and Empowerment of Women (UN Women)
  understanding, 162–3
  welfare focus, effect of, 164
ethnic cleansing, 17

feminism
  emancipation goals, 28
  empowerment of women, 25–6, 162
  femLINKpacific policy, 27
  gender equality and justice, 23–5
  gender-mainstreaming, 155
  human security, 26–9
  legal theory and practice training initiative, 73
  methodology, 21–2
  peacebuilding, 29–32
  presumption on universality, 77–8
  transitional justice mechanisms, criticism of, 75–6
  'use-value' of women, 25
Fiji, 195–223
  access to justice, 215
  Bottom-Up Governance Leadership Program, 207
  challenges, 212–13, 219–23
  conflict and insecurity, 196
  DDR process, 205, 217
  decision-making and politics, women's participation in, 206–15, 220
  domestic violence, 196, 199–201
  femLINKpacific, 27, 36, 208–9, 211, 213
  funding of initiatives, issues regarding, 221–3
  FWCC, 74, 199, 200, 203, 213
  FWRM, 73, 203, 206, 208, 210, 211, 212–13, 216
  GDI rank, 196
  gender roles and equality, 196, 200, 202, 203, 205, 214–15
  interviews, 8
  leadership initiatives, 210–12
  Male Advocates Program, 74
  media, 220–1
  military culture, issues regarding, 203–5, 217
  Pacific Plan, 197
  peace and security dialogue initiatives, 198, 206, 208–10, 212, 220
  peace education program, 218–19
  peacekeeping, 202–5
  PIFS, 198, 222
  politics, 196
  relief and recovery initiatives, 215–19
  trauma management, 202, 203, 204
  UNSCR 1325 implementation, 196–8
  violence, protection and prevention from, 198–202
  WIP program, 207
  women's movement, 210
  women's organisations, 198, 214, 219–20
  WPS Fiji CC, 196–7, 217
Fiji Women's Crisis Centre (FWCC), 74, 199, 200, 203, 213
Fiji Women's Rights Movement (FWRM), 73, 203, 206, 208, 210, 211, 212–13, 216

Formed Police Unit (FPU), 92–3, 103–4, 154

gender
    DDR programs, relevance to, 79
    feminist approach *see* feminism
    peacekeeping, relevance to, 84, 92, 104–10
    perception of term, 190–1
    power relations, 76, 78, 79, 112, 118, 146, 151–2, 163, 200
    use of term, 21
Gender Action for Peace and Security (GAPS)
    UNSCR 1325 monitoring, 46–7, 160
Gender Advisers, 46–7, 52, 59, 104–5, 106, 114, 116, 137, 154, 156, 174, 222
    GenCap program, under, 156
    personal account, 87, 180, 186, 192
    PKOs, for, 91, 94
    relief and recovery efforts, 192
    traditional justice systems, in, 180
gender and development (GAD) approach, 145–6, 148, 154, 184, 190
Gender Development Index (GDI), 28, 196, 225
gender equality
    emancipation goals, 28
    feminist approach, 23–5
    Fiji, in, 196
    gender-mainstreaming, nexus with, 150, 157–8, 166
    meaning, 23
    monitoring checklist, 160
    peace, nexus with, 15
    peacebuilding and peacekeeping, 30–1, 89, 95, 154
    priority and importance, 10, 112
    respect and dignity, 23
    rights-based approach, alignment with, 117–18
    Standardised Indicator of Gender Equality Strategies measures, 23
    Timor-Leste, in, 168, 170, 172, 174, 182, 184, 186, 189–90, 191, 193

UN Women *see* UN Entity for Gender Equality and Empowerment of Women (UN Women)
    UNSCR 1325 approach, criticism of, 45
gender inequality
    feminist approach, 23–5
    peace, nexus with, 15
gender-mainstreaming, 7, 94, 253
    deficits, 152–3
    feminist perspective, 155
    GenCap initiative, 156
    gender equality, nexus with, 150, 157–8, 166
    gender-sensitive approach, 152
    goal, 150
    'mainstream', 150
    models, 51
    patriarchal inequality, 153
    peace agreements, 153
    PKOs, application to, 102–4, 153–4, 156
    politics and, 154–5
    post-conflict peacebuilding process, 38
    principles, 150–1
    relief and recovery, relevance to, 150–8
    state involvement, 155–6
    three-pronged approach, 157–8
    UNDP initiative, 67
    UNSCR 1325, under, 37, 51
    women-specific approach, 157
gender-sensitive early warning systems
    benefits, 72
    criticism of standard systems, 71
    Solomon Islands, in, 72–3
gender-sensitive training
    benchmarks, 102
    definition, 94–5
    examples, 96–9
    gender-sensitive approach, 96–102
    male involvement, 100–1
    peacekeepers and PKOs, for, 81, 94–104, 106–7, 205, 231

pre-deployment, 95–6, 108–9, 205
principles, 99–100
purpose, 95
Gender Standby Capacity Project (GenCap), 156
gendered insecurities, 15–19
    armed conflict, 15–16
    domestic violence, 17
    ethnic cleansing, 17
    examples, 17–18
    measures, 27
    resilience, 19–20
    sexual violence, 17, 18–19
Geneva Convention 1949, 34, 255
    Additional Protocols 1977, 34
global insecurities 4, 10, 11–14 *see also* human security
    armed conflict, 11–12
    causes, 26–7
    fragility of states, 13
    poverty, 13–14, 26
Global Peace Index
    peace, defections of, 14
    rankings, 14–15

HIV/AIDS
    awareness training, 254–5
    gendered insecurity, 17
    sexual violence and, 18
human development
    measure of goals, 28
    Sri Lanka, in, 225
    Timor-Leste, in, 170–1
human rights, 255
    cultural and religious influences and, 191
    emancipation goal, 28
    female ex-combatants, concerns for, 79
    human security, nexus with, 112
    impunity for violations, 69–70, 80, 178
    interrogation methods, 'sexualisation' of, 78
    measures of security, 27
    monitoring checklist, 160

political instability and, 51
Timor-Leste, violations in, 175
Women for Human Rights, 69
human security *see also* global insecurities
    aims, 28–9
    causes, 26–7
    concept, framing of, 54
    development of concept, 26
    feminist approach, 26–9
    gender-inclusive approach, 143, 144–9, 194
    gender-specific threats, 54
    gendered views, 86
    human rights, nexus with, 112
    measures, 27
    nature, 144–5, 192
    rights-based approach, 148
    'soft issue', as, 112
    traditional focus, 26
    violence, protection from, 54–5, 192–3 *see also* violence, protection from

indigenous processes for conflict resolution, 57, 71, 115, 141 255
internally displaced persons (IDPs), 51–2, 161, 226, 232, 239, 244–5
International Civil Society Action Network, 51–2
International Colloquium 2009, 61
International Commission on Intervention and State Sovereignty (ICSS), 56
International Committee of the Red Cross (ICRC)
    protection from violence model, 62–3
    role, 5
International Criminal Court (ICC)
    Rome Statute *see* Rome Statute of the International Criminal Court
International Criminal Tribunal for Rwanda (ICTR), 60
International Criminal Tribunal for the former Yugoslavia, 59–60

International Force for East Timor (INTERFET), 169–70
interrogation methods
   'sexualisation' of, 78

Judicial System Monitoring Programme (JSMP), 180–1
jus ad bellum, 57
jus in bello, 57

Ki-moon, Ban
   gender-mainstreaming initiatives, acknowledgment of, 156
Kofi Annan International Peacekeeping Training Centre, 101

land mines
   clearing and awareness, 253
   gendered insecurity, 18
leadership *see also* decision-making, women's participation in; political participation by women
   Bottom-Up Governance Leadership Program, 207
   fragile states, 13
   gender equality, 24, 31
   levels, 20
   peacebuilding and, 23–4
   skills and training, 23
   women's participation, 3, 31, 129–30, 134, 137–8, 186, 187–9, 207, 211–12, 213, 234, 239–40, 244, 250
liberal peace theory, 146
Liberation Tigers of Tamil Eelan (LTTE), 224, 225, 226, 231, 233, 241
Liberia
   International Colloquium, 61
   NAP, 41–2, 73–4, 155–6, 174–5
   relief and recovery, women's participation in, 159
   UNMIL, 91–3

marginalisation of women, 10, 47, 58, 70, 121
masculinist militarism, 85–90, 202–3

media 126
   civic education program, 74
   influence on public opinion, 220–1
   limited access, effect of, 188
   political participation, promotion of, 234–5, 236
   rights awareness, role in, 73
   WMC, 229, 234, 235, 237, 238
Millennium Development Goals 2000 (MDGs), 14, 34
MIT Centre for International Studies, 51–2

Nagorik Uddyog, 67
National action plans (NAPs), 4, 41–3, 161
   Afghanistan, in, 68
   Australia, draft, 48, 161
   cross-learning project, 174–5
   evaluation, 43–5
   gender-responsive framework, 79–80
   Liberia, in, 41–2, 73–4, 155–6
   Nepal, in, 42–3
   peacekeeping reforms and, 108
   Philippines, in, 42
   policing reforms, 68
   Sri Lanka, draft, 226
   UNSC role, 41
   zero tolerance for sexual violence, 70
National Democratic Institute (NDI), 129, 133–4, 135
Nepal
   access to justice initiatives, 67
   Changing Our World radio program, 73
   female combatants, 103
   NAP, 42–3
   politics and peace processes, women's participation in, 121–2, 126–7, 128–9
   post-conflict program development, 73
   sexual violence support services, 69
non-combatant immunity, 57
Non-government organisation (NGO), 8
see also individual organisations

anti-violence initiatives, 74
  Fiji, in, 196–7
  gender-sensitive early warning
    systems, 72
  global activism, 35
  peace-keeping role, 20
  Sri Lanka, in, 229, 233, 247, 248
  Timor-Leste, in, 173, 190
  UNSCR 1325, support of, 43
Northern Ireland Women's Coalition
  (NIWC), 125–6

Observance by UN Forces of
  International Humanitarian Law,
  61
Office of the Special Adviser on Gender
  Issues
  UN Women, amalgamation under,
    49
Office of the UN High Commissioner
  for Refugees (UNHCR), 255
  role, 5
Oxfam Australia, 72

Pacific Centre for Peacebuilding (PCP),
  203–5
Pacific Island Forum Secretariat (PIFS),
  198, 222
Pacific Plan, 197
Papua New Guinea (PNG)
  National Law and Justice Policy and
    Plan of Action 2000, 67–8
  sexual violence support services, 69
  Stop Violence Centres, 69
  traditional justice reforms, 67–8
Paris Declaration on Aid Effectiveness
  2005
  conflict and poverty nexus, 14
  relief and recovery principles, 145
peace
  definition, 14
  emancipation goal, 28
  feminist approach, 21–32
  indicia, 27
  'liberal peace approach', 29
  'negative peace', 14

'positive peace', 14
school education programs, 218–19,
  242–3
Sri Lankan perceptions, 240–2
sustainable peace, 2, 4, 7, 14, 20, 23,
  28, 38, 52, 64, 82, 95, 118, 119,
  137, 144, 188, 219, 248
peace agreements
  challenges to women's involvement,
    124
  examples of durable, 119–20, 126
  female signatories, 116
  gender-mainstreaming, application
    of, 153
  gender-neutral language, 119
  gendered peace agreement, 119
  references to women, 122–3
peace negotiations, women's
  participation in, 6–7, 10, 19–20, 52,
    71, 76, 122–6
  Afghanistan, in, 124
  challenges, 123–4, 132, 137–40
  critical mass of women, 117
  equality-based approach, 117–18,
    119, 121
  grassroots, 116, 123, 138, 139, 168
  impunity for human rights
    violations, treatment of, 69–70,
    76
  legitimacy issues, 125–6
  mediators, as, 116
  nature of involvement, 121–2
  Northern Ireland, 125–6
  rights-based approach, 118–19
  Sri Lanka, in, 233–4
  'track 1' peace processes, 115–16
  'track 2' peace processes, 116
  traditional role and view of women,
    123
  UNSCR 1325, aim of, 37
  value, 120
'peace table'
  discussions, nature of, 122
  women's participation, 113, 122,
    140 *see also* peace negotiations,
    women's participation in

peacebuilding 3, 4, 10, 11, 14, 72
  definition, 29
  examples, 27
  feminist approach, 29–32
  informal involvement, 45
  'post-conflict', paired with, 30
  successful, 120
  UN leaders, involvement of, 47
  UNSCR 1325, under, 35, 36, 37
  variations, 29
  women's contributions and involvement, 45–6, 52, 113, 139
peaceful societies, 14–15
peacekeeping, 254
  'blue helmets', 103–4
  female ex-combatants' role, 85–6
  Fiji, in, 202–5
  gender-responsive approach, 84, 92, 104–10
  gender-sensitive training, 81, 94–104, 106–7, 205, 231
  masculinist militarism, 85–90, 202–3
  military role, 11
  NAPs, 108
  nature, 6, 84, 106–7
  peacekeepers as perpetrators, 88
  policing role, 86, 92–3
  PPC, 98–9
  Sri Lanka, in, 231–2
  Timor-Leste, in, 96–7, 181–4
  traditional role and view of women, 87, 88
  Training for Peace Project, 97–8
  UNSCR 1325 directives and implementation, 82–3, 93, 94, 105–9
  women's participation, 81, 86–9, 90–4, 102–, 102–4, 105–7, 231–2
peacekeeping operations (PKOs), 30
  definition, 83
  Fiji, in *see* Fiji
  gender equality, 89, 105–10
  gender-mainstreaming, application of, 102–4, 153–4, 156
  MONUC, 90–1, 106
  multidimensional, 83–94
  SGBV, prevention and perpetration of, 59, 87–8, 89, 95, 99, 100, 101–2, 231
  Sri Lanka, in *see* Sri Lanka
  Timor-Leste, in *see* Timor-Leste
  types, 83–4
  UN Department *see* UN Department of Peace-keeping Operations (UNDPKO)
  UN-INSTRAW, 94, 96, 99–101
  UNMIL, 91–3
  UNOMSA, 90, 91
  UNPOL, 83, 86, 93, 99, 156, 183, 184
  UNSCR 1410, 170
  UNTAET, 170, 171, 177, 178, 182
  'use-value' approach, 87, 89
Pearson Peacekeeping Centre (PPC), 98–9
Philippines, the
  anti-violence initiative, 74
  NAP, 42
  policing reforms, 68
political participation by women
  activism and affirmative action, 120, 127–31, 136, 214, 227–8, 235, 237–8
  barriers, 132–3, 138, 187–8
  capacity development programs, 133–4, 137
  Fiji, in, 206–7, 212–14
  global comparison, 128
  grassroots involvement, 194, 236, 238
  minimum representation, 133
  nature of involvement, 121–2, 126–7
  Nepal, in, 121–2, 126–9
  Northern Ireland, in, 125
  post-conflict reconstruction, 85, 117
  Rwanda, 127–8, 136
  Sri Lanka, in, 234–40
  Timor-Leste, in, 172, 173, 184–91
  UNSCR 1325, under, 107, 134
  voter registration and education, 130–1
  women's caucuses, 135–7, 156, 172, 173, 186, 237, 238

poverty
    armed conflict, nexus with, 13–14
    global insecurity, cause of, 26
    reduction initiatives, 172

Refugee Convention 1951, 255
refugees, 226, 253 *see also* internally displaced persons (IDPs)
Regional Assistance Mission to Solomon Islands (RAMSI)
    criticism, 137
    Law and Justice Program, 66
relief and recovery
    community involvement and local wisdom, 146–7
    development concept, 146
    empowerment of women, relevance to, 161–6
    Fiji, in, 215–19
    founding principle, 143
    gender-inclusive security, 143, 144–9, 194
    gender-specific, 8, 141–66
    indicators of progress, 158–61
    mainstreaming gender, 143, 150–8
    nature of, 141–2
    Paris Declaration on Aid Effectiveness principles, 145
    post-conflict reconstruction, 147–8
    rights-based approach, 143, 148
    SMART approach, 160
    'social services justice' initiatives, 148–9
    Solomon Islands, in, 147
    Sri Lanka, in, 240–6
    tasks, magnitude of, 149
    Timor-Leste, in, 192–4
    UNSCR 1325, under, 141
    UNSCR 1820, under, 141
    UNSCR 1888, under, 142
    UNSCR 1889, under, 142, 161
    women's rights and development, 144–9
Responsibility to Protect (R2P)
    framework, 56–8
    elements, 56
    purpose, 56–7

Rome Statute of the International Criminal Court 2002, 34, 256
    crimes, 34
    gender-inclusive justice, 35

Save the Children, 72
Secretary of State for Promotion of Equality (Timor-Leste), 183, 184–5, 186, 191
security *see* human security
Security sector reform (SSR), 6, 65, 78, 84, 120, 139, 142, 158, 160, 189, 217
    aim, 85
    challenges, 46, 85, 109
    gender-sensitive practices, 107, 189, 193
    policing, for, 78
    prevention of violence, 58
    UNSCR pillar, as, 31
Sexual and gender-based violence (SGBV), 35, 40
    access to justice, 69, 76
    conflict-related, 18, 58
    data collection and annual reporting, 61
    gendered-response, 78–9
    HIV/AIDS infections and, 18
    impunity of perpetrators, 40, 47, 69–70
    international response, 61
    men, against, 78
    militarised culture, in, 17, 18
    monitoring checklist, 160
    national and local response, 61–2
    peacekeeping and, 59, 87–8, 89, 95, 99, 100, 101–2, 107, 231
    policing reforms, 68
    protection against, 5, 24, 58–9, 87–8, 89, 228–9, 256
    rape, 59–61, 231
    Rome Statute of the International Criminal Court, under, 34
    security threat, as, 40, 198
    support services for women, 68–9
    UNSCR 1820, under, 40, 58, 61
    UNSCR 1888, under, 38, 58, 61

Sexual and gender-based violence (*Cont.*)
   UNSCR 1889, under, 58, 61
   war crimes prosecutions, 59–61
   weapon of war, as, 38, 76
   zero tolerance policy, 61, 70, 78, 156, 182
'sexual baiting', 201
sexual enslavement, 60, 79
Sinhala Tamil Rural Womens' Network (STRWN), 237, 241–2, 243, 247
Solomon Islands
   access to justice initiatives, 66
   gender-sensitive early warning system for violence, 72
   grassroots peace processes, women's involvement in, 116
   relief and recovery initiatives, 147
Solomon Islands Gendered Conflict Early Warning Project, 72
Solomon Islands Law Reform Commission (LRC), 66
Special Measures for Protection from Sexual Exploitation and Abuse, 61
Special Rapporteur on Torture, 55
Special Rapporteur on Violence against Women, 55
Sri Lanka, 224–51
   access to justice, 228–30
   activism and affirmative action, 227–8, 235, 237–8
   armed conflict, 11
   CEDAW, ratification of, 228
   challenges, 246–50
   conflict and insecurity, 225–6
   DDR process, 246–7
   decision-making and politics, women's participation in, 231–40
   female ex-combatants, support for, 246–7
   funding of initiatives, issues regarding, 248–50
   GDI rank, 225
   human development statistics, 225
   human security, 227
   IDPs, 226, 232, 239, 244–5
   interviews, 8
   leadership initiatives, 244
   Lessons Learnt and Reconciliation Commission, 232
   LTTE, 224, 225, 226, 231, 233, 241
   NAP, 226
   NGOs, 229, 233, 247, 248
   peace education program, 242–3
   peace, perceptions of, 240–2
   peacekeeping, 231–2
   relief and recovery initiatives, 240–6
   SGI, 226, 233–4
   STRWN, 237, 241–2, 243, 247
   training and capacity development programs, 238–9
   trauma management, 225, 227, 230–1
   UN Development Assistance Framework for Sri Lanka, 226–7
   UNSCR 1325 implementation, 226–7
   violence, protection and prevention from, 226, 227–31
   WMC, 229, 234, 235, 237, 238
Standardised Indicator of Gender Equality Strategies, 23
Sub-Committee for Gender Issues (Sri Lanka), 226, 233–4

terrorism, war against, 11
Timor-Leste, 167–94
   access to justice, 65–6, 175, 176, 177, 180–1, 192, 202
   adat justice system, 179
   CAVR, 65–6, 175, 178, 189
   CEDAW, implementation of, 176–7
   conflict and insecurity, 168–71
   criminal law development, 177–8
   cross-learning project for NAPs, 174–5
   decision-making and politics, women's participation in, 172, 173, 184–91
   Dili Declaration on Women, Peace and Security, 173, 177, 192

domestic violence, 171, 175–6, 177, 178–9, 182, 183, 184, 192–3
empowerment of women, 162–3, 172, 191
gender equality, 168, 170, 172, 174, 182, 184, 186, 189–90, 191, 193
gender-inclusive practices, 168, 194
gender-sensitive training, 96–7
grassroots activism, 168, 194
historical overview, 168–70
human development statistics, 170–1
human security, 192–3
independence, 169–70
INTERFET, 169–70
interviews, 8, 162–3
JSMP, 180–1
nation-building process, 171, 181–2, 186, 192, 193–4
NGOs, 173
peacekeeping, 87, 96–7, 181–4
policing reforms, 68
poverty reduction initiatives, 172
relief and recovery initiatives, 192–4
SEPI, 183, 184–5, 186, 191
Serious Crimes Unit, 65
Special Panel for Serious Crimes, 65
traditional and transitional justice, 65–6, 178–80, 194
UN Human Development Index ranking, 170
UNAMET, 169
UNMISET, 170
UNMIT, 84, 170, 173–4, 182–4, 186, 192
UNOTIL, 170
UNPOL, 183, 184
UNSCR 1324 implementation, 171–5
UNTAET, 170, 171, 177, 178, 182
Victim Support Division, 66
violence, protection and prevention from, 175–81
trafficking, human, 34–5, 169, 228
Training for Peace Project, 97–8
transitional justice mechanisms
challenges, 178

criticism, 75–6
definition, 63
purpose, 63–4
recommendation, 80
reconciliation and truth commissions, 64–6
truth and reconciliation commissions, 64
approaches, 65
CAVR, 65–6
examples, 64, 232

UN Department of Peace-keeping Operations (UNDPKO), 59, 87, 93–4, 154, 156, 183, 205
UN Development Assistance Framework for Sri Lanka, 226–7
UN Development Programmes (UNDP)
Liberian NAP, 41
Mainstreaming Gender Equity Programme, 67
UNDP 1994, 26
UN Division for the Advancement of Women (UNDAW)
UN Women, amalgamation under, 49
UN Entity for Gender Equality and Empowerment of Women (UN Women)
establishment, 49
role, 49
UN General Assembly (UNGA)
Declaration on Participation of Women in Promoting International Peace and Cooperation, 114
Declaration on the Protection of Women and Children in Emergency and Armed Conflict, 55
R2P framework, adoption of, 56
UN Human Development Index, 13
Timor-Leste, 170
UN Integrated Mission in Timor-Leste (UNMIT), 84, 170, 173–4, 182–4, 186, 192

UN International Research and Training Institute for the Advancement of Women (UN-INSTRAW), 94, 96, 99–101
   UN Women, amalgamation under, 49
UN Mission in East Timor (UNAMET), 169
UN Mission in Liberia (UNMIL), 91–3
UN Mission of Support in East Timor (UNMISET), 170
UN Observer Mission to South Africa (UNOMSA), 90, 91
UN Office in Timor-Leste (UNOTIL), 170
UN Organisation Mission in the Democratic Republic of the Congo (MONUC), 90–1, 106
UN Police (UNPOL), 83, 86, 93, 99, 156, 183, 184
UN Population Fund (UNFPA), 68, 183
UN Transitional Administration in East Timor (UNTAET), 170, 171, 177, 178, 182
United Nations (UN)
   barriers to female recruitment, 105
   'blue helmets' peacekeepers, 103–4
United Nations Charter, 252
   Article 41, 256
United Nations Children's Fund, 255
United Nations Convention on the Rights of the Child 1989, 256
United Nations Development Fund for Women (UNIFEM), 20
   'accountability gap', 43–4
   Fiji, in, 197, 199, 203–4, 207
   Liberia's NAP, 41
   peace negotiations, women's participation in, 20, 115–16, 120
   politics, women's participation in, 126
   Sri Lanka, in, 225–6
   Timor-Leste, in, 173, 183, 184–5, 186–7
   UN Women, amalgamation under, 49
   Women in Politics (WIP) program, 207
United Nations Fund for Women, 255
United Nations Secretary-General, 48, 254–5, 257 *see also* Annan, Kofi; Ki-moon; Ban
   action plan, 48–9
   decision-making, inclusion of women in, 115
   proposed indicators for priorities under UNSCR 1325, 50
   relief and recovery obligations, 142
   reporting obligations under UNSCR 1325, 44
United Nations Security Council (UNSC), 253, 256
   Cross-cutting report on women, peace and security, 48
   implementation of NAPs, 41
United Nations Security Council Resolution (UNSCR)
   awareness, 8
   criticism, 9, 45
   effects of implementation, 39
   impediments, 39, 51
   PeaceWomen Project analysis, 39–40
   protection from violence, 56
   UNSCR 1265, 56
   UNSCR 1296, 56
   UNSCR 1325 *see* UNSCR 1325 – Women, Peace and Security
   UNSCR 1410, 170
   UNSCR 1820, 5, 9, 35, 38, 39, 40, 50, 61, 75, 99, 141, 156, 201
   UNSCR 1888, 5, 9, 35, 38, 39, 61, 75, 142, 201
   UNSCR 1889, 9, 35, 38, 58, 142, 39, 61, 75, 142, 161, 201
   UNSCR 1960, 9, 35
United Nations Special Representatives, 5, 254
UNSCR 1325 – Women, Peace and Security, 1–2, 3, 4, 5, 6, 8, 9, 21, 22, 26, 252–7
   'accountability gap', 43–4
   achievements, 39, 43, 47–50
   aims, 37
   content, 37

criticism, 39, 43–5
decision-making, women's role in, 35, 77, 111, 112, 114–15, 139
development, 35
early warning systems for violence, 72
evaluation, 43–52
Fiji, implementation in, 196–8
gender-responsive policies, 79–80
gender-sensitive training, 94, 95, 97
impediments, 51
International Civil Society Action Network analysis, 51–2
MIT Centre for International Studies analysis, 51–2
multilingual translation, 36
NAPs, 41–2, 68, 70, 73, 79
Open Days on Women, Peace and Security, 47–8
other UN resolutions and conventions, 34
pillars, 4–5, 31, 34, 36
political participation by women, 107, 134
progress monitoring, 46–7, 50–1, 160–1
relief and recovery, 141, 160–1
Secretary-General's reporting obligations, 44
significance, 33–40
Sri Lanka, implementation in, 226–7
support, 43
Technical Working Group on Global Indicators, 50
Timor-Leste, implementation in, 171–5
understanding of, 51–2
women as peacekeepers, 82–3, 93, 105–9
'use-value' approach
women, of, 25, 89

violence, 4, 8
challenging attitudes towards, 74, 88, 178–9, 200, 229–30
data, need for, 47
disproportionate effect on women, 10, 17, 55
domestic see domestic violence
gendered power relations, 76, 78, 79, 112, 118, 146, 151–2, 163, 200
impunity of perpetrators, 40, 47, 53, 69–70, 76, 80, 178
military and peacekeepers as perpetrators, 69–70
'post-conflict' period, during, 30
protection see violence, protection from
sexual-based see Sexual and gender-based violence (SGBV)
UN Declaration see Declaration on the Elimination of Violence against Women 1993
violence, protection from 3, 5–6, 8, 24, 53–80
access to justice, relevance of, 63–70, 75–9
anti-violence initiatives and men, 74, 101, 190, 200
challenges, 75–80, 176–9
community-based protection initiatives, 75
Fiji, in, 198–202
gender-responsive DDR programs, 79
gender-sensitive early warning systems, 71–3
gender-sensitive language, 80
human security approach, 54–5, 192–3
ICRC model, 62–3
practical interpretation, 59
prevention of conflict, nexus with, 54, 62, 70–4
proactive approach, 71, 73
R2P framework, 56–8
rights-based approach, 53, 55, 80
sexual-based see Sexual and gender-based violence (SGBV)
Sri Lanka, in, 226, 227–31
structural inequalities and conflict, 70–4

violence, protection from (*Cont.*)
   Timor-Leste, in, 175–84
   UN Conventions and Resolutions, under, 55–9
vulnerability of women, 54, 62, 79, 123, 161, 169, 196, 228, 232, 246

war *see also* armed conflict; conflict
   definition, 12
   jus ad bellum, 57
   jus in bello, 57
   non-combatant immunity, 57
   society, effect on, 19, 37–8
war crimes, 34
   prosecutions for rape *see* Sexual and gender-based violence (SGBV)
war rape, 59–60
Women and Media Collective (WMC), 229, 234, 235, 237, 238
Women Building Peace: From the Village Council to the Negotiating Table, 35
Women for Human Rights, 69
Women for Peace, 27, 117, 229
Women for Prosperity (WFP), 129–30
women in development (WID) approach, 145–6, 148, 154
Women, Peace and Security Coordinating Committee (WPS CC) Fiji, 196–7, 217
Women's International League of Peace and Freedom
   PeaceWomen Project, 39–40
women's rights movements
   participation, 35–6
World Vision, 72